SENSE, SEX, AND SIN

Foundations for an Experientialist Ethics

G. Michael Blahnik

University Press of America,® Inc.
Lanham • New York • Oxford

Copyright © 1998
University Press of America,® Inc.
4720 Boston Way
Lanham, Maryland 20706

12 Hid's Copse Rd.
Cumnor Hill, Oxford OX2 9JJ

All rights reserved
Printed in the United States of America
British Library Cataloging in Publication Information Available

Library of Congress Cataloging-in-Publication Data

Blahnik, G. Michael.
Sense, sex, and sin : foundations for an experientialist ethics / G. Michael Blahnik.
p. cm.
1. Ethics. 2. Experience. 3. Sexual ethics. 4. Massage—Moral and ethical aspects. I. Title.
BJ1031.B58 1998 171'.3—dc21 98-36801 CIP

ISBN 0-7618-1240-7 (cloth: alk. ppr.)
ISBN 0-7618-1241-5 (pbk: alk. ppr.)

BJ
1031
.B58
1998

∞™ The paper used in this publication meets the minimum
requirements of American National Standard for Information
Sciences—Permanence of Paper for Printed Library Materials,
ANSI Z39.48—1984

Contents

Introductory Dialogue
1. The Experiential Being and Experiential Consistency   1
2. Cognitive and Affective Co-constituency of Experience   3
3. Ontological Componential Consistency   4
4. Sexual Experience and Ethics   6
5. *Who I Am* and Experiential Contradiction   7
6. Contextualizing Experiential Components   7
7. Christian Values and Experiential Contradiction   10
8. The "I" as Cognition and Ownership   12
9. Will as Concept vs. Faculty   18
10. The "I" in Relation to Will   35
11. Moral Convictions and Will as Concept   45
12. Responsibility and Will as Concept   47
13. Inter-Experiential Ontology   55
14. Complex Experiences and Experiential Contradiction   66
15. Interpersonal Aspects of Experience and Identity   72
16. Phases of Grappling   79
17. Phases of Determining Experiential States-of-Affair   85
18. Levels of Experiential Consistency   92
19. The Process of Morality   95
20. Acts vs. Experience and Sets-of-Experience   100
21. Reason, Will, and the Process of Morality   108
22. Levels of Experience   116
23. Truth as Objective Experiential Consistency   124
24. Physical Attraction as Sexual, Sensual, and Aesthetic   130
25. Sensuality, Sexuality, Morality, and Levels of Experience   150
26. Group Levels of Experience and the Process of Morality   161
27. Experiential Morality vs. Other Moral Systems   164
28. Sex, Love, and the Moral Process   175

INTRODUCTORY DIALOGUE

Interviewer: Could you prescribe the best way for a reader to approach this work?
Author: The best way, no. I'll have to leave that up to the individual reader. I can, though, offer *a* way that might be helpful. The work is primarily an attempt to develop the rudimentary structure of a moral philosophy based upon *experiential consistency* rather than commandments (Augustinian Christianity), rational principles (Kantian deontology), or happiness for all (Mill's utilitarianism). Experiential consistency refers to consistency between 1) the components of consciousness comprising individual experiences, 2) sets of experiences comprised of inter-related individual experiences, and 3) interpersonal experiences comprised of others' individual and sets-of-experiences. As a general rule, the more we strive for and achieve experiential consistency on all levels of experience, the more moral we act in relation to ourselves and others. This is the essential framework within which the work may be understood. But this framework is the product of 1) the practical experience of massage and 2) a philosophical exploration of the emerging areas of sexuality and sensuality within philosophy. Though I may "frame the work" in the first section entitled *The Experiential Being and Experiential Consistency*, I would not expect anyone to understand what I am talking about until they've finished reading the work. The work is a development of these two central concepts *through* a critical analysis of sensuality and sexuality (and emotionality) and *derived from* the practical activity of massage.
Interviewer: Your work originates from the practical world of experience (as we commonly use this word), "grows" within the philosophical areas of sensuality and sexuality (and emotionality), and "blossoms" into a rudimentary moral philosophy.
Author: Very succinctly put, yes.
Interviewer: Your critique of Augustinian Christian morality, Kantian deontology, and Mill's utilitarianism is brief. Is this intentional?
Author: Yes. At present I'm not concerned with critiquing other moral philosophies. There are plenty of good critiques of each philosophy currently in practice already out there. I'm more interested in developing the direction in which my thinking takes me. At this point

exploration and development are more important to me than comparative critique.

Interviewer: Not many writers of philosophy nowadays choose the dialogue style for presenting their ideas. Why have you chosen it?

Author: I like it. I find it to be a very natural way for me to express myself, whether in drama or philosophy. Also, I find the Socratic method of questioning, challenging, and probing to be a very effective way of *doing* philosophy.

Interviewer: I noticed that you do not "stay true" to what we know of Socrates, his person, his time.

Author: No. I have little concern over historical accuracy in regard to my use of Socrates. I want to extract the "essence" of the Socratic method in order to "deliver" these philosophical ideas, so I've made Socrates into a modern thinker of a slightly more "traditional" slant than myself.

Interviewer: You discuss the practice of massage mostly within the context of sexuality and sensuality. This could leave the impression that massage is a sexual field, a preconception from which this developing profession, at least in the U.S. is seeking to separate itself.

Author: Yes, it could leave that impression. Massage offers me a unique opportunity to explore philosophical distinctions between sexuality and sensuality as well as sensuality in relation to other areas of human experience, i.e. emotionality, physicality, interpersonal communication, etc., but it is not to be understood as a sexual field. I would divide massage into two major areas: 1) pain reduction and 2) pleasure production. Pain reduction involves a more mechanical type of massage, where sexual stimulation is minimal or non-existent. Pleasure production involves a more sensual type of massage, where sexual stimulation is more evident but not geared toward escalation; it is a natural physiological and/or psychological reaction and not a step toward a sexual encounter. It is within sensual massage that I find the most fertile philosophical ground for distinguishing sensuality from sexuality.

Interviewer: You spend a fair amount of time discussing the morality of extra-marital relationships, but you don't mention ideas like "open marriage".

Author: I'm not interested in arguing for or against the viability of open marriage or exploring the problems inherent within it at this time. I'm interested in developing a moral method that can deal constructively with our more powerful emotions and sensations, especially the emotion of love and the sensations constituting sexuality. Love is the most identity-affirming emotion that I know of. It says, "I accept you wholly, as you are, and I will work to maintain that acceptance." It is also not limited in its realization to one person; we can love more than one person at a time. Sex is also identity-affirming. It says, "I accept your body and the pleasure I derive from it, and you accept mine." And like love, sexual attraction is not limited to only one person. Any threat to the continuation of such mutual emotional and sexual identity-affirmation tends to be strongly opposed, i.e. fear and jealousy arise. If we can devise ways to maximize the realization of these identity-affirming emotions and sensations while minimizing the threat of losing these affirmations through disintegrating relationships, "defection" of emotion, betrayal, or abandonment, then we may take some important steps in confronting and dealing constructively with some of our most powerful emotions and sensations. My argument in relation to extra-marital relationships is directed to that end. It is not an argument for legitimizing adulterous relationships but for separating essentially adulterous relationships from essentially moral extra-marital relationships.

1. The Experiential Being and Experiential Consistency

SOCRATES: Have you given more thought to yesterday's discussion, my friend?

MASSAGE THERAPIST: Most assuredly, Socrates. You did promise to act the role of mid-wife and help deliver this philosophical idea, did you not?

SOCRATES: Of course. That is the least I could do.

MASSAGE THERAPIST: Good. You remember, Socrates, that in our last discussion I defined **experience** as a *necessary combination of cognition, affect, behavior, sensation, and the physical world, as owned* (Blahnik, 1997). Cognition includes all understandings, thoughts, ideas, images, cogitations, etc. Affect includes all feelings and emotions, whether strong or subtle, sustained or fleeting. Behavior includes our outward bodily comportment that is visible to others and our inward physiological motion that sometimes is visible to others, most times not. Sensation includes the contact we have with our environment and our own bodies through our senses. The physical world refers to the physical situation within which we are located. And ownership refers to the intimate connection between our thoughts, feelings, behaviors, sensations, and physical environment and ourselves. Without this connection we are merely conscious beings, but with it we are selves. Without it we merely go through life, but with it we are aware of ourselves going through life.

SOCRATES: I remember clearly.

MASSAGE THERAPIST: Now I'd like to introduce to you the idea of an experiential being. An **experiential being** is a being who is simultaneously cognitive, affective, behavioral, sensual, and is located within an environment, as owned. An experiential being is the personification of experience. In relation to my profession, an experiential being is not the same as "my body" or the client's "body". It is, rather, our body's relation to our thoughts, feelings, behavior, and sensations of our environment as owned.

SOCRATES: So when you apply a massage stroke to a client, you are applying it to an experiential being and not just a body.

MASSAGE THERAPIST: Exactly.

SOCRATES: I'm curious. Is it not the body that is being massaged?

MASSAGE THERAPIST: Yes.

SOCRATES: And is it safe to say that thoughts and feelings are not usually conceived as being things that are capable of being massaged?

MASSAGE THERAPIST: I see where you are headed with this, Socrates. Please don't play intellectual games with me. It is not just a body being massaged but a "client's body", or a "person's body". And it is the "client" or the "person" who possesses thoughts and feelings. So when a therapist massages a client's body, she massages the client, as a whole, i.e. an experiential being.

SOCRATES: I'm sorry. I was playing with you a little. But I really do have a serious point to raise about this issue. Need the therapist always massage an experiential being? That is, are all people experiential beings at all times to all people?

MASSAGE THERAPIST: Yes and no. Ontologically, all people are experiential beings in that all are constituted by cognitions, feelings, behavior, and sensations of a physical environment, as owned, but one person need not treat another person as an experiential being at all times. Often times we will **primatize** one or more components of experience, either our own or another's (others'), or both simultaneously. To the extent that one component of experience is primatized to the exclusion or near exclusion of the others is the extent to which experience becomes inconsistent on intra-experiential, inter-experiential, and/or interpersonal levels of experience. And to the extent that experience is inconsistent is the extent to which it is, or can be, immoral. And this is the link between experiential consistency and the experiential being: our affirmation of ourselves and others as experiential beings prompts moral experience; our denial of ourselves and others as experiential beings prompts immoral experience.

SOCRATES: I see I have my work cut out for me. It will probably take the rest of our conversation to get a good understanding of these new ideas of yours.

MASSAGE THERAPIST: I trust you will be able to help me provide you with this understanding.

SOCRATES: I will do my best. First, I'd like to make sure I understand what you mean by "experience". I have some understanding already, based on our previous discussion, but I'd like to apply this understanding to the areas of sensuality and sexuality, and use massage as a practical application of these ideas.

MASSAGE THERAPIST: An outstanding idea. Lead on.

SOCRATES: If a female heterosexually-oriented massage therapist massages a male client to whom she is physically attracted, and she actually thinks something like, "he has an attractive back", then is she treating him as an experiential being or is she primatizing the physical aspect of her experience (i.e. his back)?

2. Cognitive and Affective Co-constituency of Experience

MASSAGE THERAPIST: Let me address this by asking you some questions first. If she thinks something like "he has an attractive back", what possible feelings could she have in relation to that thought? That is, while she is having the thought, what possible feelings would co-exist with it?

SOCRATES: Well, she might feel appreciation or attraction or lust...something like that. Is that what you mean?

MASSAGE THERAPIST: Yes, exactly. Now when she has this thought, would you say that she must feel something at the same time she has the thought?

SOCRATES: That she must feel attraction or some such thing?

MASSAGE THERAPIST: Yes.

SOCRATES: Well, it seems natural for there to be some sort of feeling co-existing with the thought, but I don't know if it is necessary for one to exist.

MASSAGE THERAPIST: Could you give me one example of a thought that does not co-exist with some sort of feeling?

SOCRATES: Certainly. If I have the thought 2+3=5, I'm not feeling anything in relation to it.

MASSAGE THERAPIST: I think if you look more carefully you will find the feeling. For instance, what is your general feeling in regard to our conversation? Are you interested in it? Curious about it? Bored with it?

SOCRATES: Interested in it.

MASSAGE THERAPIST: When I asked if you could give me an example of a thought existing without a feeling, would you say that you were interested in this "challenge"?

SOCRATES: Yes.

MASSAGE THERAPIST: So when you conceived the "example" thought of 2+3=5, you felt interest in relation to it?

SOCRATES: Well, yes, I suppose I did. But that was within the context of our conversation, which I find interesting. If I were to conceive the thought outside this context, I may not experience any feeling in relation to it.

MASSAGE THERAPIST: For example?

SOCRATES: Balancing my check book. I may conceive 2+3=5 as a mundane part of my activity.

MASSAGE THERAPIST: Does the activity interest you? Frustrate you? Bore you? Are you apathetic about it? Disinterested?

SOCRATES: You're saying that I must feel "something" in relation to the thought, even if the something is disinterest or possibly indifference.

MASSAGE THERAPIST: Exactly. The thought may very well not be associated with a strong feeling, but it is must be associated with some sort of feeling. Nor need the *content* of the thought be associated with the feeling, but the thought itself must. Without feeling we have nothing to "sustain", "support", or "enliven" our thoughts. We are, in effect, robots.

SOCRATES: Though I am hesitant to concede this point to you at this time, I admit I cannot think of an example to refute your claim.

MASSAGE THERAPIST: But your inability, and mine, to think of a refutation of this claim certainly does not mean that there are no examples that would refute it.

SOCRATES: Exactly so. With that in mind, I'll go ahead and concede the point to you. But I do have another question that I need to address, if you will indulge me.

MASSAGE THERAPIST: Most assuredly.

3. Ontological Componential Consistency

SOCRATES: Must the feeling that I feel be consistent with the thought I conceive? Could I not think, for example, "you have wronged me" without feeling anger, irritation, or some related feeling? That is, if you act in such a way that prompts me to think "you have wronged me", can I not feel love or compassion toward you, even though you have wronged me?

MASSAGE THERAPIST: No, not in relation to that particular thought. The feeling of compassion is inconsistent with the thought "you have wronged me". It cannot sustain the thought. If you look more carefully at what actually happens in situations like these, you'll find that the consistent feeling does occur, if only for a brief moment. When a person interprets another's behavior as a personal injustice done to him, he will feel some form of anger, resentment, etc. But such a feeling may be inconsistent with an established value, such as "I should feel compassion for those who have wronged me". This value may actually occur in some form as a thought that replaces the thought of "you have wronged me". But this new thought is not supported by the feeling of compassion. Rather, it is supported by the feeling of duty or obligation. The person still feels anger, but it is so peripheral in consciousness that he does not recognize it. And he misidentifies his new feeling of duty as compassion. So in answer to your question, I'd say that a feeling must be consistent with a thought, if only for a very short period of time; and a feeling may or may not be consistent with a claim (i.e. a linguistic behavior). The man in our example must feel some form of anger in relation to his thought of injustice, but he need not recognize it. And he need not feel the feeling he claims to feel. But the thought that constitutes his claim must be associated with a consistent feeling in order to be sustained in consciousness. And that feeling, in this example, is duty or obligation.

SOCRATES: Let me see if I understand you correctly. If I conceive the thought "you've wronged me", I must feel something consistent with the thought in order for the thought to be sustained in consciousness.

MASSAGE THERAPIST: Yes.

SOCRATES: So, if I, as a massage therapist, conceive the thought "she has an attractive back", I must feel something consistent with the thought.

MASSAGE THERAPIST: Yes.

SOCRATES: I must feel attraction, appreciation, or some related feeling.

MASSAGE THERAPIST: Yes.

SOCRATES: Are you going to maintain, also, that if the thought is sexual, then the feeling that accompanies it must also be sexual?

MASSAGE THERAPIST: Yes.

4. Sexual Experience and Ethics

SOCRATES: So a massage therapist who feels a sexual feeling in relation to a client is simply feeling consistently with her own thought.
MASSAGE THERAPIST: Yes.
SOCRATES: So why does it seem to me and to others that sexual feelings are inconsistent with individual morality and professional ethics?
MASSAGE THERAPIST: When a massage therapist touches a part of a client's body that she thinks is attractive and that she feels attraction to, her feeling is consistent with her thought. Also, I might add at this point, that her behavior of touching is consistent with her thought and feeling. But now, given the values of the particular therapist, she conceives the thought that her sexual thought and feeling are unprofessional. In other words, she thinks something like "I shouldn't feel attraction to his back". This new thought is associated with the feeling of duty or obligation, or some related feeling. The feeling of duty replaces the feeling of attraction in consciousness just as the thought "I shouldn't feel attraction to his back" replaces the thought "his back is attractive". The new thought occurs because of **who the therapist is in this situation**, i.e. *the sum total of all previous experience which defines the individual*. This therapist, for example, is a person who, upon experiencing a sexual feeling in relation to a client, will tend to experience a negative judgment in relation to it. This negative judgment is the result of the sum total of previous experience and exemplifies the person's value and moral system. So when it seems to you that a therapist's having sexual feelings in relation to a client is inconsistent with your morality or professional ethics, it is because you, to some extent, are defined by that morality.
SOCRATES: Let me see if I understand you. I experience that some of what you say about sexuality and massage makes sense. It makes sense that we are sexual as well as sensual and moral beings, and that we cannot or at least should not deny this fact. But I also experience that what you say contradicts a moral system that I value, or at least part of it. The two experiences are *who I am in this situation*.
MASSAGE THERAPIST: Socrates, you have not only understood me well, but you have added insight to that understanding!
SOCRATES: You need not get all excited, my friend. I don't intend to become your pupil.
MASSAGE THERAPIST: Of course not. My apologies.

5. *Who I am* and Experiential Contradiction

SOCRATES: If who I am consists, at least in part, of these two contradictory experiences, then how am I to determine which moral system is valid, the one I have experienced to be valid for all these years or the one you are developing right before my eyes, and with my help!

MASSAGE THERAPIST: The only answer I have for you is to keep on pursuing answers. Explore with me, help me, challenge me, be with me, and I will do the same with you. Perhaps between the two of us we can discern a truth or two about this complex problem.

SOCRATES: A most thoroughly stimulating proposal! Lead on.

MASSAGE THERAPIST: In the system I've developed so far, the experiential being is necessarily constituted, in part, by a sensual aspect or component. Sexual sensations are understood as a form of sensation. In addition, the massage therapist is "sexed"; so too is the client. There is no getting around this. Our experience consists of thoughts, feelings, behavior, sensations, the physical environment, and ownership of them. I've already argued that our thoughts require feelings to co-exist with them, and that these two components of experience must be consistent, at least for a short period of time. If each of us is, in part, sexual, then our thoughts and feelings will, at times, be sexual. If personal morality or professional ethics denies the validity of this aspect of our experiential being, then it negates a necessary and integral part of our wholeness. And, as I've maintained before, it is the *whole* person that is being treated in massage, not the whole person minus his or her sexuality. Also, it is a *whole* person treating another person, not a whole person minus his or her sexuality. To the extent that a morality or ethic denies the validity of any integral aspect of the whole human being is the extent to which that ethic itself is immoral, because, as I shall show, such denial constitutes and prompts further inconsistent experiences.

6. Contextualizing Experiential Components

SOCRATES: I'm sorry, my friend, but I must object to your reasoning here. I'll grant that we are sexual beings, as well as sensual, physical, intellectual, emotional, spiritual, and psychological beings. But there are situations appropriate for the expression of all these aspects of our being. In the office we express our intellectual aspect, in the theater the emotional aspect, in the church the spiritual aspect, and in the bedroom the sexual aspect. The profession of massage is not a sexual profession, as is pornography or prostitution. Hence, sexuality has no place in it. To the extent that sexuality has become a part of it is the extent to which an ethic or morality is needed to eliminate or transfer sexuality to situations appropriate to its expression.

MASSAGE THERAPIST: Your argument, Socrates, is not wholly without merit, but in order for it to be acceptable to me I need to refocus and contextualize it. By that I mean your idea of "compartmentalizing" integral aspects of ourselves by matching them with their corresponding social or interpersonal situations needs to be placed within the context of the experiential being as a whole human being, regardless of the situation within which we find ourselves. This means that an experiential being interacts within an office situation, a theater, a church, a bedroom, and a massage room. The experiential being consists of all the aspects you mentioned (physical, intellectual, sexual, etc.) It is the *component* co-constituting the experiential being that is appropriately primatized, emphasized, or expressed within the situation. The other components do not simply disappear, as if they don't exist. Rather, we necessarily "carry them with us wherever we go." For instance, in the office we are sexual as well as intellectual beings. This is so clearly evidenced in the physical attractions we feel toward others in the office. In fact, we cannot dissociate any aspect of ourselves within any social or interpersonal situation. We can only *agree to primatize some aspect of ourselves over others and then develop rules and regulations, policies and procedures, and ethical codes by which to conduct ourselves.*

SOCRATES: So in an athletic situation, let's say track, the emphasis would be on the physical aspect of the experiential being, i.e. musculature, bone, physical motion, physical skill, etc., but the psychological, spiritual, and sexual aspects of the experiential being must be recognized as relevant or integral to the athletic situation.

MASSAGE THERAPIST: Yes.

SOCRATES: But if one athlete is attracted to another athlete, it is certainly not appropriate for the first athlete to express that attraction within the athletic situation - at a practice, let's say.

MASSAGE THERAPIST: This would be a matter to be addressed by an ethical code. Those involved in making the code for conduct addressing this situation establish the parameters of acceptable and non-acceptable conduct. Also, we have our own personal code of conduct that may or may not coincide with the code created by the code makers. But if you are saying that we must either not experience the attraction or express it at all on the track field, then I'd definitely have to disagree with you. I've so far argued that thought and feeling, as components of experience, must co-exist and be consistent with each other. Now, I'd like to argue that behavior must also co-exist and be consistent with thought and feeling. Using our example, the athlete thinks "she's attractive" and feels attraction in relation to her. He must also behave consistently with how he thinks and feels. That is, his "internal behavior" (physiology) and his "external behavior" (comportment) must, at least momentarily, support his attraction to her. He may look at her a little longer than he would if he weren't attracted to her, his nervous system may be a little more stimulated than if he were not attracted to her, etc. In some way, his internal and external behavior must support his thought and feeling in order for the thought and feeling to be sustained in consciousness.

SOCRATES: Let's say I look around the track field and my gaze lands on Sally. I stop my looking around behavior and replace it, so to speak, with "looking at" behavior. I am thinking "she's attractive" and I feel attraction.

MASSAGE THERAPIST: Sounds good.

SOCRATES: I then become aware of myself looking at her and think that maybe I shouldn't stare, so I look away. I still feel attraction and I still think she's attractive, but I've decided not to pursue this area of experience because I don't think that staring or leering at someone's body is very respectful. Wouldn't I be behaving inconsistently with how I think and feel?

MASSAGE THERAPIST: How so?

SOCRATES: I think "she's attractive", and feel attraction, but I behave by looking away. It seems that if you are right, then I should continue to stare at her.

MASSAGE THERAPIST: Not at all. When you reflected upon yourself you thought something like "I shouldn't stare at her". Along with this thought you felt something like "duty" or "obligation" to do what is right, and you acted accordingly by looking away. Granted, you still probably feel attraction and would consider her to be attractive if you thought about it, but this pair of components recedes into the periphery of consciousness. What is now *focal* is your negative judgment and feeling of "duty".

SOCRATES: So this is another example of a moral system entering consciousness to halt some sort of experience or desire.

MASSAGE THERAPIST: Yes. This "moral system" and the desire-experience are both integral parts of *who we are*. So if you are saying that the athlete shouldn't experience the girl as attractive, I'd say that you would be espousing a moral idea that is untenable and impossible to actualize. The experience happens. We cannot "unhappen it" before it happens.

7. Christian Values and Experiential Contradiction

SOCRATES: No, I'd grant you that the experience of attraction is wholly natural, even in athletic situations. I'm just arguing that we can act inconsistently with how we think and feel. In fact, I'd have to maintain that contemporary Christian morality is designed, in part, so that we "can" act in opposition to how we think and feel. St. Augustine argues for a morality that has come to be accepted by many as "common moral sense". This morality rests on the assumption that desire after transient or changing things (vs. unchanging or eternal things) is the source of evil or "immoral", and our acting upon that desire is the cause of evil. Using our example, generalizing now, if a man is attracted to a woman, he is "desiring" to some degree. He might not desire to go to bed with her, but at least he desires to look at her or think about her.

MASSAGE THERAPIST: So attraction is a form of desire.

SOCRATES: Yes.

MASSAGE THERAPIST: Now is the woman a "transient or changing thing"?

SOCRATES: This is an important consideration. From the Christian perspective, if I may be so bold to say, the woman's body, qua body, is transient. It will get old, die, and decay. But her "soul" is not transient; it is unchanging.

MASSAGE THERAPIST: By her soul do you mean "who she is", her "self"?

SOCRATES: I would like to use it that way, yes. I'm not concerned with the soul as something that exists without a body, so let's not open that can of worms here.

MASSAGE THERAPIST: Yes. Go on.

SOCRATES: So if a man desires a woman's body alone, he is desiring a transient thing. Whereas if he desires a woman's soul or self, he is desiring an unchanging or eternal thing. This type of desire is applauded by Christian morality.

MASSAGE THERAPIST: So a man who desires a woman's body alone is experiencing a "source of evil".

SOCRATES: Yes.

MASSAGE THERAPIST: And a man who desires a woman's soul or self is experiencing a "source of good".

SOCRATES: I'd have to say so, yes.

MASSAGE THERAPIST: The word "desire" throws me a bit. Can I replace it with "attraction".

SOCRATES: Yes.

MASSAGE THERAPIST: Good. If a man is attracted to a woman's body alone, then he is experiencing a source of immorality. He need not "be" or "be acting" immorally at this point.

SOCRATES: Right.

MASSAGE THERAPIST: And a man who is attracted to a woman's "soul" or "self" is experiencing a source of good.

SOCRATES: That does seem to be consistent.

MASSAGE THERAPIST: Go on.

SOCRATES: Therefore, when a man is attracted to a woman's body alone, and acts upon that attraction, he commits an immoral act. Much of Christian morality is designed to guide our desires toward eternal things like soul, justice, wisdom, love, etc. and away from transient things like flesh, money, power, etc.

MASSAGE THERAPIST: So if we apply this to our massage therapist, she may be attracted to a client's "self" or "soul" but not to his body alone, if she is disposed to acting morally.

SOCRATES: Yes.

MASSAGE THERAPIST: Could you explain what it means to be attracted to a self?

SOCRATES: Well, from the Christian point of view, the self would be the soul that resides within our body and is "breathed into us by God" and is our closest link to God, which lends it its eternal quality.

MASSAGE THERAPIST: Now, I'm confused. Are we going to use "self" to mean *who we are* or some metaphysical thing that inhabits our body.

SOCRATES: Your question is very appropriate indeed. As I am giving you this account of Christian morality, I too am ambivalent. The "self-as-who-we-are" is much more intimately connected to our bodies than is the "self-as-soul". The soul, according to Christian metaphysics, arises separately from the body and is "put" or "placed" in some manner into the body by God. But such metaphysical notions have been thoroughly criticized and rejected by science and modern philosophy. Modern understanding is that the self is equivalent to or at least derived from the structure of our evolved brain. Because of our cerebral cortex we are able to be self-reflective, to be aware of ourselves as separate from, though intimately connected with, our environment. Our "soul", then, "arises" from our body. If there is no cerebral cortex, there is no soul, i.e. no self, just "animal" consciousness.

MASSAGE THERAPIST: Yes, and the modern understanding of self puts into question the Christian idea of "desiring eternal things." For if the self is necessarily dependent upon the brain for its existence, then when the brain dies, so too does the self.

SOCRATES: And then we are back to our old "can of worms".

MASSAGE THERAPIST: Yes, so may I propose a way around this problem?

SOCRATES: Please.

8. The "I" as Cognition and Ownership

MASSAGE THERAPIST: I think we have a solution to the problem in the idea of the experiential being and experience, as I've developed them so far. Experience consists of cognition, affect, behavior, sensation, the environment, and the "I" in relation to all these other components. In this idea of experience, the "I" is not equivalent to an agent. The "I" does not think, feel, believe, or sense the environment. There is no "I" or "self" that is detached from the thinking, feeling, behaving, and sensing that goes on. Hence, the "I" is not something that arises from outside of the body and is placed into us by God.

SOCRATES: Then where does it come from?

MASSAGE THERAPIST: Let's accept the modern evolutionary perspective here and maintain that the self is derived from or necessarily connected to our evolved brain.

SOCRATES: Though this whole perspective is subject to criticism.

MASSAGE THERAPIST: Of course. We'll make it a tentative acceptance.

SOCRATES: Ok.

MASSAGE THERAPIST: Within the notion of experience, *the "I" is equivalent to the function of ownership*. I'll use our massage therapist to clarify. When the therapist thinks "this muscle is tight", she feels

(let's say) concerned, she behaves outwardly by stroking the muscle and inwardly through the physiology of her body, and she senses the skin and underlying muscle tissue of the client within the massage room environment. At this point, the therapist's attention is focused on something other than herself. Her experience is, at this moment, non-reflective. If through some bizarre neuro-chemical event, she were rendered physically unable to reflect upon herself or be aware of herself doing what she's doing, then she would just continue to behave, however she behaves, without being aware of herself behaving, much like we say "lower" animals do. But our massage therapist, being human and normally developed, becomes aware of herself within this process of massaging the client's muscle, and she thinks, "Am I doing this right?" At this point, her experience shifts from non-reflective to self-reflective. In the non-reflective experience her **focal consciousness** consists primarily of the client's muscle. In the self-reflective experience her focal consciousness consists primarily of herself in relation to her client. But if we look closely at what happens here, as the philosopher David Hume did when he tried to locate the self, we find something very interesting. When the therapist becomes aware of her "self", her experience actually consists of her thought, "am I doing this right", her feeling of doubt, her behavior (let's say) of lightening her stroke, her sensations in relation to the client's skin and underlying muscle, all within the environment of the room. In this experience there is no "self" having a thought. We can only determine such a thing after the fact or after the experience, when we reflect upon the experience itself. But as the experience occurs, there is no self that has the thought, or the feeling, or performs the behavior, or senses the skin. Rather, there is the thought "am I doing this right" and the ownership of that thought. The "I" in the thought is necessarily co-existent with the rest of the thought. We can't pull the "I" out of the thought "am I doing this right" and still have the thought. For instance, if we thought something like "is this being done right", we would, in effect, be experiencing an act of massage being performed but not by ourselves - a dissociated experience, if you will. In other words, the self-reflective nature of the thought would be destroyed. What I am contending, then, is that the "I" in the thought cannot exist without the rest of the thought. The therapist cannot be aware of herself (in this example) without the "vehicle" of thought. She as a "self" is not "having a thought"; rather, a thought which consists, in part, of herself ("I") happens and is owned.
SOCRATES: What do you mean by "is owned"?

MASSAGE THERAPIST: What actually occurs in this self-reflective experience is the thought "am I doing this right". This thought "could" register in consciousness without being owned by the therapist in the sense that she could attribute its origin to a source outside of herself. For instance, she could experience the thought as being put in her head by a Martian. In this sense, her thought would not be her own. This type of thought is equivalent to a schizophrenic hallucination. In the non-schizophrenic person, the thought "am I doing this right" is owned by the person thinking it. But this ownership is peripheral in consciousness; it is assumed. When the therapist thinks the thought, she is not focally aware of the thought being hers; whose thought it is is never in question. But the thought is owned [by her], though the "her" is not to be found in focal consciousness. Only the linguistic "I" is found in focal consciousness. And the "I" is inseparable from the rest of the thought (linguistic expression) that includes it. Therefore, there is no "I" or "self" that exists separate and distinct from its "cognitive package" (at least in this example).
SOCRATES: Let me see if I understand you. If I look in a mirror, I do not see my "self" pure and simple. Rather, I see "my face", "my hair", "my nose" etc.
MASSAGE THERAPIST: Yes.
SOCRATES: The face, hair, and nose represent part of the physical environment component of my experience, and the "seeing of them" represents the sensual component of my experience.
MASSAGE THERAPIST: Yes.
SOCRATES: When I look at my face in the mirror, my experience consists of the thought (perhaps) of "I've got bags under my eyes", the feeling of fatigue, the behavior of looking into the mirror and its corresponding physiology, the sensation of seeing the image of my face, and the image itself within the environment of the room within which I am looking at myself.
MASSAGE THERAPIST: Sounds good.
SOCRATES: So when I am looking at my face, it is not "I" who is looking, but rather the "I" of my thought "I've got bags under my eyes" is being owned.
MASSAGE THERAPIST: Yes.
SOCRATES: If at a later time I remember that I was looking at my face in the mirror, this memory-experience would consist of the image (let's say) of myself (body) looking at myself (face) in the mirror. The

image exists in consciousness but not any "I" or "agent" separate from the image. Only the image-as-owned.

MASSAGE THERAPIST: Yes! We cannot reflect upon ourselves without **cognitivizing** some component of our consciousness. In the examples used so far, we cognitivize the cognitive component of our experience. In the first example, the therapist thinks "am I doing this right". She doesn't think "is this being done right" as if that which is being done is being done by someone else; rather, she cognitivizes her thought to include herself. She thinks "am I doing this right." In other words, she "thinks" herself into existence. Her "self" is an integral part of her thought. She cannot detach her "I" from her thought without destroying the integrity of her thought. Nor can she, as an agent separate from her thought, own her thought. And this is a very important point. When she thinks "am I doing this right," "she" is not owning the thought. Rather, the thought "is owned". She is "living" a thought which includes her "I" as an integral part. Her ownership of her thought is a subjectless ownership. The ownership is functional; it is a process, an event that has no subject performing it. It is just happening. This process can be represented this way:

cognition: "is the client uncomfortable"
affect : concern
behavior : stroking part of body
sense : skin, underlying muscle, client's body moving
environ : client's body, massage room
"I" : ownership

At this point the therapist's experience is non-reflective. She is not focally aware of herself doing what she's doing; rather, she is aware of the client's body moving in relation to what she is doing. The "I" in this analysis represents the ownership of the other components of consciousness. That is, the thought "is the client uncomfortable" is not just some thought that pops into her head from some unknown source; it is "her" thought. The concern she feels is "her" concern, etc. She's not at the moment aware of herself thinking the thought or feeling the concern; she is just thinking and feeling it; and the thought and feeling are "hers". Now, the client's movement need not prompt her to be self-reflective, but let's say it does. Now her experience can be represented:

cognition: "am I doing this right"
affect : doubt
behavior : lightening the pressure of the stroke
sense: : skin, underlying muscle, client's body movement

environ : client's body, massage room
"I"   : ownership

Notice. In the second experience (the self-reflective one), the "I"-as-ownership still exists as it did in the first experience (the non-reflective one). But the cognitive component has changed significantly. In the first experience the cognitive component consists of the client's body; in the second experience the cognitive component consists of "I"-in-relation-to-behavior-in-relation-to-the-client. In this experience the cognition includes the "I" or self. Her "self" exists inasmuch as the "I" (which is herself) is cognitivized (or made into thought). And there is no agent or "other self" doing the thinking. There is only the thinking-as-owned. The cognitivization of the self occurs because of who the therapist is in this situation. She need not have reflected upon herself at this point, but she does. She need not think "am I doing this right", but she does. And she does so not because she wills herself to do so but because of who she is in this situation. The "I" that occurs in her cognitive component of consciousness is a part of experience. Her ownership of her "I"-in-cognition transforms her consciousness into experience, i.e. it makes her consciousness hers. In all of this there is no separate and distinct "I" or "self" that thinks, feels, acts, or senses the physical environment. There is only the "I" or self *in context*, i.e. as cognition that is owned.

SOCRATES: I must admit, I have difficulty understanding these points you're trying to make.

MASSAGE THERAPIST: The point to be made is this: there is no "self" that exists separate and distinct from the components of experience. "We" do not think; "we" do not feel, "we" do not act or sense our environment. When "we" think, what exists is a thought-as-owned [by us]; when we feel, it is a feeling-as-owned [by us] that exists. And when we reflect upon ourselves, it is a special type of thought that is owned [by us], i.e. a thought that includes "us". This special type of thought is just a thought; it is not "us". Neither is owning this thought "we" owning; rather, it is merely "owning", i.e. a function or process without an agent doing the owning. What this means in relation to morality is this: when the therapist thinks that her client's back is attractive, her experience would be represented:

cognition: his back is attractive
affect   : attraction
behavior : stroking back
sense   : skin, underlying muscles, contour of back

The "I" as Cognition and Ownership

environ : client's back, massage room
"I"   : ownership

In this experience the therapist is not aware of herself in any focal way. Her consciousness is dominated by the client's back. Her thought, feeling, behavior, and sensation are owned. Then she becomes self-aware. Her experience changes to:

cognition: "I shouldn't think this"
affect   : duty
behavior : altering stroke slightly
sense   : client's back, underlying muscles
environ : clients' back, massage room
"I"   : ownership

Between the first and second experience there exists nothing. The therapist doesn't exist outside of her own experience. Her experience "contains" her and not the reverse. When experience shifts from non-reflective to self-reflective, it is experience that changes. The therapist's "self" changes as experience changes. What this means is that the self is a function of experience.

SOCRATES: When you say "a function of experience", do you mean that the self is not an agent that "moves its body", "feels its feelings", "thinks it thoughts" or "senses its environment"? Rather, it is merely our "connectedness" to some aspect or component of our consciousness, a consciousness composed of cognition, affect, behavior, sensation, and the physical environment?

MASSAGE THERAPIST: Yes. A connectedness of ownership. These components of consciousness are ours.

SOCRATES: So if I raise my arm it is not "I" who is raising my arm; rather, it is "the raising of my arm as owned [by me]."

MASSAGE THERAPIST: Though it sounds awkward, yes. As Bertrand Russell pointed out: it is only a habit of language or mind that we refer to ourselves as agents of our own experience. We've structured our language to reflect a "subject-object" syntax. This is the way we communicate with each other. But if we really look at the experience of raising our arm, we find that the subject (agent, "I") exists, let's say, in the following manner:

cognition: understanding of raising arm
affect   : interest
behavior : raising arm
sense   : teacher, room
environ : room

"I"   : ownership

This experience is non-reflective; we are merely raising our arm, as in trying to answer a question in a classroom. We are focally aware of the teacher at this moment and peripherally aware of raising our arm. The "I" that exists in the experience refers to our peripheral ownership of the other components of consciousness. We own our understanding of our behavior (cognition); in other words, we know what we are doing and the situation within which we are doing it, though we are not focally aware of our doing it. The "I" in the experience is not a performing agent, as if it somehow controls the act. Rather, it is a part of the act itself, that part which determines the act as ours. Now if we reflect upon ourselves, our experience consists of:

cognition: I'm raising my arm
affect   : interest (slightly altered)
behavior : raising arm (with slight self-reflective behavior)
sense   : teacher, room, arm (if in field of vision)
environ : room
"I"   : ownership

In this self-reflective experience the "I" of ownership is peripheral and the cognitive "I" of "I'm raising my arm" is focal. I own the cognition which consists in part of the cognition of myself, i.e. the cognitivized "I". The "I" of ownership is not an agent that owns; I do not suddenly "jump out of my experience" and claim ownership of my cognition (and other components of consciousness). Rather, "I" refers to the function of rendering the cognitive "I" as mine. In neither non-reflective nor self-reflective experience does the "I" exist as an agent which performs the act. Hume's and Russell's insight is verified by such an experiential analysis. There is no pure self as agent.

SOCRATES: So when you say that the self is a function of experience, you mean that we cannot separate any self from our components of experience without destroying the experience altogether. We must be a part of experience, either peripherally as ownership or focally as cognition and simultaneously as peripheral ownership.

MASSAGE THERAPIST: Well put, Socrates. That is exactly what I mean.

9. The Will As Concept vs. Faculty

SOCRATES: I'm curious. Now how does all this tie into our discussion of Christian morality and massage? For St. Augustine and many subsequent Christian thinkers, desire is the source of sin and will is the cause of sin. But all desire is not the source of sin, only desire for transient changing things, like flesh, money, power, material goods, etc. Desire for eternal unchanging things, like justice, wisdom, and love are sources of good. So when the massage therapist desires the body of the client, she experiences a source of sin. And if she acts upon that desire, she causes or commits sin. Therefore, if she feels this desire, she should reject it, suppress it, or direct it toward eternal unchanging things, like love, or avoid the occasions that prompt such desire.

MASSAGE THERAPIST: So if the massage therapist is attracted to the client's body, she is experiencing a source of sin. And if she acts upon that attraction, she causes or commits sin.

SOCRATES: Yes.

MASSAGE THERAPIST: If this is so, then the Christian position seems to contradict the idea of the experiential being as I've developed it so far. But perhaps the contradiction is only apparent. Perhaps the two positions are very similar.

SOCRATES: How so?

MASSAGE THERAPIST: If we are attracted to an experiential being, then we are attracted to a whole person and not merely his/her body. If the massage therapist is attracted to the client's back, and that back is an integral part of his experiential being, then such attraction is, or at least can be, wholly moral.

SOCRATES: Your reasoning might be sound if the experiential being is an eternal unchanging thing, like justice, wisdom, or love.

MASSAGE THERAPIST: Yes, I admit that the notion of "eternal and unchanging" is hard to apply to anything these days. But if I may take some liberties with these terms, I'd like to apply them to the concept of the experiential being by saying that "who we are", though subject to change, is still the same throughout our lives. It is "our" identity. I may change in many ways throughout my life, but I will always, barring identity-shattering psychotic events, be myself. It is my identity, no matter how it is described, that remains the same. Hence, there is an unchanging quality to it. It is this "unchanging" identity that is attracting the massage therapist, and not merely the changing transient body.

SOCRATES: In this way the massage therapist can be attracted to the client's body because it is integral to the client's self, which is "unchanging".

MASSAGE THERAPIST: Yes.

SOCRATES: So physical attraction is moral even in the Christian sense.

MASSAGE THERAPIST: Yes. But the Christian idea, at least as you've presented it here, of feeling desire and not acting upon it is clearly false. As I've argued before, when we think, we necessarily feel, act, and sense our environment. So when we feel desire, we cannot help but behave in relation to it. And that behavior must, at least for a moment in time, be consistent with the feeling. The athlete must actually look at the girl while he is feeling attraction. He may quickly turn his glance away, but such behavior would be consistent with a new feeling, i.e. duty. In like vain, the massage therapist who feels attraction to her client will act, if only for moment, consistently with that feeling. She may prolong her glance, shift her glance from one part of his body to another, touch his body, etc. If she then thinks "I shouldn't feel this way", she will feel another feeling, e.g. duty, in relation to the new thought. Therefore, the Christian notion, as you present it, is clearly false: we cannot help but act in accordance with our thoughts and feelings.

SOCRATES: You present an interesting argument, my friend, though I can't help get the feeling that you're twisting my words to fit your purposes. To put it in the philosopher's vernacular, your argument seems like so much sophistry. If we desire to do something that we judge to be immoral, then we need not act upon that desire. We could choose to act an opposite way from the direction our desire points us. And when we do so act, we still feel the desire. So our acts of restraint are inconsistent with our desire or feeling. And this restraint, at least as I understand this part of Christian morality, is evidence of a good and moral person. The good Christian is the one who can restrain herself from what desire directs her to do.

MASSAGE THERAPIST: I'll show you that what I say is not sophistry and that your notion of Christian restraint needs to be relocated within the framework I am developing here. Could you give me one clear example of the desire/restraint idea you're arguing for?

SOCRATES: Certainly. A man wants to shoplift a radio. He's looking at the radio, thinking "I want to take that", feeling the desire to take it, and sensing the radio and its physical environment. He then thinks that he shouldn't take it, that it would be wrong for him to do so. So he walks away, even though he has not lost his desire to have the radio. He has acted properly or morally because he has restrained his desire to steal and has walked away.

MASSAGE THERAPIST: Good. I can see a number of serious problems with your description. The initial experience consists of something like this:
cognition: "I want to take that radio"
affect : desire (to take)
behavior : looking at the radio, body readying itself to take
sense : radio, physical environment
environ : store
"I" : ownership
Then his experience shifts to:
cognition: "I shouldn't take it; it's wrong
affect : duty
behavior : looking away from radio, body relaxing
sense : other visual stimuli within environment
environ : store
"I" : ownership
If the man is not the type of man who would conceive the negative judgment of the second experience, he would think something else, perhaps "Is there anybody looking?" But let's say he is the type to judge his intention or impending behavior as wrong or immoral; so he has the thought. If the duty that the man experiences in the second experience is the type of duty that is characterized by commitment, i.e. he is immediately convinced that his impending behavior is wrong, then his behavior of looking away from the radio and the relaxing of his body are connected with his feeling. He has, in fact, lost his desire to "take" the radio. Hence, his body acts in accord with what he actually feels, i.e. committed duty. He may still experience pangs of wanting to possess or have the radio as he walks away from it, but this desire is not the same as the desire to take the radio. In other words, I think you described your example inaccurately. The feeling of committed duty virtually replaces the desire to take, and the behavior of walking away is consistent with it. The desire to have the radio experienced as he walks up the isle occurs in conjunction with a thought like "I really want that radio", and this thought and feeling are consistent with his "preoccupied" behavior as he walks up the isle. As the man walks up the isle his **compound experience** consists of the following:
cognition: "I really want that radio"
affect : desire, want
behavior : a pre-occupied look, perhaps a slowing of walking pace
sense : the store environment

environ   : the store
"I"   : ownership
And:
cognition: just go home
affect   : committed duty
behavior: restoring focused look, perhaps a stronger pace
sense   : outside of store (sight)
environ   : the store
"I"   : ownership

In this compound experience the thoughts, feelings, behavior, and sensations are **intra-experientially consistent** though they are **inter-experientially inconsistent** or **contradictory**. Therefore, when the Christian says that restraining one's desires is an accurate description of these events, let alone a praiseworthy act, he/she is patently wrong. Nowhere in the above analysis does restraint even occur in consciousness.

SOCRATES: Oh, my! My dear friend. You are very adept at sophistry! All you've done is create an "analysis" that does not admit of restraint. That does not mean that restraint does not exist. For instance, if the man desires to have the radio and he acts by leaving the store, he is restraining his desire to have the radio.

MASSAGE THERAPIST: I think your mind, Socrates, is pretty firmly embedded in your moral system, as it should be, but such a persistent mind-set is getting in the way of your understanding me as I hope or wish to be understood. I'll reiterate my argument. The man does not restrain his desire; he acts consistently with another "desire", i.e. committed duty. The desire of wanting to have the radio may continue to register in consciousness, but it does so in accordance with his thinking "I really want that radio" (or some similar thought). This thought and feeling accompany another behavior (pre-occupied look, slower pace), but this thought, feeling, and behavior are not strong or significant enough to alter the behavior of walking out of the store. Rather, the feeling of committed duty is much stronger. Hence, what you call restraint is non-existent. Restraint only exists when it registers in consciousness. For example, if the man is thinking, while walking up the isle, "I'm not going to go back to that radio, even though I want to", he is thinking a "self-restraining" thought. He conceives of himself as restraining himself. Now he is in position to "pat himself on the back" for doing his Christian duty. But now restraint is a cognition that is part of a new experience, and this experience consists of something like this:

cognition: "I'm not going to go back to that radio, no matter how much I want it"
affect : determined duty
behavior: strengthening of pace, determination in body motion
sense   : outside of store, door
environ : store
"I"   : ownership

In this experience the affect is determined duty. This form of duty differs from committed duty in that it is less focused. Analytically, we can say that the desire for the radio influences committed duty by weakening it, challenging its focus. The man's focal consciousness is subject to the interplay of his desire for the radio and his desire to do his moral duty. We tend to refer to these types of compound ambivalent experiences as self-restraining and attribute this quality not only to the experience but also to the person. Not only is the act one of self-restraint, but the person acting is expressing his capacity for self-restraint; and such a capacity is applauded by Christian morality.

SOCRATES: Yes, exactly so.

MASSAGE THERAPIST: But don't you see, Socrates, this term we use, i.e. self-restraint, is an evaluative term applied after-the-fact. The man's experience does not admit of self-restraint. He is not acting against his desire to steal; he is acting consistently with his desire to do his moral duty. In the case of committed duty, he experiences very little ambivalence. In the case of determined duty he experiences more ambivalence. This ambivalence is due to the strength or power of the respective experiences. In both instances the power of duty exceeds that of desire to steal or possess the radio. It is the inherent power of these experiences that accounts for the man's walking out of the store, not his capacity for self-restraint. Later, when he reflects upon this event, he can think "I acted with self-restraint" and feel pride in relation to it, but such an experience (thought and feeling) is had after-the-fact. It is "imposed" upon the experience, and the capacity of self-restraint is accepted as a mark of integrity possessed by the man.

SOCRATES: Well, I know from my own experience that what you say is simply not so. Just yesterday I had this tremendous desire to eat a piece of pie. I had the pie on the table, fork in hand. But I said to myself, and I actually used these words: "Restrain yourself, Socrates. You don't need the fat." And I put the pie away. And even though later I had thoughts of eating it, I resisted the temptation and didn't eat it.

MASSAGE THERAPIST: If I can show you that even if you use the word "restrain", you are not acting inconsistently with how you think, feel, and sense, will you accept the validity of what I am arguing?
SOCRATES: Let's hear the argument first. Then I'll let you know.
MASSAGE THERAPIST: I'll analyze the event into a specific compound experience, though in reality the experience may be more complex than how I characterize it.
SOCRATES: Go ahead.
MASSAGE THERAPIST: Your first experience consists of:
cognition: I want this pie
affect : desire (to eat pie)
behavior : looking at pie, fork in hand
sense : pie, environment
environ : kitchen
"I" : ownership
So far so go?
SOCRATES: So far so good.
MASSAGE THERAPIST: Then you think "Restrain yourself, Socrates. You don't need the fat".
SOCRATES: Yes.
MASSAGE THERAPIST: Your new experience consists of:
cognition: "Restrain yourself, Soc..."
affect : duty
SOCRATES: Hold right there! I feel desire! Desire to eat the pie.
MASSAGE THERAPIST: Yes, I agree. But is the feeling of desire-to-eat-pie consistent with the thought "Restrain yourself, Soc..."?
SOCRATES: No! And that is my point! The thought and the feeling conflict.
MASSAGE THERAPIST: So how do you experience such a thought? How is such a thought sustained in consciousness?
SOCRATES: I'm not sure what you mean.
MASSAGE THERAPIST: If I think "You have wronged me", I feel anger, not joy. Joy does not support or enliven my thought of being wronged. How could I conceive the thought of being wronged if I feel only joy? Such a thought would be meaningless, groundless.
SOCRATES: You mean that if I think "Restrain yourself, Soc...", I cannot be feeling just desire to eat the pie. I must feel something consistent with my thought in order for my thought to exist.
MASSAGE THERAPIST: Yes! If the actual thought in consciousness is to have any value or meaning at all, it has to be supported by a

consistent feeling. In your example, I'm saying it is supported by duty, i.e. to do what is right. It could be supported by guilt, fear, or any number of feelings, depending on who you are in this situation.

SOCRATES: My thought of "Restrain yourself, Soc..." is not associated with my feeling of desire to eat the pie?

MASSAGE THERAPIST: Associated, yes. It occurs in a contiguous experience. Contiguous experiences tend to have intimate associations with each other. But it is not supported by the feeling of desire to eat the pie. How would a desire to eat the pie co-exist with and sustain the thought "Restrain yourself, Soc..."? If you only desired to eat the pie, and the pie was "in eating distance", and you had the capacity to eat the pie, and there were no environmental factors to interrupt your experience, then why would you "not" eat the pie? There's nothing to stop you!

SOCRATES: I stop myself.

MASSAGE THERAPIST: No! You *think* "Restrain yourself, Soc..." If this thought is to have any impact upon you at all, it cannot be associated only with desire to eat the pie; it would have no meaning, no value, no force, no power. The thought would be frivolous at best, if it could exist at all. In order for it to exist, to be sustained in consciousness, it must be supported or enlivened by a consistent feeling, e.g. duty. "Restrain yourself, Soc..." is equivalent to "I shouldn't eat the pie. I don't need the fat." The "shouldn't" indicates a duty not to eat the pie - a duty to oneself or someone else. In this case, let's say, it indicates a duty to oneself. This sense of duty or obligation to one's self supports the thought. It gives it meaning and power. It is these two experiences that exist, each having its own strength. The desire of the first experience "influences" the duty of the second experience, but it does not support it in consciousness. In fact, it contrasts with it. Hence, the Christian who maintains she is acting against her own desire (or restraining her desire) is misinterpreting the actual state of affairs. She is, in fact, acting consistently with another desire, i.e. the desire to do one's duty to oneself.

SOCRATES: My dear friend. It seems that you would have us do away completely with the idea that we can control our desires. For according to you it is not "we" that control anything; rather, if anything, experience controls us.

MASSAGE THERAPIST: I prefer to conceive of it as: "we" are an inextricable part of experience. But, yes, a "part" is what we are; we do not "run the show". We may think we do; we may act like we do; we may tell others that we do; but we don't. When we think we control our desires, that is exactly what we are doing, i.e. thinking. This thought is always supported by some affect, some behavior, some sensation, and the physical environment within which the thought takes place. For instance, after the man in your shoplifting example leaves the store, he may think "I wanted it, but I didn't take it" He is conceiving a "desire-controlling" thought, just as he conceived a "self-restraining" thought in the store. It is the desire-controlling thought that exists, not an agent controlling the desire. We determine after-the-fact that we "controlled our desire". But such a determination is merely another cognition (thought, judgment) supported by (let's say) the affect of confidence, and the corresponding behavior and sensations of the physical environment. And not only is it merely a thought, it is an inaccurate thought because it fails to address the desire or affect that really accounts for our behavior "in opposition to the desire that occupies our consciousness (to steal or possess the radio, to look at the girl, to touch the client, etc.)"; that is, it fails to address duty.

SOCRATES: Your argument is, no doubt, interesting, my friend, but the implications of such a view are quite unsettling to me. If we can "do away with" self-restraint and self-control, or controlling our desires, by reducing them to components of experience, then it seems that we can do away with any sort of self-induced or self-initiated behavior. In other words, we can do away with free will.

MASSAGE THERAPIST: I think your unsettledness is not without foundation, for this implication is, in fact, valid. In defining experience as the necessary combination of cognition, affect, behavior, sensations of the physical environment, and the "I", free will is understood no longer as a faculty subject to an agent's manipulation but as a concept we use to refer to certain types of experience.

SOCRATES: Could I cut through unnecessary verbiage by giving you a clear simple example of free will and then allow you to explain to me how it can be reduced to components of experience and understood as a concept rather then a faculty?

MASSAGE THERAPIST: Yes, by all means.

SOCRATES: I raise my arm. See?

MASSAGE THERAPIST: I see.

SOCRATES: I raised my arm not because I had to, not because someone else or my circumstances forced me to do so, but because I chose to do so. I exercised my free will and chose to raise my arm.

MASSAGE THERAPIST: Just prior to raising your arm, what were you thinking? What thought, idea, image, understanding, or cogitation occupied your consciousness?

SOCRATES: I thought of raising my arm.

MASSAGE THERAPIST: Did you think of doing anything else?

SOCRATES: What do you mean?

MASSAGE THERAPIST: Did you think, let's say, of picking your nose?

SOCRATES (laughs):: No, no I didn't.

MASSAGE THERAPIST: Of winking at me?

SOCRATES (laughs): No.

MASSAGE THERAPIST: Did you think of anything other than raising your arm?

SOCRATES: No, I guess not. That was the only thought that entered my mind.

MASSAGE THERAPIST: Ok. Now, what were you feeling as you conceived this thought?

SOCRATES: What did I feel?

MASSAGE THERAPIST: Yes. I've maintained that we must feel something consistent with our thought in order for that thought to be meaningfully sustained in consciousness. So, what did you feel?

SOCRATES: Interest, I suppose. A challenge. I wanted to give you a task to see how you'd handle it.

MASSAGE THERAPIST: Ok. And how did you behave - what was your body doing - as you conceived the thought?

SOCRATES: As I conceived it? I was just sitting here.

MASSAGE THERAPIST: Would you say that your physiology was activated in that your body was readying itself to raise its arm?

SOCRATES: That sounds a little strange, but, yes, I'd say that something was going on inside of me so as to enable me to raise my arm.

MASSAGE THERAPIST: And you were looking at me when you conceived it?

SOCRATES: Yes.

MASSAGE THERAPIST: While you were in this room.

SOCRATES: Of course.

MASSAGE THERAPIST: Were you aware of yourself conceiving it, or did you just conceive it?

SOCRATES: I just conceived it.

MASSAGE THERAPIST: Ok. Experientially, here's what I see as having happened: at the moment of conceiving the thought your experience consisted of the following:
cognition: raise arm
affect : interest
behavior : sitting, body readying itself to raise arm
sense : massage therapist, environment
environ : room
"I" : ownership
Would you say this is an accurate analysis?
SOCRATES: Yes, it seems so.
MASSAGE THERAPIST: Would you maintain that at this point you exercised your faculty of free will and raised your arm?
SOCRATES: Yes.
MASSAGE THERAPIST: Let me ask you. Given the above experience, could you "not" have raised your arm?
SOCRATES: Of course.
MASSAGE THERAPIST: How?
SOCRATES: I'm not following you.
MASSAGE THERAPIST: You say you could "not" have raised your arm. You were thinking "raise arm", feeling interest, readying yourself (body) to raise your arm; there were no sensations and nothing in your environment to distract you from raising your arm. How would you "not" raise your arm?
SOCRATES: I would simply choose not to.
MASSAGE THERAPIST: Why? What possible reason would you have to choose not to raise your arm?
SOCRATES: Where are you going with this?
MASSAGE THERAPIST: You said, given the experience as analyzed above, you could somehow choose not to raise your arm. If there is nothing in consciousness to indicate an alternative course of action to that of raising your arm, then how can you choose "not" to raise it?
SOCRATES: I can simply decide not to do it.
MASSAGE THERAPIST: So you can think something like "No, I'm not going to raise my arm".
SOCRATES: Yes.
MASSAGE THERAPIST: What if you didn't think that thought? What if you never thought any thought or had any understanding of an alternative course of action enter consciousness? Nothing in any other

area of your experience changed so as to affect your immediate course of action. You never reflected upon yourself or what you were doing, which might have inhibited your action slightly. How could you have done anything other than what constitutes your immediate consciousness, i.e. raise your arm?

SOCRATES: I'm not sure how to answer that question.

MASSAGE THERAPIST: Let me put it another way. If you are not directly aware of yourself thinking of raising your arm, feeling interest in doing so, or of your body readying itself to act, but you still own these components of consciousness in that you assume that the thinking, feeling, and acting are yours, then can you in any way "remove" yourself from this experience so as to look at your components of consciousness and manipulate them in some fashion?

SOCRATES: Again I'm not sure how to answer you. If you're asking whether or not I can think of raising my arm and then change my mind, I'd say, 'yes'.

MASSAGE THERAPIST: But this is exactly what *you cannot* do. If *you* could change your mind, you'd have to jump out of your experience, select from a list of possible alternative thoughts, place the alternative thought into your consciousness, jump back into your experience and own the new thought. And this, I maintain, is impossible for you to do. *You* cannot change your mind; rather, a new thought can enter consciousness that virtually substitutes itself for your thought of raising your arm. And *you* have done nothing to bring this about. I offer that it happens because of who you are in this situation and not because of any act of will.

SOCRATES: I cannot change my mind? Do you know how silly that sounds?

MASSAGE THERAPIST: I'm very aware of how silly it sounds. I'm also very aware of how true it is. What is held often times as common sense is merely long-established bias, *a way* of understanding accepted uncritically as *the only way* of understanding.

SOCRATES: So what you are saying is this: free will is virtually non-existent within immediate experience, that components of consciousness exist in consciousness (through no will of our own), sustain themselves in consciousness (through no will of our own), and leave consciousness (through no will of our own). Only after-the-fact do we conceive of the idea or concept of free will to explain or understand what happened. Hence, free will is an *explanation* of experience rather than a human faculty employed by individual selves.

MASSAGE THERAPIST: Basically, yes. If you will indulge me. I'd like to subject this claim to an experiential analysis to see if it survives.
SOCRATES: That is fine, but I'd also like to consider it critically from other points of view. After all, your method of analysis is a part of the philosophy you are espousing, and it may serve only to verify in a circle.
MASSAGE THERAPIST: By all means, look at it critically from whatever angle you please.
SOCRATES: Go ahead.
MASSAGE THERAPIST: Initially you conceived the thought "raise arm".
SOCRATES: Yes.
MASSAGE THERAPIST: Did you choose to think this thought?
SOCRATES: Of course.
MASSAGE THERAPIST: No, understand me correctly. I'm not asking you to consider *now* whether or not you chose to think the thought. I'm asking you to consider whether or not you chose to think the thought *then*, i.e. when you actually conceived the thought.
SOCRATES: Yes, I chose to think the thought.
MASSAGE THERAPIST: How?
SOCRATES: What do you mean? I just chose to think it.
MASSAGE THERAPIST: It's clear to me, Socrates, that these *ways of understanding* are persistent. You're still not understanding me. Let me put it this way. Here's your experience analyzed:

cognition: raise arm
affect   : interest
behavior : sitting, body readying to raise arm
sense   : massage therapist, environment
environ : room
"I"   : ownership

Now, did your idea *come to mind* or did you select it from a number of other ideas or at least one other idea?
SOCRATES: Oh, I'm beginning to see what you mean now. No, I did not select it. There were no other ideas that I was considering. The idea just came to mind.
MASSAGE THERAPIST: Ok. "Could" you have chosen to think the thought or have the idea?
SOCRATES: Could I have entertained other ideas and chosen from among them?

MASSAGE THERAPIST: No. This particular idea of "raising arm". "Could" you have chosen that?
SOCRATES: I don't see how I could have chosen it.
MASSAGE THERAPIST: Yes. It seems that if you could choose the idea, you'd somehow have to separate yourself from your own experience of having the idea, consider a list of ideas which includes the idea of "raising arm", select the latter, insert it into your experience, and then rejoin your experience.
SOCRATES: I'm beginning to understand what you are saying now. No, I could not have chosen to think the thought. It simply *came to mind*.
MASSAGE THERAPIST: Did you choose to feel your feeling of interest?
SOCRATES: No, I just felt it.
MASSAGE THERAPIST: And your behavior? Your body readying itself to raise your arm?
SOCRATES: In all honesty, I don't see my physiological behavior to be chosen; my physiology will act in accordance with my thought and feeling. But it seems that how I comport myself, my entire body, the body observable to others, is a matter of choice.
MASSAGE THERAPIST: How so?
SOCRATES: I didn't have to sit there. I could have stood up, for instance, and conceived the idea. I could have crossed my legs. I could have performed any number of behaviors.
MASSAGE THERAPIST: Again, I'd ask, why would you perform any other behavior than that which you performed? Why would you cross your legs?
SOCRATES: Possibly because I felt a little uncomfortable sitting with my legs uncrossed, and crossing them would relieve the discomfort.
MASSAGE THERAPIST: Then this discomfort would have *registered in consciousness*. You would have been aware of it.
SOCRATES: To some degree, yes.
MASSAGE THERAPIST: But such an example is not an indication of choice or free will either, because you would not have chosen the thought of crossing your legs; it simply would have come into consciousness as a response to your awareness of your discomfort. The discomfort could have prompted other thoughts (e.g. twisting your leg a bit), but it didn't. Within this situation, given who you are, you thought of crossing your legs. Nor was the crossing of your legs a matter of choice between it and just sitting there, legs uncrossed. You didn't think

"should I cross my legs or keep them uncrossed?" You simply crossed them, or kept them uncrossed, as the case may be.

SOCRATES: So there was no actual choice that registered in consciousness.

MASSAGE THERAPIST: No.

SOCRATES: Therefore there was no choice at all? Is that what you're saying?

MASSAGE THERAPIST: Yes.

SOCRATES: May I interrupt your analysis momentarily to point out that what you are saying contradicts the common sense notion that we can always either *do X* or *not do X*? At any given moment, no matter what we're doing, unless subject to the laws of physics, we can always *not* do it.

MASSAGE THERAPIST: Yes, and this common sense notion is patently false. When you raise your arm, you cannot simply "not raise your arm" without doing something else. For instance, when you raise your arm a bit, stop and put it down, the stopping and putting down of your arm are behaviors. You cannot *not* behave. You can alter the course of your intended behavior, but you cannot negate behavior altogether, barring suicide.

SOCRATES: Let's say, then, that "doing X" = raising arm and "not doing X" = putting arm down. I can either do X or not do X; I can either continue raising my are or put it down.

MASSAGE THERAPIST: Yes, but only if both ideas occur in consciousness in relation to each other. That is, you could be thinking "raise arm" while raising it only to think "No, this won't make my point". Then you think again "No, raise it". Here you have a battle going on. Two opposing though related **sets of components of consciousness** constitute your consciousness. These types of experiences we tend to refer to as **making a choice**, and we use them as clear evidence of our reasoning and the use of free will to act in one way or the other, or in some related way.

SOCRATES: Yes.

MASSAGE THERAPIST: I'll deal with that one later. If the idea "No, this won't make my point" is accompanied by the feeling of confidence, then the behavior of altering your course of action is consistent with the new idea or thought. You put your arm down not because you choose to do so over against raising it, but because this behavior is consistent with your new cognition, affect, etc. You don't will the new thought into consciousness; nor do you will the new feeling of confidence, the new behavior, or any other components of consciousness into consciousness. They occur, I maintain, because of who you are in this situation. In the former instance, where we battle with ourselves, trying to decide which course of action we should take, it is not *we* who are battling. Rather, the battle occurs and *we* are an integral part of it. Let's look again at the analyzed experience:

cognition: raising arm
affect   : interest
behavior: sitting, body readying itself to raise arm
sense   : massage therapist, environment
environ : room
"I"   : ownership

When this experience occurred, did you have any control over how strong an experience it was when it entered consciousness?

SOCRATES: Strong in what sense?

MASSAGE THERAPIST: Well, sometimes I'll experience a thought that totally occupies my focal consciousness. I'm not thinking of anything else. I'm not even aware of myself thinking it. These thoughts tend to be quite powerful or strong.

SOCRATES: I see. I'd say that I did not control the strength of the experience at the point it first entered consciousness. But after that, yes. I do have some control over this experience.

MASSAGE THERAPIST: I'll address your idea of control later. For now, let's say that you did not control the strength of your experience, just as you did not control or choose the components that constituted the experience.

SOCRATES: Yes.

MASSAGE THERAPIST: Would you say the same for the second experience which can be rendered thus:

cognition: "No, this won't make my point"
affect   : confidence
behavior: stopping motion of arm, reversing direction
sense   : massage therapist, environment
environ : room
"I"   : ownership

SOCRATES: Yes, I'd say that when the experience occurred, I had no control over how strong it was.

MASSAGE THERAPIST: If the strength of the two experiences is *out of your control,* at least for a period of time, then you virtually have

no choice as to which of these experiences, if either, is stronger than the other.
SOCRATES: Initially, no.
MASSAGE THERAPIST: So if the second experience is much stronger than the first, you may very well continue the behavior initiated by the second experience, i.e. put your arm down.
SOCRATES: I suppose.
MASSAGE THERAPIST: But you will maintain that you need not continue that behavior. You *could* do something else.
SOCRATES: Yes.
MASSAGE THERAPIST: What else could you do?
SOCRATES: I could, for instance, extend my arm to the side.
MASSAGE THERAPIST: You could do this without there being an idea or understanding of such an arm extension in consciousness?
SOCRATES: No, I do conceive of extending my arm.
MASSAGE THERAPIST: Then the conception is a cognition supported by an affect, behavior, sensations, and the environment. And the conception is not willed into consciousness; nor is the strength of the experience determined by you.
SOCRATES: My friend, your persistence is getting a little exasperating.
MASSAGE THERAPIST: An ironic thing for your to say, Socrates.
SOCRATES: I suppose. But nevertheless, every time I come up with an example of the use of free will you re-frame it in terms of **components of consciousness, experience, and relationships between experiences.**
MASSAGE THERAPIST: Because that is my claim, Socrates. *Free will does not exist as a faculty; it is reducible to components of consciousness, experience, and relationships between experiences.* Free will is a concept we use to refer to actual experience. We do not possess it; it occurs in experience as interrelated components of experience.
SOCRATES: If that is so then how do you account for those experiences in which we "battle with ourselves", in which we struggle to decide one way or the other. It seems clear to me that such a struggle is "ours". We struggle with our thoughts and feelings in order to determine which behavior we should engage in.
MASSAGE THERAPIST: Such is our explanation.
SOCRATES: But the explanation does not reflect what is actually happening.

MASSAGE THERAPIST: Not in immediate experience, no.
SOCRATES: Explain, please.
MASSAGE THERAPIST: Let's compare our two experiences:
cognition: raise arm
affect   : interest
behavior : raising arm
sense   : massage therapist
environ : room
"I"   : ownership
And:
cognition: No, this won't make my point
affect   : doubt
behavior : slowing of the arm
sense   : massage therapist
environ : room
"I"   : ownership

I have altered the second experience to reflect indecision. Before, the thought was supported by confidence. The feeling virtually eliminated any indecision. The negation of the behavior of raising your arm was certain and clear. In this new second experience, you're not sure of either behavior, i.e. raising or stopping your arm. You did not choose either set of components to constitute your consciousness; nor did you choose how strong each set would be. Now, according to the "common sense" understanding of free will, you could somehow decide which of these alternative courses of action to perform.
SOCRATES: Exactly so.

10. The "I" in Relation to Will

MASSAGE THERAPIST: Tell me, is there an "I" (self) between these experiences that manipulates them according to its will? Or do these experiences occur contiguously in relation to each other, allowing no room for such manipulation?
SOCRATES: I think that there is something between these experiences that allows us to experience them as experiences-as-ours. That is, if we were to separate experience into **sets of components of consciousness as ours**, as you have done, then there must be something, it seems to me, that ties these experiences to each other. I will call that something the self or "I". But whether or not this "I"

manipulates components of consciousness according to its will is another issue, one I'd like to explore with you.

MASSAGE THERAPIST: I'd gladly address that issue with you, but first I want to look at the issue of whether or not the "I" exists between experiences. I think this issue is subject to the same criticism that the issue of choosing one's thoughts is subject to. That is, there seems to be no way we can separate ourselves from our experience in order to manipulate that experience. Using our example, in the first experience of thinking of "raising arm", the "I" is the ownership of the cognition. Our focal consciousness consists, let's say, primarily of the cognition itself; the idea dominates our consciousness. We peripherally own our affect, behavior, and sensations of our environment. But for some reason another thought enters consciousness. Perhaps just as we initiate movement of our arm upward, we think (though not necessarily in language form), "Is this going to work?" This thought is associated with the feeling of doubt and the behavior of slowing our arm motion or some other form of hesitation. The thought was not chosen to exist in consciousness; nor was its strength or duration in consciousness determined, at least initially, by us. What possible function could a self outside of experience serve that experience itself does not already supply?

SOCRATES: The function of synthesizing one experience with another. We may not choose to think that particular thought, but we can be the synthesizing agent between experiences.

MASSAGE THERAPIST: But upon what grounds would you make such an assertion. Where in experience is the synthesizing "I"? Could we explain the ownership of both experiences to be inherent in experience itself? That is, the "I" of the first experience is the same as the "I" of the second experience because the first experience is "owned into the second experience". In this sense, the "I" does not perform a synthesizing function; rather, experience itself is synthesizing due to the function of ownership and the content of the cognition. We know that the two cognitions are ours by virtue of the function of ownership, and we know that the first cognition is inextricably related to the second cognition by virtue of that same ownership. Consistency of ownership between experiences exists because it is the nature of ownership to be consistent and not because "we" in any way make it consistent. Also, as we mentioned in our last discussion, the content of the first cognition of "raise arm" is *carried over* into the second cognition of "No, this won't make my point" via 1) the "my" cognition in focal consciousness and 2) an *identification-memory* in peripheral consciousness. An identification memory refers to the cognitive periphery of experience that links us to past experience, i.e. we are capable of calling our "I" into focal consciousness in relation to our past experience.

SOCRATES: When the cognition "raise arm" occurs in consciousness, the "I" functions as ownership of that cognition; hence, we know non-reflectively that the cognition is ours.

MASSAGE THERAPIST: Yes.

SOCRATES: Then the cognition "No, this won't make my point" occurs in consciousness. The "I" maintains its ownership function.

MASSAGE THERAPIST: Yes.

SOCRATES: I'm still unclear about how the "I"-as-ownership connects the two experiences.

MASSAGE THERAPIST: The experiences are discrete only for the sake of analysis. We might otherwise understand experience to be a continuous flow of **sets of components of consciousness-as-owned.** The sets of components change, whereas the ownership, though varying in clarity, strength, and intensity, barring dissociative and related experiences, remains the same. Ownership is what makes components of consciousness *ours*. We "own" only inasmuch as already owned components of consciousness are owned [by us]. That is, after we own a set of components, we may conceive of ourselves as owning beings who have owned that set of components. But such a conception is just another set of components-as-owned. Therefore, the function of ownership serves to connect our components of consciousness, which exist in analyzable sets, by grounding each set in ownership itself.

SOCRATES: If that is so, then how do we make decisions? When we battle with ourselves over two distinct courses of action, how do "we" decide which course to pursue?

MASSAGE THERAPIST: In immediate experience the "we" that supposedly decides is reduced to specific components of consciousness. If we think initially "raise arm" and then think "No, this won't make my point", and the respective experiences are equal in strength, we may very well land up hesitating, leaving our arm raised half way, with a thoughtful expression on our face. The anticipated direction of our behavior or course of action has been halted, and we momentarily don't know which way to go. We are *indecisive*. This is an adjective describing the conflict between two courses of action (i.e. two experiences primarily characterized by conflicting cognitions). At this point "we" don't suddenly remove ourselves from this conflict in order

to decide which course to take; this is impossible. Rather, we *live through* the process of experience as it moves toward *resolution*.
SOCRATES: Why can't I just say "Yes, it will work", feel confidence, and continue to raise my arm?
MASSAGE THERAPIST: You could - if you are that type of person who would experience that set of components of consciousness within this situation.
SOCRATES: But "I", as agent, couldn't decide on the course of action.
MASSAGE THERAPIST: No. You cannot will this *decision-experience* into consciousness. You cannot distance yourself from the conflicting experiences and choose which one you want. Your very "wanting" is beyond your control. You don't will your deciding thought ("Yes, it will work") into existence; you don't will your deciding feeling (confidence) into existence; nor do you will your behavior of continuing to raise your arm into existence. Your arm raises up, to be sure, and you are *in control* of that raising up behavior, but this *in control* is merely the concatenation of components of consciousness that has reduced the courses of action to only one, i.e. raise arm. Your behavior is merely consistent with the other components of consciousness. We tend to refer to these types of experiences as **decisions**, and we tend to credit ourselves as being agents with the power to make such experiences occur in consciousness. The fact is, we do not have that power. Decisions are the result of a process of experience in which conflicting courses of action (cognitions) are reduced to a single course of action. And at no point in this process is there an agent willing or choosing one course of action over another.
SOCRATES: So you are *not* saying that we have no control over which course of action we will take, but that such control is a function of experience rather than a capacity of a self or agent.
MASSAGE THERAPIST: Yes, exactly.
SOCRATES: *Control* is rendered experientially as the connection between cognition ("Yes, this will work"), affect (confidence), behavior (raising arm), and sensation of the environment.
MASSAGE THERAPIST: Yes.
SOCRATES: And the "I" is the ownership of these components rather than a controlling agent.
MASSAGE THERAPIST: Yes.
SOCRATES: So in applying this thinking to our massage therapist, we can argue thus: When she thinks "his back is attractive", and feels

attraction to it, strokes his back, senses his skin and underlying musculature, and is, let's say, non-reflective, she 1) acts naturally in that it is human nature to feel attraction to some members of the species (while not being attracted to others), 2) acts morally in that she treats the other as an experiential being rather than merely a body, 3) is not *choosing* to act in this manner but rather is acting consistently with the other components of consciousness (and owning those components), and 4) is not an *agent* performing the act but rather is part of a *process* of owning components of consciousness that she did not choose to have enter consciousness.

MASSAGE THERAPIST: That sums it up quite nicely.

SOCRATES: I'm sorry, my friend. I can accept the naturalness of attraction, and I could even, to some extent, accept the moral nature of the act, but I simply cannot accept this agentless, choiceless action. Call it a persistent habit of thought or mind-set, but the idea of her having no choice whether or not to stroke his back seems simply absurd to me.

MASSAGE THERAPIST: Does having a choice mean having alternative courses of action in which we may engage?

SOCRATES: Yes. I'll grant you that simply *not doing X* is not a legitimate alternative, but only when we consider immediate experience. If the therapist thinks "his back is attractive", etc., she has already decided to perform the action of stroking his back. Such behavior is a part of her routine of administering a massage. The thought of his back being attractive and the feeling of attraction may alter the administering of the stroke somewhat, but it does not prompt her to consider the option of not stroking his back. This consideration has already been decided upon when she determined her course of action in relation to this client, or clients in general. In other words, she exercised her free will in determining how she was going to massage this client, either individually or in general.

MASSAGE THERAPIST: Your argument seems attractive, Socrates, because the strength of the free will mind-set is compelling. But if you were to analyze her experience of determining her course of action, you would find exactly what I have been saying. Let's say that the client has back pain that he wants the therapist to address. Communicating this to the therapist prompts her to think "Fine, I'll concentrate my effort on his back." She thinks this because of who she is in this situation and not because she chose to think it.

SOCRATES: The thought comes naturally to her mind.

MASSAGE THERAPIST: Yes. Also, she feels confidence in relation to her thought. From your "common sense" point of view, she has made a decision. But a decision between what and what? Only one course of action entered consciousness. She never considered not concentrating on his back or concentrating primarily on his shoulders and secondarily on his back; she only thought of concentrating on his back.

SOCRATES: Yes, but there exists time between the point when this thought occurs and when the actual behavior of stroking his back occurs. Within this time there exists the possibility of her deciding not to concentrate on his back.

MASSAGE THERAPIST: You can say this only from a **third-person point of view**. That is, we are immediately engaged in the act of discussing and philosophizing about a situation; we are not engaged in that situation itself. If we were engaged in it, we would not experience any possibility of "not concentrating on his back" unless we had the thought of doing something else, i.e. concentrating on his shoulders primarily and his back secondarily. No thought, no choice. No choice, no exercise of free will.

SOCRATES: But she is not *forced* to do what she does. She doesn't *have to do* what she does.

MASSAGE THERAPIST: I never said she did. I agree with you one hundred percent. She is not forced to concentrate on his back. Just because she conceives the thought of doing so, she need not realize that thought in subsequent action. Between the time she conceives the thought and performs the action, any number of things might happen to alter her consciousness. For example, she may think that his back pain is due primarily to structural problems in posture. She may then concentrate primarily on these structural areas and secondarily on his back muscles. But this alteration of consciousness is not the product of her choice; she doesn't choose to think the thought; the thought occurs because of who she is in this situation. The thought may be accompanied by a feeling of confidence, which would, in effect, eliminate the thought of concentrating on his back from consciousness. Or it may conflict with the other thought, thus producing a **compound set of experiences** that we refer to as **reasoning**. She is an integral part of these sets of experience, but she is not the agent directing the flow of these experiences.

SOCRATES: So, according to you, we neither choose our actions nor are compelled to act because of internal and/or external forces.

MASSAGE THERAPIST: Yes.
SOCRATES: You're thinking is both non-determinist and non-free will.
MASSAGE THERAPIST: Yes.
SOCRATES: And the most you can offer as explanation for our actions is that we act according to *who we are in a given situation.*
MASSAGE THERAPIST: Yes.
SOCRATES: So the therapist strokes the client's back not because she has chosen to do so either prior to the actual stroking or at the moment of stroking but because of who she is in this situation.
MASSAGE THERAPIST: Yes.
SOCRATES: And also because there exists no alternative courses of action (thoughts), feelings, behavior, sensation of the environment, or self-reflection that would significantly alter her consciousness so that she may do otherwise.
MASSAGE THERAPIST: Yes. What you've said adds something important to what I've said so far. The fact that the components of consciousness do not change significantly, and that we are not agents in control of this "lack of change" lends credence to the notion that our behavior is neither causally determined nor the product of free will.
SOCRATES: I admit, my friend, that your argument has prompted my mind to go in all sorts of directions. There's much I would like to discuss with you in relation to free will and determinism, but I don't want to get too far from our main topic.
MASSAGE THERAPIST: Yes, I think what I've said so far can serve as a basis upon which our discussion of sensuality, sexuality, morality, and massage can be constructed.
SOCRATES: My question is this: If our massage therapist is attracted to the client and acts in accordance with that attraction, she does so necessarily.
MASSAGE THERAPIST: Yes. Her feeling of attraction must be accompanied by a consistent behavior, even if only for a short period of time.
SOCRATES: And she does not will this behavior into existence.
MASSAGE THERAPIST: No.
SOCRATES: And when she suddenly thinks that it might be wrong for her to act "further" by stroking the client's hips, let's say, while feeling attracted to him, she is caught in a conflict between experiences.
MASSAGE THERAPIST: I will agree with that as long as you keep in mind that the "she" that is caught is our *third-person* way of referring

to her experiences, and she "is caught between experiences" is also a *third-person* notion. In immediate experience "she" equals ownership of herself-as-cognition, and "between" experiences equals the **trans-experiential function of ownership**.

SOCRATES: Fine. Now there are two distinct courses of action for the therapist: stroke the hips or refrain from doing so (and do other parts of the body).

MASSAGE THERAPIST: Yes.

SOCRATES: If she refrains from stroking his hips, she will be acting consistently with her thought of refraining and her feeling of, let's say, nervous discomfort.

MASSAGE THERAPIST: Her attraction is so strong that it is uncomfortable for her.

SOCRATES: Yes. So in refraining she is not choosing to stroke his hips; rather, she is acting consistently with her thought of refraining, etc.

MASSAGE THERAPIST: Yes.

SOCRATES: And this **series of experiences**, i.e. from initial conflict to final resolution is called **reasoning**; the final resolution is called a **decision**; and the act of doing something else is called an exercise of **free will**.

MASSAGE THERAPIST: That sounds acceptable.

SOCRATES: So she does not possess a will. Rather, she possesses (owns) components of consciousness.

MASSAGE THERAPIST: Even this possession is agentless, at least in immediate experience.

SOCRATES: Yes. The components of consciousness are owned [by her].

MASSAGE THERAPIST: Yes.

SOCRATES: She does not choose the strength of her alternative-course-of-action experiences.

MASSAGE THERAPIST: No.

SOCRATES: Can she direct herself in relation to one course of action over another?

MASSAGE THERAPIST: For instance?

SOCRATES: Can she force herself to refrain from stroking his hips even when her attraction to them is very strong?

MASSAGE THERAPIST: She has a strong attraction to his hips and wants to stroke them but thinks "I shouldn't act on such a feeling". But the prohibitive experience is weak, so she forces herself to stop, i.e.

to act in relation to the prohibitive experience, even though the attraction experience is stronger.
SOCRATES: Yes.
MASSAGE THERAPIST: How could she do this?
SOCRATES: She does this by asserting her will, or am I stuck again in the pesky free will mind-set?
MASSAGE THERAPIST: I'd say so, yes. Because experientially here is what I see happening: Her first experience of attraction is accompanied by behavior in the direction of stroking the hips. Then the second, prohibitive experience occurs. But the experience is weak; it is short-lived in consciousness or it "influences" the strong experience by "altering its clarity" or "diminishing its strength".
SOCRATES: Ok.
MASSAGE THERAPIST: So why would she suddenly "side" with the prohibitive experience?
SOCRATES: Because it's the right thing to do.
MASSAGE THERAPIST: Again, you say this from the *third-person point of view*. Does she *think* "It's the right thing to do"? Does this thought or understanding (cognition) constitute part of her consciousness?
SOCRATES: I'm not sure what you mean.
MASSAGE THERAPIST: I'm saying that *she* cannot suddenly "side" with the prohibitive experience without experiencing a strong prohibitive experience. For instance, she initially is attracted; the attraction is "challenged" by the weak prohibitive experience; this experience may alter her behavior slightly, e.g. she hesitates. And then something else happens in consciousness. Let's say the client moves his body in a way she experiences as very sensual. This new experience looks like this:
cognition: he is so sexy!
affect   : excitement
behavior : definite hesitation
sense   : looking at hips, etc.
environ : client, room
"I"   : ownership
This experience prompts the next experience:
cognition: I can't do this
affect   : duty (guilt, etc.)
behavior : directing hands elsewhere on the body
sensation: other parts of body

environ : room
"I" : ownership

SOCRATES: Are you saying that these types of experiences must occur before she can "side" with the original prohibitive experience?

MASSAGE THERAPIST: Yes. Otherwise, there is no experiential support for her so "siding". She would "side" without thinking, feeling, or sensing the environment in any way that would support her behavior of "siding". She would have, in effect, extracted her "self" and her behavior from the rest of her experience, performed the act without any thought, feeling, or sensation in relation to it, and then rejoined her experience. And this, I contend, is impossible.

SOCRATES: So our accounts of her having the free will to overcome her desires are basically uninformed. We do not see all there is to see in experience before we make our judgments regarding free will.

MASSAGE THERAPIST: Exactly so, yes. If we really look hard at what exists in immediate experience, we will see that a "self" never really reasons, decides, or acts in relation to alternative courses of action. *Reason is reduced to a series of conflicting courses of action, the course of which is "determined" by who we are in this situation and not by free will; decision is reduced to a specific experience which renders all preceding experiences functionally insignificant; and **will** is reduced to experience prompted by and consistent with the "decision-experience".* (In practice, the decision-experience could be equivalent to the "acting-experience" if there is not a perceivable length of time separating the reasoning process from the act.)

SOCRATES: Am I to conclude from all this that the massage therapist really does not decide not to refrain from massaging the client's hips?

MASSAGE THERAPIST: "She" doesn't decide, but a decision-experience is owned by her. We refer to such experiences after-the-fact as our having made a decision. Nor does "she" reason, but reason-experiences are owned by her. Nor does she will her behavior, but her "willed-experience" is owned by her. We claim ourselves as agents more so out of convenience or convention than because we actually are agents.

SOCRATES: So let's say that the therapist experiences a strong desire to stroke the genitals of the client, which prompts a weak prohibitive experience. She hesitates slightly. Now, does she have to stroke his genitals simply because she has a strong desire to do so?

MASSAGE THERAPIST: No. Her desire does not *cause* her to act *in the future* upon that desire, but not because she has the free will not

to act on the desire, but rather because something might very well occur in consciousness that would inhibit or prohibit her from doing so. This "something" could range from an attack of guilt or panic to the client saying "Oh, no you don't".
SOCRATES: But if there existed in consciousness no inhibitive or prohibitive components that would significantly alter the course of her experience...
MASSAGE THERAPIST: Then she would so act.
SOCRATES: She would have to?
MASSAGE THERAPIST: There would be nothing stopping her. According to our definition of experience and behavior, she's got to behave in some manner. She cannot not act. And her behavior needs to be consistent with other components of consciousness constituting her experience. If the *natural course* of her experience is not in some significant way altered, then she will so act.
SOCRATES: Even if the act is against her moral convictions.

11. Moral Convictions and Will as Concept

MASSAGE THERAPIST: Well, with the introduction of moral convictions, at this point, we need to consider this matter a bit further. Are you using "moral convictions" the same way we used "values" previously?
SOCRATES: Yes, I suppose I am.
MASSAGE THERAPIST: So the therapist is *seized by an uncontrollable desire* and can't help but act on it.
SOCRATES: Yes.
MASSAGE THERAPIST: And later she regrets it, feels guilty, gets reported to the ethics board, and loses her license.
SOCRATES (laughs): Well, yes.
MASSAGE THERAPIST: So what's the point?
SOCRATES: My point is that even though she, as you maintain, was not forced to act upon her desire, she would so act if there were no inhibitive or prohibitive factors occurring to alter her *natural course of experience*.
MASSAGE THERAPIST: Yes.
SOCRATES: If she does not *choose* to act upon her desire but rather acts consistently with it, then she should not be responsible for her behavior. After all, she had no real choice. Her alternative courses of action "worked themselves out", rendering only one course of action.

So she had no choice in the matter. Hence, she is not responsible for acting as she did. Why should she be punished by guilt and the revoking of her license?

MASSAGE THERAPIST: Within the philosophical model I am building, *free will exists as a concept abstracted from immediate experience, referring to specific experiences or sets of components of consciousness as owned.* Free will is no longer to be understood as a faculty for our use. The *self exists in part as a function of ownership which is inextricably connected to some component of consciousness.* The self is not a separate and distinct agent. Therefore, the self does not use faculties. Rather, it is an inextricable part of experience. Where experience goes, so too does the self. Experience is, in this sense, "larger" than the self or the "I"; it contains the "I"; the "I" exists as a "part" or "component" of experience. But this does not mean that the "I" is a "passive agent determined by the power of experience". Simply because we rid ourselves of free will as a faculty of the "I" does not mean we have to accept a deterministic model of behavior that would relieve us of responsibility. The massage therapist who experiences a strong desire to stroke the genitals of a client need not actually do so. But if nothing occurs in consciousness to alter the direction of experience, then she will perform the act. Now, let's say that she already accepted the ethical demands of her profession and she believes that touching a client in this manner is unethical. Upon touching him, then, her consciousness is constituted by components that, in effect, reject the validity of her action. Such an experience might look like this:

cognition: what did I do?!
affect   : shock
behavior : directing strokes toward other areas of body
sense   : skin
environ : room
"I"   : ownership

At this point the therapist experiences the shock of what she's done. She experiences what she has done as morally or ethically wrong, but the full recognition of the immorality of the act has not yet occurred in consciousness. She knows she has performed a particular act; she knows the act is wrong (for her); and she's only beginning to realize that she performed an immoral or unethical act. As her experience progresses it looks more like this:

cognition: I acted immorally
affect   : guilt

behavior : stroking other parts of body (self-consciously)
sense : skin
environ : room
"I" : ownership

Now, the full impact of her act exists in consciousness. She fully accepts that "she" performed the act; she judges the act as immoral; and she feels guilty in relation to it. Is she responsible for her act? If she accepts that "she" performed the act, then she is responsible for the act.

SOCRATES: But now you seem to be contradicting yourself. How can "she" accept that she performed the act when there is no "she" (i.e. "I"-as-agent) performing?

12. Responsibility and Will as Concept

MASSAGE THERAPIST: Good question! Within the immediate experience "she" is *not* an agent; she is an inextricable part of the whole experience; her behavior occurs in accordance with the other components of consciousness. That experience could be rendered thus:

cognition: stroking genitals (understanding)
affect : desire
behavior : stroking motion
sense : skin, genitals
environ : room
"I" : ownership

At this point her "I" is only the function of ownership; she is aware of what is going on, but she is not self-reflective. Immediately after passing over the genitals, (let's say) the "shock-experience" registers in consciousness. This experience consists in part of the cognition "What did I do!" Here the "I" exists in *two* parts of consciousness, i.e. in cognition and as the function of ownership. Her "I", in effect, has been **cognitivized**, and this cognitivized "I" is owned [by her]. Her cognition also consists of "some" behavior-as-performed-by-her. The cognitivization of the "I" (self-reflection), in conjunction with the cognitive act-as-performed, all of which is owned [by her], constitutes her responsibility in this situation. She *knows* that she performed the act, not that her desire forced her to perform it, not that someone else forced her to perform it, and not that her material situation determined her behavior. Rather, she cognizes "I did something". Inasmuch as she cognizes this, or something similar, she will hold herself responsible for her behavior.

SOCRATES: Simply because she recognizes that she performed the behavior does not necessitate her accepting responsibility for the behavior. Many a murderer would know that they performed the act, but they will go to their graves proclaiming their innocence and, hence, non-responsibility for their actions. Or they will know they did the act but blame their action on something else, i.e. the victim, the circumstances, their being drunk, an unjust society, poor family upbringing, etc.

MASSAGE THERAPIST: The murderer who blames other things for his act is doing so after-the-fact. If the murder-experience consists of the owning of the cognitivized "I"-as-agent-of-the-act, then the person is responsible for the act. If the murderer later denies responsibility by placing the blame elsewhere, then he is engaging in experiences we refer to as subterfuge, prevarication, self-delusion, or rationalization. These "denial" experiences in no way reject the validity of his responsibility-experience. They merely emphasize how this person deals with or reacts to his responsibility-experience. In fact, we can argue that he engages in denial experiences "because" he has experienced his own responsibility for his behavior, and he is the type of person who disowns his experience in these situations. If he had not experienced responsibility in relation to his behavior, then he probably would not have denied his responsibility. Rather, he simply would not have recognized the act as being his or, if his then not of his doing, i.e. not of his agency.

SOCRATES: I'm curious. You argue that the "I" is not an agent, the "I" does not behave or act. Rather, the "I" is ownership, or the "self" which is cognitivized in the cognitive component of consciousness.

MASSAGE THERAPIST: Yes.

SOCRATES: But now you say that in order for there to be responsibility in relation to a given act or behavior, the person responsible must experience him or her self as an agent.

MASSAGE THERAPIST: Exactly so, yes.

SOCRATES: A non-agent experiencing oneself as agent?

MASSAGE THERAPIST: That's one way of putting it, yes.

SOCRATES: How can this be?

MASSAGE THERAPIST: When we reflect upon ourselves, some component of consciousness co-exists in focal consciousness with the "I". When the massage therapist thinks "What did I do!", her "I" is focalized cognition. Her "I" is cognitivized, but it is also "I"-as-agent. She does not think "What was done here", thus being dissociated from the behavior; nor does she think "What is my relation to this act", thus questioning or not knowing her connection to her behavior. Rather, she thinks "What did *I do!*". Her agency is an integral aspect of her cognition. She cognitivizes her "I" as agent, not her "I" as spectator or passive recipient of some overpowering force. And by saying "She cognitivizes..." I am only using our common declarative syntax in communication. *She*, as an "I" does not cognitivize her "I" or anything else; her "I" *is* cognitivized in the self-reflective experience that is not the product of her choice or will. Her self-reflective experience occurs as a natural course of affairs given who she is in this situation. *She* is an agent only inasmuch as her "I" that is cognitivized as an agent is owned. Her agency is a constituent of her cognitive component of consciousness and not a separate entity manipulating that (or other) component(s) of consciousness.

SOCRATES: So if the massage therapist's cognitive component of consciousness consists of her "I"-as-agent, e.g. "I did such and such", then she is responsible for her behavior.

MASSAGE THERAPIST: Yes.

SOCRATES: Is this the only condition that must be met in order for her to be responsible for her behavior? Can she ever *not* experience herself as agent and still be responsible for her behavior?

MASSAGE THERAPIST: It seems clear to me that any behavior that is not recognized as inextricably associated with a cognitivized "I"-as-agent is not to be associated with responsibility either. We refer to these agentless-behaviors as involuntary and tend not to assign responsibility to them. But there seem to be situations whereby we can be responsible for behavior in which we do not experience ourselves-as-agents. For instance, we could act under the influence of a drug and not experience ourselves as agents, but we could have experienced ourselves as agents while ingesting the drug, and therefore be responsible for putting ourselves in position to act involuntarily. Also, we can claim that we didn't experience our behavior as connected to us-as-agents, only to have others determine our agency for us. In other words, we claim innocence, but our peers claim otherwise.

SOCRATES: So as long as we experience or can be shown to have experienced ourselves as agents in relation to our behavior, we are, either directly or indirectly, responsible for our behavior.

MASSAGE THERAPIST: Yes.

SOCRATES: So our massage therapist is responsible for stroking the genitals of her client.

MASSAGE THERAPIST: Completely. She is responsible for all her strokes inasmuch as she cognitivizes her "I"-as-agent in relation to them.

SOCRATES: So if she is engaged in a stroking motion, and the client suddenly moves his body so that his genitals are in the path of the stroke, and the therapist does not have time to recognize what has happened and alter her course of action, and she strokes the genitals, she is not responsible for her action because she has not cognitivized her "I"-as-agent in relation to the stroke-of-genitals.

MASSAGE THERAPIST: Yes.

SOCRATES: But let's say that even though she could not alter her stroke in time to avoid the client's genitals, she still cognitivizes her "I"-as-agent in relation to the stroke-of-genitals. Is she still responsible for her behavior?

MASSAGE THERAPIST: I believe you are asking a more complex question than you imagine.

SOCRATES: How so?

MASSAGE THERAPIST: I believe you are referring to those times when we assume guilt not in direct relation to our action itself but to our entire experience, which in immediate experience is rendered as an *agented act after-the-fact*. That is, when the massage therapist actually strokes the client's genitals accidentally, her cognition is agentless. Only when she becomes aware of what has happened does agency fill her cognition. In effect, the massage therapist experiences her agentless behavior as *agented*.

SOCRATES: But it was not really agented?

MASSAGE THERAPIST: No.

SOCRATES: So she is not really responsible.

MASSAGE THERAPIST: Not directly, no.

SOCRATES: Indirectly? For engaging in massage behavior in general in relation to this client?

MASSAGE THERAPIST: Yes. She is not responsible for stroking the client's genitals, but she is responsible for being in a situation whereby such accidents are more likely to occur then in many other situations; but this doesn't directly apply here.

SOCRATES: Therefore we can experience responsibility for behavior when, in fact, there is no responsibility.

MASSAGE THERAPIST: I'd rather locate responsibility within rather than outside of experience. Responsibility has no objective existence outside the objectivity inherent within experience. I'd rather say that the massage therapist's initial experience was agentless, but her subsequent experience consisted of her judgment of her previous experience as agented. Her cognition consisted initially of an understanding that her hand moved over her client's genitals, and subsequently of "What have I done!" The cognitivized "I" in the second experience serves as agent of the past action that the word "done" refers to. In the first experience, her understanding of what is happening is owned, but there is no *she* performing the act in consciousness. Hence, responsibility is not an experiential existent, at least in relation to this particular act. Then when she thinks "What have I done!", she, in effect, introduces her agency into consciousness in relation to an agentless act. She assumes responsibility where there is none.

SOCRATES: You say that responsibility is not an objective reality and that it should be located within the inherent objectivity of experience.

MASSAGE THERAPIST: Yes.

SOCRATES: What exactly do you mean by that?

MASSAGE THERAPIST: I mean that *responsibility* does not refer to an existence that somehow transcends human experience. There is no "superhuman" responsibility under which human experience is subsumed, unless that superhuman responsibility is a meta-experiential construct.

SOCRATES: No God to determine for human beings just who is responsible for what.

MASSAGE THERAPIST: Exactly.

SOCRATES: Experience determines who is responsible for what, and experience even determines what God says about who is responsible for what. Beyond that we cannot go.

MASSAGE THERAPIST: Yes. Nor does *responsibility* lie in some super-experiential reality, i.e. the objective universe, i.e. nature. The concept does not refer to a reality that somehow transcends experience. When our experience consists of an owned agented cognition, responsibility lies within our own experience. There exists an **experiential state-of-affairs** or an **objective reality within experience**. I may subsequently judge this experience through another experience that denies my responsibility, as our murderer does. But this does not change the fact of my responsibility-experience. Another person may judge my experience (behavior in this situation) as one in which I am not responsible, but that does not change the reality of my responsibility-experience. In other words, anyone, including myself, might judge, evaluate, or somehow attempt to alter the reality of the responsibility-experience "after-the-fact", but the actual experiential state-of-affairs exists on its own merit. It exists as such as experience. So you and I could argue over whether or not I own responsibility for a given act, but our arguments do not alter the experiential objectivity of the experience. Our experience exists as such, as a fact. How we and others relate to, understand, respond to, or experience our experience involves other experiences that are valid or objective in and of themselves but not necessarily accurate in relation to the initial objective experience.

SOCRATES: So when the massage therapist's experience consists of an agented cognition, she is objectively responsible for her behavior; but this objectivity is wholly a part of her experience, and not a part of any super-experiential reality that we can "tap into" or "access".

MASSAGE THERAPIST: Yes.

SOCRATES: Let's say that the experience occurs objectively. It consists of the requisite agented cognition. This experience, as behavior, is witnessed by an observer. The observer's **judgment experience** of the initial experience (behavior) is opposite of the original experiencer's judgment-experience of the experience. The original experiencer judges his experience as non-agented, and therefore he argues that he has no responsibility in relation to it, whereas the observer's judgment-experience of the original experiencer's experience is that it does consist of an agented cognition. How do we determine which judgment-experience is accurate? And isn't the original experiencer in the better position to determine the content of his own experience?

MASSAGE THERAPIST: Your question is a very important one. It points to the interpersonal quality of experiential reality. Since the original experiencer is capable of misjudging his own experience, his judgment cannot always be accepted outright. If an interactor's judgment-experience includes a cognition contradictory to the cognition of the original experiencer's judgment experience, and if the relationship between the two people is somehow necessary (e.g. co-workers) or valued (e.g. spouses), then they will interact in such a way as to determine mutually the correct judgment of the experientially objective original experience.

SOCRATES: So the determination of experientially objective reality rests upon consensus. The "objective" reality does not really stand on its own; it is subject to consensually determined judgment-experiences.

MASSAGE THERAPIST: The original experience both stands on its own *and* is determined (confirmed/disconfirmed) by judgment-experiences. The objectivity of the initial experience is the experience as objectively related components of consciousness. If the experiencer were able to stop his experience in "mid-flow" and extend in time the components that constitute his experience, he would be able to own himself in relation to those components. For instance, if he were raised to believe or experience that any experience of anger was unacceptable or wrong and that he was a bad person for expressing such anger, then he might actually experience anger for a very brief moment and express it with consistent behavior (e.g. "angry eyes", tensed muscles), but any further "angry" expressions are unacceptable to him. Therefore, he immediately engages in "repressed behavior" that appears to the less insightful as "good" or "benevolent" behavior rather than "repressed anger". And the experiencer judges his "repressed behavior" as benevolent. In this example, the objectivity of the initial experience lies in the actual relationship between components of experience. The experience may look like this:

cognition: "stop doing that"
affect : anger
behavior : narrowed eyes, tensed muscles
sense : other person
environ : room
"I" : ownership

At this point the "I" is not cognitivized; it merely functions as ownership. The experiencer's "energy" is directed away from himself; his experience is non-reflective. Then this experience occurs:

cognition: This is not right for me to do/feel (understood)
affect : guilt
behavior : brief hesitation, altering course of behavior
sense : other person
environ : room
"I" : ownership

Here the "I" is cognitivized (not right for *me* to do) in relation to the act/feeling (depending upon which component is focalized in consciousness). At this point the person is responsible for his behavior, but his experience quickly shifts to:

cognition: I should act benevolently (understood)
affect : duty
behavior : smiling, widening eyes

sense   : other person
environ   : room
"I"   : ownership

Here the "I" owns the cognitivized "I" in relation to the behavior that is being engaged in. This immediately passes into:

cognition: I'm acting benevolently
affect   : affirmation, acceptance
behavior : smiling, modulated voice
sense   : other person
environ   : room
"I"   : ownership

Now the "I" owns the cognitivized "I" in relation to "benevolent" behavior and an accepting affect. This experience constitutes the judgment-experience. It is this "benevolent" behavior that is being experienced as acceptable and right, even though the angry behavior actually occurred in experience. If the anger-experience were to be somehow prolonged in time, then the experiencer could theoretically experience himself in relation to it and then fully realize his guilt. But because of *who he is in this situation,* he cannot do so. But simply because he cannot do so does not mean that his anger-experience never occurred. And the interactor, if insightful, could experience that anger in the behavior of the experiencer and, hence, her experience will contradict the judgment-experience of the experiencer. And her experience will be more accurate in relation to the objective experiential occurrence.

SOCRATES: But there is no objective way for her to determine that her judgment-experience is any more accurate than his, because she can't get out of her experience to determine objective criteria.

MASSAGE THERAPIST: If you understand *objective* to mean apart from or outside of human experience, then yes there is no way to so determine. But if you understand it to refer to an *experiential state-of-affairs*, then there is a way to so determine its objectivity.

SOCRATES: How is that?

MASSAGE THERAPIST: By experiencing its objectivity. In our example, the interactor's experience will be objective to the interactor. That is, she will experience her experience to entail the actual experiential state-of-affairs as experienced by the experiencer.

SOCRATES: And the experiencer will also experience his judgment-experience to match his original experience. That is, his judgment-experience will confirm his original-experience, at least in his own mind.

MASSAGE THERAPIST: Yes. And any determination of *who is right* might be left at that, i.e. each may go away believing he/she is right. But subsequent interaction with each other or with others may very well determine which, if either, judgment-experience was more accurate in relation to the original experience. Let's say that these two continue to interact, and this issue that "divides" them continues to surface. The experiencer's behavior becomes problematic for the interactor; she may become irritated with it. So she confronts the experiencer with her judgment in relation to his behavior. A discussion ensues which over a period of time continues to *confirm the rightness* of the interactor's judgment-experience. She continues to experience her experience as right (i.e. matching the experiential objectivity of the original experiential state-of-affairs). The experiencer, on the other hand, experiences *disconfirmation-experiences.* That is, he begins to doubt the validity of his judgment-experience (at least part of it), and he begins to confirm the validity of the interactor's judgment-experience. As discussion and interaction continue, the experiencer comes to experience the validity of the interactor's judgment-experience, and now they are in agreement with each other over the experiential objectivity of the original state-of-affairs.

SOCRATES: But this could have worked otherwise. That is, they could agree that the experiencer's judgment-experience was more accurate in relation to the original experiential state-of-affairs.

MASSAGE THERAPIST: Yes.

SOCRATES: Then their judgment-experience would be wrong?

13. Inter-Experiential Ontology

MASSAGE THERAPIST: The experiencer's judgment-experience and subsequent confirmation-experiences *in relation to the anger-experience* are inaccurate. And likewise, the disconfirmation-experiences of the interactor in relation to her original judgment-experience, and subsequently her *confirmation-experiences* of her new judgment-experience (having been convinced by the experiencer) are inaccurate. For the experiencer, the error lies in the relationship between his judgment-experience (and subsequent confirmation-experiences) and the original experience. For the interactor, the error lies in the relationship between her *disconfirmation-experiences* (and her subsequent *confirmation-experiences*) and her original judgment-experience.

SOCRATES: I'm curious about this notion of *relationship between experiences*. If an experience consists of cognition, affect, behavior, sensation, the physical environment, and the "I", then what exactly is this apparently ontological category of *relationship between experiences*?

MASSAGE THERAPIST: An example. Your experience consists of the following:

1) cognition: you're behavior is irritating (understood)
    affect   : irritation
    behavior : tightened jaw, narrowed eyes
    sense   : me
    environ : room
    "I"   : ownership

This experience prompts a self-reflective experience which is a negative judgment of the irritation experience. This experience is rendered:

2) cognition: my anger is bad (understood)
    affect   : guilt
    behavior : loosening of jaw, widening of eyes
    sense   : me
    environ : room
    "I"   : ownership

This **self-judgment experience** is prompted to occur very quickly after the irritation-experience because of who you are in this situation. For whatever reasons, you've developed this type of **experiential pattern**: irritation (anger) -- owned evaluated anger -- (which prompts):

3) cognition: I should do what is right (understood)
    affect   : duty
    behavior : beginning to smile, modulate voice
    sense   : me
    environ : room
    "I"   : ownership

This experience quickly prompts the self-judgment experience:

4) cognition: my smiling and calm voice are good
    affect   : approval
    behavior : smiling, speaking calmly
    sense   : me, voice, smiling muscles
    environ : room
    "I"   : ownership

Which leads directly to another *self-judgment experience:*

5) cognition: I'm acting benevolently
    affect   : satisfaction
    behavior : smiling, speaking calmly, confidently
    sense   : me
    environ   : room
    "I"   : ownership

Your first experience, referred to as the irritation-experience, is non-reflective; you feel irritation and express it accordingly, but you're not aware of yourself feeling and expressing as you do. Your second experience, referred to as the (first) self-judgment experience, consists of a cognition constituted by the cognitivized "I" ("my" anger), the cognitivized feeling of anger (though the label of "anger" certainly need not be clearly cognized), and the negative judgment ("...is bad"). The cognitivization of the previous experience and the affect of anger (which, of course, persists into the second experience) is not supported by anger but by guilt. If you were a different person, it might be supported by a stronger form of anger (i.e. if you were the type to get angry with yourself when you realize that you're angry). But we're saying that you're the type to feel guilt for feeling anger. Your irritation-experience *prompts* your self-judgment experience because it is natural for you to become self-aware after irritation-experiences exist for a certain length of time at a certain intensity, and for you to judge it as bad. The length of time and intensity of the irritation need not be specific in order for the self-judgment experience to occur, i.e. there need not be a threshold that needs to be crossed before a self-judgment experience can occur, but, let's say that within a range of time and intensity, the self-judgment experience usually does occur. Because of who you are in this situation, your self-judgment experience exists for a very short period of time, just long enough for you to own the relationship between your "I" and your anger. This occurs by owning the cognitivized "I", anger, and judgment. This experience passes very quickly from consciousness and is replaced by a *series of experiences* leading to the "final" self-judgment experience. This final self-judgment experience consists of a cognition that is constituted by the cognitivized "I", which is not merely understood but *focalized*. Your self-judgment experience also consists of an understood or *peripheral* cognition. This is why you tend not to recognize yourself as being angry when someone asks or confronts you with it: your cognition is peripheral in consciousness; so, too, is the guilt that supports the cognition. What is focal may very well be "me". That is, your focal consciousness consists of me (and my behavior) and your peripheral consciousness consists of all the other components of experience, including the *ownership of the cognitivized "I"* (i.e. self-reflection). Before you experience yourself as acting benevolently, your focal consciousness consists of the cognition "my smiling and calm voice are good", which then passes into the full-blown self-judgment "I am acting benevolently", which is supported by the affect of satisfaction and expressed in increased smiling, voice modulation, etc. Though your self-judgment experience is constituted as noted, its relationship to your original self-judgment experience is one of *focal vs. peripheral experience*. The self-judgment experience is focal; the cognitivized "I" is focally consistent with the judgment of benevolence in relation to behavior. The original self-judgment experience, as it occurred in consciousness, consists of peripheral cognition (my anger is bad), peripheral affect (guilt), and focal environment (me). The cognition and affect never reached focal consciousness, but they could, by definition, be focalized, i.e. they could be made explicit within experience, though not necessarily clearly and distinctly. So if I confronted you with what I experience to be your behavior of repressing your anger, you would "search your consciousness and memory" and find virtually nothing. Though, I will argue, the self-judgment experience, in fact, existed; you were not clearly cognizant of it as *residual existence-as-memory* in the periphery of your final self-judgment experience. The original self-judgment experience has receded even further, we can say, into the periphery of consciousness. Hence, when you try to find evidence of repressed anger or guilt, you find only (mainly) benevolence. But even now you cannot accurately analyze your own experience, because you cannot locate and identify the peripheral components of your experience, i.e. you cannot identify your residual anger or residual guilt.

SOCRATES: Do you mean that the irritation I felt at first still exists within the final self-judgment experience, but in the periphery of consciousness? And it is so peripheral or "out-of-focus" that I can't find it? Hence, when you ask me about repressing my anger, I simply deny it, without much question or doubt?

MASSAGE THERAPIST: Yes.

SOCRATES: Let me see if I understand you rightly. Initially, I'm irritated (angry); then because of who I am in this situation, I reflect upon my experience, and in doing so, judge my component of experience (anger) as bad, and feel guilt in relation to the judgment.

This self-reflection or self-judgment occurs primarily in peripheral consciousness; I am only partly or unclearly aware of it. But if I were able to stop my experience at this point, and prolong my components of experience in time, I might very well focalize these peripheral components *as-they-are* and not just as I judge them later to be. And when I reach the self-judgment experience, these peripheral components of anger and guilt (and negative evaluation) are very much overshadowed or overpowered by my self-satisfaction and judgment of benevolence that your confrontation seems quite wrong if not absurd to me.

MASSAGE THERAPIST: Yes. That seems a quite accurate summary.

SOCRATES: Therefore, a person who typically "represses" his anger actually experiences the anger, then evaluates it, and finally rejects it in favor of a more acceptable feeling - all of this is done very quickly.

MASSAGE THERAPIST: Usually, yes.

SOCRATES: Then what is this *inter-experiential level of ontology* you're referring to?

MASSAGE THERAPIST: The self-judgment experience exists *on its own* as an experience, but it also exists *in relation to* the first two experiences. The irritation-experience is non-reflective; it is simply "felt anger". When you reflect upon it or own your "I" in relation to it, your awareness consists of a negative judgment. Your cognitivized "I" is related to a feeling (anger) that is evaluated as bad. This self-reflective experience is the first step in this series of experiences of establishing your identity, or *who you are*. You experience this self-reflective experience because of who you are, *and* you simultaneously establish or reinforce (in this instance) who you are. Your self-reflective experience immediately prompts an experience that contradicts your self-reflective experience. In this new self-reflective experience your consciousness consists primarily of smiling and modulating your voice. These components occupy focal consciousness. The *benevolent* behavior is insincere. You still feel anger, but this conflicts with your duty to do what is right. Your anger and negative evaluation of my behavior still exist in peripheral consciousness, but your duty to do what is right "outweighs" it. Your duty to do what is right is stronger than your anger at this moment; therefore, you smile and modulate your voice, take notice of this behavior, and judge yourself as acting benevolently. Your self-judgment may dominate your consciousness so much so that when I confront you about repressing your anger, you cannot help but deny it and disagree with me. My confrontation prompts your experience to change to something like this:

cognition: am I angry?
affect : curiosity
behavior : reflective stare
sense   : around room
environ : room
"I"   : ownership

This quickly shifts to:

cognition: "calm" body behavior
affect : equanimity
behavior : peaceful stare
sense   : around room, me
environ : room
"I"   : ownership

And then to:

cognition: I'm not angry
affect : confidence
behavior : talking to me
sense   : me
environ : room
"I"   : ownership

My confrontation serves to push your anger even further into the periphery of consciousness. So when you reflect upon yourself you find no trace of it. Your self-judgment experience (I'm not angry) confirms your other self-judgment experience (I'm acting benevolently), and both contradict the initial *experiential state-of-affairs*, i.e. the irritation and first judgment experiences. The experiential state-of-affairs (experiential objectivity) is what it is; your self-judgment experiences consist of focal and peripheral components; the focal components "outweigh" the peripheral components and, hence, tend to "cover" them or "obscure" their clarity and distinctness; but the peripheral components are strong enough to exert a good deal of influence upon the focal components; hence, the behavior appears insincere to the perceptive interactor. But not only are the self-judgment experiences "self-contained"; they are also interconnected. The "I'm not angry" self-judgment serves as a *confirmation-experience* in relation to the "I'm acting benevolently" self-judgment. And the two self-judgment experiences contradict the initial "irritation-" and "guilt-" experiences. It is this relational contradiction between experiences or sets of experiences that renders

the judgment as inaccurate. Also, the judgment experience itself could possess peripheral components (e.g. anger, guilt) that are not recognized as significant, which may or may not be the case.
SOCRATES: When I experience the irritation-experience, there exists an *objective experiential state-of-affairs,* analyzed into the components above.
MASSAGE THERAPIST: Yes.
SOCRATES: This is true, whether I realize it, agree to it, confirm it later - or not.
MASSAGE THERAPIST: Yes.
SOCRATES: And this objective experiential state-of-affairs consists of components - some focal, some peripheral.
MASSAGE THERAPIST: Yes. *Experience always consists of focal and peripheral components.*
SOCRATES: Focal components are those that "dominate" consiousness; peripheral components are those that are receded in consciousness but could be focalized given the right circumstances.
MASSAGE THERAPIST: Yes.
SOCRATES: So in my *irritation-experience,* focal consciousness consists of you and your behavior; that's what I'm clearly aware of.
MASSAGE THERAPIST: Yes.
SOCRATES: I'm not clearly aware of my irritation, my tightening jaw, narrowing eyes, aspects of the room, or myself in relation to my behavior.
MASSAGE THERAPIST: Exactly.
SOCRATES: Therefore, all of these components are peripheral.
MASSAGE THERAPIST: Yes.
SOCRATES: Then my experience shifts to the guilt-experience.
MASSAGE THERAPIST: Yes.
SOCRATES: Why?
MASSAGE THERAPIST: Because of who you are in this situation. You tend to feel guilt when you get angry.
SOCRATES: At least when I am aware that I am angry.
MASSAGE THERAPIST: Yes, though the awareness is peripheral.
SOCRATES: Yes. So I evaluate my original experiential state-of-affairs (my irritation-experience) negatively.
MASSAGE THERAPIST: Yes.
SOCRATES: If so, then my irritation-experience and guilt-experience are both componentially consistent in themselves but opposed to one another in relation to each other.

MASSAGE THERAPIST: Yes.
SOCRATES: But then my experience shifts to the *duty-experience*, thinking "I should do what is right".
MASSAGE THERAPIST: Yes.
SOCRATES: Why does it shift in this way?
MASSAGE THERAPIST: You've experienced something that you tend to disapprove of, i.e. anger. You're not the type to dwell on this disapproval and busy yourself in self-rejection.
SOCRATES: But I am the type to "rectify the situation" immediately by performing acceptable behavior.
MASSAGE THERAPIST: Yes.
SOCRATES: So I feel a duty to "change myself" rather than wallow in my guilt.
MASSAGE THERAPIST: Yes.
SOCRATES: So far my experiences are still componentially consistent.
MASSAGE THERAPIST: Yes.
SOCRATES: Then I become aware of my behavior, which I am approving in relation to.
MASSAGE THERAPIST: Yes.
SOCRATES: At this point it is my approved behavior that is focal in consciousness and not the *residual anger* from my previous experience, which in this experience is peripheral.
MASSAGE THERAPIST: Yes. The anger is still a part of the experiential state-of-affairs, but you're only peripherally aware of it.
SOCRATES: So I can call this anger into focal consciousness.
MASSAGE THERAPIST: Theoretically, yes. In your situation *you* probably could not do it on your own, but if the circumstances were right, you could so experience it focally.
SOCRATES: What would constitute the *right circumstances*?
MASSAGE THERAPIST: Perhaps if I acted so as to escalate your anger, you explode, then we discuss my observation of evidence of your anger initially; you might come to see when you do, in fact, get angry and how you deal with it.
SOCRATES: So the anger exists in my self-judgment experience (I'm acting benevolently), but I can't focalize it myself.
MASSAGE THERAPIST: Right.
SOCRATES: But it is focalizable.
MASSAGE THERAPIST: Yes, but not immediately and clearly. For instance, you could focalize a painting on a wall above a chair that you are currently looking at simply by shifting your attention from the chair

to the painting. But if you were to shift your attention from *me* to your irritation, you might experience an *unclear* or perhaps *neutral emotion*, an emotion you might have trouble naming.
SOCRATES: In owning the cognition "I'm acting benevolently" I am, in effect, *constructing* who I am in this situation as well as acting in accordance with who I am.
MASSAGE THERAPIST: Your focal cognition "I'm acting benevolently" occurs because of who you are in this situation, not because you choose it and not because psychological or bio-chemical forces cause you to think it, *and* you "construct" who you are when your cognition dominates focal consciousness to the total exclusion of significant peripheral components (e.g. anger). But such a "construction" is based, at least partially, on inter-experiential inconsistency.
SOCRATES: The cognition "I'm acting benevolently" is not just a description of a part of my experience. I am not simply commenting upon my behavior; I am *characterizing* it. I am naming it and owning it in relation to me.
MASSAGE THERAPIST: Yes. And it is this characterization that is simultaneously a distortion of the immediate experiential state-of-affairs and an inaccurate "conclusion" of a series of interrelated experiences.
SOCRATES: I ignore the peripheral content of my immediate experience (e.g. anger), and evaluate the focal content (i.e. benevolent behavior) positively.
MASSAGE THERAPIST: Virtually, yes.
SOCRATES: And my immediate experience is intimately related to my initial experience. It is part of a series of experiences that help construct, confirm, or fortify who I am. But the judgment of my acting benevolently is not consistent with my irritation-experience in relation to who I am.
MASSAGE THERAPIST: Yes, I think that's a good way to understand this inter-experiential ontological aspect of experience. The irritation-experience exists on its own terms; your self-reflective judgment exists on its own terms *and* in relation to the irritation-experience. The self-reflective judgment alters the irritation-experience by adding the "I" to cognition, which may slightly modify the other components (e.g. increase or decrease intensity, alter focal component, etc.) or, as is so in your case, radically modify the experience, i.e. affect changes from irritation to guilt (guilt overpowering irritation, though, in

this situation, it does not dispel it). It is your irritation-experience upon which your self-reflective judgment experience *works*. At this point you do not experience any experience that separates you from your experience. That is, you do no see yourself as owner of your experience; you just live it. But when you experience your duty-experience, your cognition shifts from *what is* to *what ought to be*. It is at this crucial point that the continuity of experience breaks down. Anger is not recognized as anger; negative evaluation of anger is not recognized as negative evaluation of anger. Rather, they are converted into experience *away from the experiential state-of-affairs* or that which *rejects the validity of the experiential state-of-affairs*. The duty-experience, in effect, breaks experiential continuity, radically alters the irritation and guilt through the imposition of duty, shifts focus from *what is* to *some state-of-affairs that is not but should be*, and sets up the basis upon which self-judgments will be made. This basis is the **agented cognition**-*in-relation-to-a-potential-state-of-affairs*. You not only "should" do your duty, but you "can" or "are capable of" doing it. When you engage in and become aware of the behavior that is consistent with your duty, you experience approval of the behavior, which leads to the self-judgment experience fortified by satisfaction. Prior to the duty experience your cognitions are not agented; therefore, responsibility is not an issue, at least not focally. The movement from the irritation-experience to the guilt-experience is movement from non-reflective reaction to the environment (e.g. me) toward a peripherally self-reflective experience with "me" as the focal component, and your negative judgment (i.e. my anger is bad), your affect of guilt, your behavior of loosening jaw and widening eyes, and other sense-physical components as peripheral components.

SOCRATES: Am I agented at this point?

MASSAGE THERAPIST: Yes, but only peripherally. You do cognize the "badness of your anger", but such an evaluation is not clear and distinct; it is "out of focus". So too are your feeling and behavior. They are as "out of focus" as are some of the environmental aspects of the room within your field of vision.

SOCRATES: But I "can" focalize my feeling, cognition, and behavior if necessary.

MASSAGE THERAPIST: Yes, if circumstances permit. If for some reason you could not "flit" from this experience to the next, and had to "remain" with the components constituting consciousness, then, yes, you could focalize these other components. But also, focalization of

these components would not ensure your clearer understanding of them. For instance, you could focalize your anger and understand it as a slight bothersomeness. In the words of psychology, you might minimize the strength of your feeling. And the same is possible for your cognition and behavior, i.e. you "could" focalize them, possibly in this manner:
cognition: understanding my words (e.g. are you angry)
affect : irritation (slightly decreased in intensity)
behavior : tightened jaw, narrowed eyes (slightly modified)
sense : me
environ : room
"I" : ownership
This immediately shifts to a self-reflective experience:
cognition: am I irritated [understood]
affect : slight trepidation
behavior : self-reflective pose (a hesitation)
sense : me
environ : room
"I" : ownership
Your irritation still exists in this experience; it's just not represented analytically. It might be beneficial to think of the trepidation-experience as "superimposed" upon the irritation-experience, each affecting the other so that when subsequent experience occurs, it will occur in relation to both experiences. For instance, when you respond to my question, you say, "no, I'm not irritated". The irritation of the initial experience still persists into the second experience, but it has been greatly decreased in intensity. The self-reflective experience serves to de-intensify the first experience by shifting focus from my behavior to you. The slight trepidation you feel (though you may not recognize it) *shares* affective consciousness with your irritation, decreasing the intensity of the irritation. But in this series of experiences your components are distinct. Your trepidation acts directly upon your irritation, prompting it to move further into the periphery of consciousness, and then is virtually replaced by a confidence that supports the cognition "no, I'm not irritated". Your trepidation-experience, though very short-lived, is **intra-experientially consistent**; all components support each other. But the second experience is less clear and distinct. It could be rendered analytically as:
cognition: [my saying] "no, I'm not irritated"
affect : [doubt] confidence

behavior : smiling, modulating voice
sense   : me
environ : room
"I"   : ownership

Here your experience is **complex**. You simply don't think "no, I'm not irritated" and feel confidence. Rather, you cognize yourself thinking or actually saying this. You not only own your words but you own your awareness of saying your words. You are confident inasmuch as your cognition is consistent with your inter-experiential state-of-affairs, but you are doubtful inasmuch as it is inconsistent with it. The mixed feelings support the complex cognition, which is supported by the insincere smiling and modulated voice. In this sense your experience is **intra-experientially inconsistent** or complex. What is inconsistent is your ownership of only one aspect of the experience, to the near total exclusion of ownership of the other aspect. Your focal consciousness consists of [my saying] "no, I'm not irritated", but you are focally aware of the "linguistic content" of it, i.e. "no, I'm not irritated". The "my saying" aspect of the cognition is peripheral in consciousness. (Note: I'll use brackets to denote peripheral consciousness.) It is supported by the affect of doubt, which corresponds to the insincere quality of the behavior. So your experience, in effect, is shifting away from a clear and distinct, consistent, experiential state-of-affairs to a complex state-of-affairs that is not recognized as a complex state-of-affairs. Rather, it is being recognized as a clear and consistent state-of-affairs. This recognition is inconsistent with the actual experiential state-of-affairs. So, in a sense, I agree with your insightful analysis, Socrates. An experience in itself can be inconsistent, i.e. intra-experientially inconsistent when its focal component is *split* into focal and peripheral aspects, whereupon the focal aspect is accepted as all there is in focal consciousness and the peripheral aspect is virtually expelled from focal consciousness.

14. Complex Experiences and Experiential Contradiction

SOCRATES: So if I may apply these ideas, as they are so far developed, to our massage therapist, I could say something like this: If the massage therapist has a desire to touch a part of a client's body and then thinks that she shouldn't or that her duty is not to act upon her desire, then her duty-experience *breaks the consistency of her experience,* at least as it is established up to this point.

MASSAGE THERAPIST: Not necessarily. Her duty-experience may be intra-experientially consistent. She may be very clear as to what she should or should not do in relation to her desire. Duty-experiences break the consistency of experience when they prompt an **intra-experiential split** between actual states-of-affair and accepted experiential states-of-affair, as we just discussed, or when they prompt **inter-experiential contradictions** that go unrecognized.

SOCRATES: Could you apply these notions of *intra-experiential split* and *inter-experiential contradiction* to a concrete example involving our massage therapist?

MASSAGE THERAPIST: Yes. If she were to experience sexual desire, reflect upon herself peripherally and judge the desire as bad, alter her behavior, reflect upon her new behavior and judge it as good, and then characterize her behavior as good in relation to her agented cognition, while disregarding the "my doing..." aspect of her agented cognition (i.e. [my doing] my behavior is moral or good), *then* she is engaged in an intra-experiential split. Her focalized cognition is split into two parts: 1) "my doing...", which is not accepted or recognized as focal, and 2) "...my behavior is moral or good", which is accepted as focal. Hence, she characterizes her behavior as moral or good but feels somewhat doubtful, funny, awkward, or insincere in doing so. Her behavior is not clear and distinct; her mind is a little "fuzzy"; her feelings are somewhat mixed or ambiguous; she does not (cannot?) fully own the actual focal cognition, which is a type of meta-cognition (e.g. my doing my behavior...); nor does she fully own her feelings of doubt, or the insincerity of her behavior. These aspects exist in experience and may be experienced by the client in a way that she is immediately or currently unable to do.

SOCRATES: She cannot focalize that which is already focalized?

MASSAGE THERAPIST: Contradictory though it seems, I'd have to say 'yes'. The "my doing..." aspect of her cognition is an aspect of her focal consciousness; it is a part of the experiential state-of-affairs. But she cannot give it its proper due; she cannot own it as-it-is. She cannot see herself as questioning the validity of her experience, or in this case, the validity of her behavior. For that is what the meta-cognition of "my doing my behavior..." is, i.e. a question or doubting of validity of one's behavior. Rather, she, in effect, accepts the agented evaluative cognition (i.e. my behavior is moral or good) as the whole of her focal cognition and virtually disregards the meta-cognitive aspect.

SOCRATES: She doesn't choose to do this though.

MASSAGE THERAPIST: No, the meta-cognitive aspect serves partially to constitute the cognition; it does not constitute an alternative cognition. It is easily overridden and eventually replaced by further experience which serves to confirm the accepted or recognized cognition.

SOCRATES: Confirmation-experiences continue the approval of her behavior as she continues to massage her client.

MASSAGE THERAPIST: Yes.

SOCRATES: Will the confirmation-experiences successfully eliminate the "my doing...", the doubt, and the insincere behavior that constitutes this intra-experiential split or intra-experiential inconsistency?

MASSAGE THERAPIST: Not in relation to this particular area of experience. The self-deception may be strong, but the inconsistent aspect will not be totally eliminated.

SOCRATES: And what about **inter-experiential inconsistency**?

MASSAGE THERAPIST: Let's say that sexual desire constitutes the affective component of the therapist's experience, prompting a self-reflective duty-experience. There exist two distinct experiences in conflict with each other. They may be rendered as follows:

cognition: I want to touch him sexually
affect   : sexual desire
behavior : "pre-occupied" stroking
sense   : client's body
environ : massage room
"I"   : ownership

And:

cognition: I shouldn't touch him sexually
affect   : duty
behavior : more committed stroking
sense   : client's body
environ : massage room
"I"   : ownership

Here the massage therapist's experiences are intra-experientially consistent, but together they conflict.

SOCRATES: Inter-experientially inconsistent experiences are conflicting courses of action that register in consciousness; they may alternate in occupying focal consciousness, or one may completely replace the other, but they do not necessarily admit of complex experiential components.

Complex Experiences and Experiential Contradiction 69

MASSAGE THERAPIST: Exactly. The componential structure of inter-experientially contradictory experiences is often intra-experientially consistent. Each component supports the other. It is the *relationship* between the two types of experience that is contradictory; and this contradictory aspect is a part of the objective experiential state-of-affairs.

SOCRATES: I'm beginning to see what you mean by this claim of inter-experiential ontology. Not only do the components of each analyzed experience exist but the relationship between the components themselves *and* the relationship between the experiences themselves also exist.

MASSAGE THERAPIST: Yes.

SOCRATES: This notion of inter-experiential conflict or inconsistency seems to me to lead back to the idea that the "I" has an ontological status separate from that of experience.

MASSAGE THERAPIST: How so?

SOCRATES: If I experience two distinct experiences alternating in consciousness, one occupying focal consciousness now, now the other, then am "I" not the locus or center within which this conflict takes place? Am "I" not the glue which holds the experiences together, within which the "battle" rages?

MASSAGE THERAPIST: That is the way we discuss it; that is the way poets express it; that is the way our language arranges it syntactically; and that is the way I will often express it, but it is simply not the way it is. Refer to the **compound experience** above. Both experiences are self-reflective; the therapist is aware that she wants to touch her client sexually and that she shouldn't do so. This compound experience is, necessarily, represented in this fashion, though it is simplified and somewhat misleading. In actual immediate experience the conflicting experiences are usually not so well delineated, and they may be interrupted by **complexification** or *peripheral influences*. But for the sake of explication, I'll represent them in this fashion.

SOCRATES: I'll accept that.

MASSAGE THERAPIST: In the desire-experience the cognitivized "I"-as-wanting-to-touch-him-sexually is owned. This experience prompts the duty-experience. That which connects the two experiences is the function of ownership, not any transcendental "I". If she were a different person, she might not experience a duty-experience as she does. She might very well experience a calm acceptance of her sexual desire, allow herself to feel it awhile as she strokes parts of his body until the desire dissipates. But because of who she is in this situation she experiences the duty-experience; or more accurately, the duty-experience is prompted by the desire-experience, both of which consist of components that are owned. The cognitivized "I" of the duty-experience is the same "I" of the desire experience. This sameness is an aspect of the peripheral consciousness of the duty-experience, a residual cognition or a form of memory. This cognitive link between the experiences-as-owned is part of an experiential state-of-affairs in this compound experience. The "I" is not above, or the locus of, this state-of-affairs; the state-of-affairs is partially constituted by the "I" through cognitivization of the "I", its simultaneous function of ownership, and the cognitive peripheral link between experiences, i.e. identification-memory.

SOCRATES: I realize that you've explained this before, but I cannot help think that your explanation seems so much like the caricatured mythical battle between the devil and the angel, one the force of desire or evil, the other of reason or good. The two forces battle while the human being is but a pawn being pushed this way and that, until the forces resolve their discrepancy.

MASSAGE THERAPIST: In a sense the caricature is accurate. The strength of each experience is not determined by the person. The therapist cannot *make* her desire-experience weak prior to experiencing it so that she might not have to deal with it.

SOCRATES: She cannot get outside of her experience to do so.

MASSAGE THERAPIST: Right. The experience occurs because of who she is in this situation. When she reflects upon herself in relation to it, she is not in position to do anything about it unless a new experience conflicts with it. If there is no conflict, then there is no reason to do anything about it. So it is the existence of the duty-experience that provides the inter-experiential conflict; and, again, she has no control over the strength of the duty-experience. As mentioned, the duty-experience could, given another person, be so strong as to "resolve" the conflict as soon as it appears in consciousness. So the *forces* of her experiences are beyond her control. But these forces are not *outside* of her experience, nor is *she* outside of her experience. She may "feel" like a pawn being pushed and pulled by forces outside of her, but the feeling is very much a part of experience. If she were a different person, these "forces" might prompt a feeling of challenge or excitement; she might be actively involved in the relationship between the forces.

SOCRATES: If the strengths of her conflicting experiences are roughly equal, can she not just opt for the one over the other?
MASSAGE THERAPIST: How could she?
SOCRATES: Can she not just think "I'm going to do my duty and not act on my desire"?
MASSAGE THERAPIST: Sure. But if she thinks this, then the thought would be supported by the other components of experience. So she would probably have mixed feelings - a "blend" of desire and duty complexified by conviction. In other words, she'd be telling herself what she's going to do, but the cognition would be supported by mixed emotions (and would be intra-experientially inconsistent), so any action she would perform in relation to "duty" would be a "cover" or a "false front". She would not have reached a decision in the matter. The strengths of her conflicting experiences (which include herself) would not have resolved themselves; rather a new experience, i.e. her conviction-experience would occur, but such a conviction would be false. This false conviction-experience can be rendered analytically as:
cognition : I'm doing my duty
affect   : false conviction
behavior   : false behavior
sensation : altered sensation of client's body
environ   : room
"I"   : ownership

In a false conviction-experience such as this the therapist's cognition is a mixture of her previous cognitions, i.e. "I want to touch him sexually" and "I should not touch him sexually". The "conviction" is hollow. There exists an aspect of doubt within the cognitive component of experience, supported by mixed feelings rendered as false conviction, supported by mixed behaviors rendered as false behavior (insincere behavior). So in this case, a compound experience, composed of two relatively distinct though conflicting experiences, prompts a complex, intra-experientially inconsistent experience. In other situations inter-experientially contradictory experiences may prompt other relatively distinct experiences until the conflict is resolved. For instance, the environment may change so as to introduce a distracting element, e.g. a knock on the door, a voice, a phone ringing. The shift in the environmental component of consciousness could easily prompt the dissipation of desire, which entails the alteration of cognition, behavior, and sensation. Or the sensual component of consciousness may change if the therapist, while ambivalent, strokes an area of the client's body that feels or looks unusual, fascinating, or repulsive. This alteration may serve to decrease the power or completely replace the desire.

SOCRATES: And the "falseness" of her conviction may or may not be recognized by her, depending upon the peripheral/focal quality of her doubt accompanying her conviction.

MASSAGE THERAPIST: Yes.

SOCRATES: So compound experiences may lead to complex experiences or other compound experiences, and this process will continue until the conflict is resolved.

MASSAGE THERAPIST: Optimally, yes. But actually the person could die before the problem is resolved.

SOCRATES: Do you mean that a person who represses his anger or desire may continue to do so until he dies?

MASSAGE THERAPIST: Yes.

15. Interpersonal Aspects of Experience and Identity

SOCRATES: Now what, specifically, is this *interpersonal aspect of experience*? Are we talking about an ontological aspect of experience that somehow transcends "personal experience"?

MASSAGE THERAPIST: Let me understand exactly what you are asking. By "personal experience" do you mean "my" experience and "your" experience, both constituted by our respective sets of components, e.g. cognition, affect, behavior, sensation, environment, and the "I"?

SOCRATES: Yes.

MASSAGE THERAPIST: And by "interpersonal aspect of experience" do you mean some aspect of experience that exists *outside of these sets of components* that may or may not "enter" into these sets?

SOCRATES: Well, I'm not sure. You mentioned before that there is an important interpersonal aspect to this whole notion of an objective experiential state-of-affairs.

MASSAGE THERAPIST: Yes, I know what you are referring to, but I'd like to get an understanding of terms so I know where to start.

SOCRATES: Well, that's as much as I understand.

MASSAGE THERAPIST: Ok, then I'll start here. I would drop your notion of "personal" in "personal experience" because it's redundant. All experience, as I've defined it, is personal in the sense that it is composed of the aforementioned components, and, contrariwise, all experience is impersonal for the same reason. Experience is what it is; I

am a part of it in the way that I am a part of it. My "I" functions on basically two levels: 1) componentially, and 2) as ownership. When my experience is non-reflective, my "I" functions primarily as ownership; when my experience is self-reflective, my "I" functions both componentially and as ownership.
SOCRATES: By "componentially" you mean the "I" is cognitivized or made a part of your cognitive component of consciousness.
MASSAGE THERAPIST: Yes. But there is a type of self-reflective experience through which my **identity** is formed; and this I referred to before as a **characterizing**. I'd like to call it a **characterizing-experience** or **pseudo-identity-experience**, depending upon the situation.
SOCRATES: You're referring to the "I am acting benevolently" experience that we discussed before.
MASSAGE THERAPIST: Yes. If you remember, the experience was rendered this way:
cognition: I'm acting benevolently
affect   : satisfaction
behavior : smiling, speaking calmly and confidently
sense   : me
environ : room
"I"   : ownership
Prior to that your experience was:
cognition: my smiling and calm voice are good
affect   : approval
behavior : smiling, speaking calmly
sense   : me
environ : room
"I"   : ownership
In this experience you own your behavior and approve its goodness, but you have not yet assigned that behavior to your "character" or "identity". If this experience were extended in time it might look like a type of dissociative experience where you are aware that your behavior is yours, you're aware that it is good in itself, i.e. as behavior, but you're not quite aware that it is good as "your" behavior or, which amounts to the same thing, that you are performing a good behavior. In other words, the "I'm acting benevolently" experience is *agented*; you are responsible for the behavior.
SOCRATES: So it is the **agented cognition** that is equivalent to an **identity-experience**.

MASSAGE THERAPIST: Yes. But this experience is only one of the necessary types of experiences in the formation of identity. You can experience yourself as acting benevolently, but that does not mean that others will experience you in that way. In our example, my experience of your behavior consists of the judgment that you are repressing your anger. I experience a contradiction between your actual feelings and your behavior or how you are expressing those feelings.

SOCRATES: But, according to what we've said so far, when I first feel anger, the anger exists as a component of consciousness, i.e. as an objective experiential state-of-affairs. As experience proceeds, the anger recedes further into the periphery of consciousness. But anger is not the only affect in consciousness; duty shares consciousness with anger and serves to "push" anger further into the periphery. So when you experience a contradiction between my feelings and my behavior, your experience reflects only part of the experiential state-of-affairs. You recognize my anger, you cognize my modulated behavior, and you cognize a contradiction between the two, but you fail to recognize the duty involved, and hence you fail to fully understand the consistency within my experience.

MASSAGE THERAPIST: I agree. But this, I believe, is how we tend to interact with each other. Our respective experiences in relation to a given experiential state-of-affairs, are, I would venture to say, seldom, if ever, completely congruent with the experiential state-of-affairs. Nevertheless, we do tend to be accurate enough in relation to experiential states-of-affair so as to point out truths that are not recognized in any significant way by those who participate in the states-of-affair.

SOCRATES: So I may experience **confirmation-experiences** in relation to my identity-experience, and thus solidify, as much a possible, my identity, whereas you may experience a contradiction in me, and possibly confirmation-experiences in support of that **contradiction-experience.**

MASSAGE THERAPIST: Yes.

SOCRATES: Well, if I continue to confirm my identity in this manner and go away from our interaction, comfortable with the idea that I am right about myself and you are wrong, and you go away comfortable in the knowledge that "you" are right and I am wrong, then how are we to resolve this issue? Is it resolvable? Is there an absolute right or an absolute wrong? Or are we "blocked" from ever "recovering" the experiential state-of-affairs?

MASSAGE THERAPIST: I will expand upon what I briefly said before in regard to this idea. The short answer to your question is that we are not blocked from recovering the experiential state-of-affairs, but we can only recover it *within* our immediate experiential state-of-affairs. In relation to our example: your components of experience exist *as such*; my components of experience, that include you, exist *as such*. So far, our respective experiences *are* experiential states-of-affair; they are experientially objective. We can, at least in theory, analyze our respective experiences into their respective components and come to full agreement as to their content and componential relationship. But we can only do so *within* experience. Our comparative analyses serve as confirmation-experiences in relation to our original experiential state-of-affairs, i.e. we validate the objectivity of our experience through experience on two levels: 1) to ourselves and 2) to the other. If the relationship between you and me is important to each of us (e.g. co-workers), then the likelihood of our repeating these experiences, whereby my experience of you contradicts your experience of you, is great. Such repetitions tend to create stress. From my point of view I would have difficulty getting the "truth" out of you, and from your point of view you would be frustrated by my "criticism" of you. In such cases a third party may be necessary to serve as arbiter until the issue is resolved or an agreement is reached to productively interact even though the issue would not be completely resolved. If a third party is not needed, then through a process of **mutually assertive interaction**, we will come to resolve our differences by altering our respective points of view in relation to each other and to ourselves, and hence alter our identities.

SOCRATES: Could you describe this "mutually assertive interaction" and how, specifically, it alters our respective points of view and identities?

MASSAGE THERAPIST: Yes. I believe you to be expressing your anger. If I tell you this, you, in all likelihood, will become defensive or simply deny it. In other words my simply analyzing your behavior in this manner is not assertive behavior; it is analytic and accusative, and, as you said before, it misses understanding the rest of your experience sufficiently enough to prompt a rejection of what validity it, in fact, has. This is not to say that such confrontive behavior is not ever effective in producing self-enlightenment in people; psychotherapy is replete with instances whereby a well-timed analytic confrontation is very effective. I'm just saying that, in general, people tend not to be enlightened by such confrontation; in fact, such confrontations usually serve to stimulate even more animosity than already exists between those involved. But an assertive response to "repressed-anger behavior" is usually more effective and much closer to the truth or experiential states-of-affair.

SOCRATES: And what constitutes an assertive response?

MASSAGE THERAPIST:: I might say, "It bothers me when you act like that."

SOCRATES: If you said that to me when I was "repressing my anger", would I not become more "repressed" and say, "Oh, I'm sorry that you feel that way", while I smile condescendingly?

MASSAGE THERAPIST:: You might very well respond in that manner. But I will not understand myself as having stimulated your response. I will understand that my assertiveness has prompted a response, and not the optimal one from my point of view, but I will also understand that my behavior is not in any way an attack on you; rather, I'll understand it as an accurate rendering of my experiential state-of-affairs. So my experiential state-of-affairs is consistent with my immediate experience (assertive confrontation).

SOCRATES: Can you clarify that for me?

MASSAGE THERAPIST:: Yes. You act angrily and cover it quickly with "benevolent" behavior; I interpret your series of behaviors as evidence of repressed anger. My experience "includes" your experience inasmuch as my experience consists of components constituted by aspects of you. For instance, my response to your angry-benevolent series of experiences might be rendered thus:

cognition: "you're repressing your anger"
affect   : disdain
behavior : listening, critical posture
sense   : you
environ : room
"I"   : ownership

Now I simply express my thought to you. This expression-experience is rendered:

cognition: "you're repressing your anger"
affect   : disdain
behavior : speaking
sense   : you
environ : room
"I"   : ownership

This immediate experiential state-of-affairs is connected with the contiguous past state-of-affairs.
SOCRATES: Yes, I see that. But what if I react to your judgment of me in such a way that contradicts your judgment?
MASSAGE THERAPIST: If I express this thought to you now, while feeling disdain, your anger may recede further into the periphery of consciousness and you may feel a slight incredulity in relation to my "analysis", and therefore deny the validity of the remark outright, and feel quite justified in doing so. Or your anger might proceed closer to focal consciousness while your behavior gets more pseudo-benevolent. Or you could respond in a different manner altogether. Your response depends upon who you are in this situation. However you respond, I will experience your response in the manner determined by who I am in this situation. Let's say that you get angrier and more pseudo-benevolent. Your voice gets "syrupy sweet", your eyes reflect a self-righteousness, and your posture is condescending. I, in turn, feel repugnance in relation to your behavior. My repugnance-experience which, let's say, consists of the cognition "you phony", the affect of repugnance, the behavior of "rejecting" facial gestures, body posture, etc. My repugnance-experience is *componentially consistent* "and" it serves as a *confirmation-experience* in relation to the experiential state-of-affairs of my initial response to your angry-benevolent series, i.e. my disdain-experience. My immediate repugnance-state-of-affairs is inter-experientially linked via the function of ownership and the cognitive periphery of consciousness to the past disdain-state-of-affairs as a confirmation of that past state-of-affairs.
SOCRATES: Yes, I understand what you're saying here also. But you're still within your own experience. You're still locked into understanding the "objectivity" of the situation as "your" understanding of it and not as how it is.
MASSAGE THERAPIST: Apparently, I haven't spoken clearly enough yet. The objectivity in this situation is experiential through and through. Your initial anger-benevolence series of experiences exists objectively. It consists of sets of components of consciousness in relation to an "I" or function of ownership. Each component exists as it is, and each is related to the other as it is, and each set of components is related to other sets of components as it is. Therefore, when I experience your anger-benevolence series of experiences, my experience "consists" in part of you, especially your physical body and behavior. You are interpersonally linked to me via components of my experience.

Your experience, which consists in part of me, is objective. It is "there" for the world to see, hear, intuit, i.e. to experience. Likewise, my experience, which includes you as a component, exists objectively for you and the world to experience. If my experience of your experience contradicts your experience of your experience, then there exists objective interpersonal grounds for interpersonal interaction that will, optimally, render an immediate experiential state-of-affairs mutually consistent with the past experiential state-of-affairs.

SOCRATES: Yes, it is this interpersonal aspect of experience that I'm interested in. You say that this too has objectivity; it is ontological, at least experientially ontological.

MASSAGE THERAPIST: Yes. Let's say that my judgment of your anger-benevolent series of experiences is only consistent with "part" of your experiential state-of-affairs. For instance, I think and say, "you're repressing your anger" and feel disdain in relation to it. My judgment reflects or is consistent with a "part" of the experiential state-of-affairs. In fact, you are "repressing" your anger. But you are also expressing some doubt in relation to your "covering" or "repressing" behavior. It is this doubt that I do not experience. Your doubt is not a significant aspect of my experience. This, I believe, is what often happens between people. The experiential state-of-affairs is only partially experienced or "received" by the other, so when this partially received experience is reflected back to the original experiencer, the reaction is often one of rejection, denial, or some similar reaction, which often results in a further distorting of experience from the original experiential state-of-affairs.

SOCRATES: I can understand that such judgment-experiences that only capture part of the experiential state-of-affairs often result in distancing one person from another; I'd like to know how assertive-experience rectifies this problem and fosters truth in communication and a more accurate rendering of the experiential state-of-affairs. I surmise this is what you are going to contend.

MASSAGE THERAPIST: Yes, it is. Assertiveness is, basically, a consistent rendering of an objective experiential state-of-affairs which includes another person or persons. When I say "I think you are repressing your anger" instead of "you are repressing your anger", I am addressing *my* objective experiential reality. Whether or not my experiential state-of-affairs consists of your entire experience or only part of it is of secondary importance. What is primarily important is that my immediate assertive-experience is consistent with my past judgment-experience.

SOCRATES: But if the judgment-experience is only partially accurate in understanding or experiencing the other's objective experiential state-of-affairs, then why should it be important to render the assertive-experience consistent with it? Isn't that just heaping one mistake or partial truth upon another? After all, if you tell me that "you thought" I was repressing my anger, I probably wouldn't act much differently if you just said that I was repressing my anger.

MASSAGE THERAPIST: That may be so. The assertive "owning of one's experience (thoughts, feelings, behaviors, and sensations) by rendering a judgment in "opinion form", or as psychologists say, "I"-statements, doesn't guarantee a non-rejecting or "positive" response. Often times such renderings are merely disguised judgments, and the other person understands them to be so and, hence, reacts negatively. Even those assertive-experiences that are not disguised judgments may prompt negative reactions at first. But, I argue, that true assertive-experiences will maintain **consistency over time** and initial negative responses will eventually be **worked through** and the experiential objectivity of the assertion will remain in tact.

SOCRATES: So I may "smother you in pseudo-benevolence" for assertively informing me about how you feel about my behavior, but this will not significantly alter your position, because your expression is an honest and consistent rendering of "your experience" and not a judgment of "my experience".

MASSAGE THERAPIST: Yes, exactly.

SOCRATES: Also, if I'm the type to get angry for being confronted assertively, I may initially blast you for your "false judgment", but over time I will come to realize that your opinion is just that, i.e. your opinion, and it may very well have some truth to it, as well as some untruth, inaccuracy, or incompleteness.

16. Phases of Grappling

MASSAGE THERAPIST: Yes. I refer to the process of *working through an assertive confrontation* as **grappling**. This process can be divided into phases: **initial reaction phase**, **self-reflective phase**, and the **resolution phase**. I divide it like this to simplify the actual processes that tend to occur; the actual process is quite variable.

SOCRATES: Would you explain further?

MASSAGE THERAPIST: Yes. The initial reaction phase simply refers to how the *confrontee* reacts to the genuine assertive confrontation. If I tell you that your (repressed) behavior agitates me, you may react indignantly, angrily, apathetically, sarcastically, apologetically, etc., depending upon who you are in this situation. I then must "deal with" your reaction. If you get angry and verbally attack me, I must be ready to accept your reaction as a genuine expression of yourself, even if it involves a personal attack upon my character. This phase may last quite a while and be repeated several times before it completes itself. Your reaction may prompt me to feel guilty, depressed, angry, retaliatory, etc. All of these responses indicate that the phase is not quite complete.

SOCRATES: Yes, I was thinking as you were speaking that such an assertive confrontation may only prompt "negative" reactions, which would, in turn, prompt "negative" reactions and create a vicious circle.

MASSAGE THERAPIST: Yes, and this often happens when the *confronter* is not quite ready to genuinely confront the confrontee. It may take several efforts before the confronter can assertively confront the other and accept the other's response with **functional equanimity**. That is, the confronter need not be stoic in his reaction to the confrontee's response, only self-accepting enough not to engage in behavior that would continue the vicious circle pattern.

SOCRATES: Ok. The confronter is capable of handling the confrontee's responses and, hence, he's made a genuine assertive confrontation. Then what?

MASSAGE THERAPIST: Then the confrontee is in position to grapple with the truth of the confrontation. In this phase the confrontee reflects upon himself in relation to the confronter's implied connection between the confrontee's behavior and the confronter's assertive confrontation. He may ask himself "Am I really angry?" "Do I cover up my anger?" "Is he agitated because I act hypocritically?" The confrontee *sorts out the truth* or attempts to establish what exactly is the experiential state-of-affairs. He may come to accept the whole of the confrontation or only parts of it while rejecting other parts. If he accepts the whole, he has resolved the issue with himself. Then he communicates that resolution to the confronter and a **mutual resolution** is reached. If he accepts parts and rejects parts, communicates this to the confronter who himself grapples with the confrontee's assertive confrontation, and, let's say, accepts the confrontee's understanding of the state-of-affairs, then a mutual

resolution is reached. Or the process may occur in a variety of similar ways.
SOCRATES: When mutual resolution is reached, the objective experiential state-of-affairs is determined, but such a determination is, necessarily, an immediate determination and may or may not correspond identically to the actual state-of-affairs that occurred before.
MASSAGE THERAPIST: Yes.
SOCRATES: And if a third person were used to determine the experiential state-of-affairs in cases of contradictory (vs. mutual) determinations, then the third party's determination also would be immediate and not necessarily identical with the experiential state-of-affairs.
MASSAGE THERAPIST: Yes, again.
SOCRATES: If each participant involved in this interaction is necessarily "locked into" immediate experience, then how can we determine whose immediate experience, if anybody's, "matches" the original state-of-affairs?
MASSAGE THERAPIST: We determine this through the **process of experience**. Through the process of experience all interactors will optimally be satisfied in regard to the structure of immediate experience that purports to "match", at least functionally, the original state-of-affairs.
SOCRATES: And of what does this process consist?
MASSAGE THERAPIST: Since experience is a necessary combination of cognition, affect, behavior, sensation, and the physical environment, then any attempt to exclude any of the components of experience from experience will prove detrimental to experience. For instance, if the confronter is assertive, she (let's say) is fully recognizing all aspects of experience. She accepts her affect and utilizes her cognition executing her confrontational behavior, all of which is supported by and consistent with the sense-physical situation. Also, her behavior is evaluated as right, though she may feel some fear or nervousness in confronting the other. Now let's say that the confrontee reacts to the confrontation in a predominantly "rational" or cognitive manner, de-emphasizing or not even recognizing his (let's say) affect. This type of thing often occurs in business situations where the confrontee is in a position of power and doesn't have to deal or grapple with the truth of the confronter's confrontation. The interaction could be represented thus:
cognition: "I'm upset over your criticizing me in front of my peers"

```
affect    : resentment
behavior  : verbal confrontation
sense     : confrontee, room
environ   : room
"I"       : ownership
```
The confrontee responds thus:
```
cognition : "What I said needed to be said"
affect    : resentment, duty (to act appropriately or professionally)
behavior  : controlled verbal response, modulated voice, controlled
            body posture
sense     : confronter, room
environ   : room
"I"       : ownership
```
The confrontee feels resentment over being "challenged" by the confronter, but he doesn't express this resentment clearly in his behavior. Rather, his behavior expresses the combined affect of resentment and duty, though only duty is recognized or evaluated by him (when he self-reflects). In fact, he may not even recognize the duty he feels. He may evaluate his behavior as professional and hence appropriate and his cognition:behavior as wholly right, while de-emphasizing or even implicitly denying the existence of the duty which supports and instills them with meaning and importance. In other words the affect of duty is not given its full place in experience; it is cognitivized in that the confrontee's self-evaluation consists nearly exclusively of his cognition:behavior, which he evaluates as professional. Now how the process of experience would determine the experiential state-of-affairs in this situation depends in part upon the empirico-phenomenal situation. How is the confronter related to the confrontee? Employer-employee? Wife-husband? Co-worker-co-worker? Peer-peer? How is the power between them distributed? If the power is relatively equal, that is, if the continuation of the relationship is mutually needed or desired, then the process of experience is likely to resolve itself in mutual agreement. And this agreement will be reached at the deepest level possible, i.e. at the **identity-experience level**.

SOCRATES: You've brought up lots of ideas here that require explication.

MASSAGE THERAPIST: Yes.

SOCRATES: First, if the power between the interactors is relatively equally distributed, and each seeks or needs the continuation of the

relationship, then the confrontee will not use his power to rid himself "completely" of the challenge that the confronter poses with her confrontation.
MASSAGE THERAPIST: Yes.
SOCRATES: But the confrontation will disturb him.
MASSAGE THERAPIST: Yes. He may cognitivize or intellectualize the disturbing affect, but this does not mean that the affect is gone or that it has lost its strength.
SOCRATES: It's "covered up".
MASSAGE THERAPIST: A way of putting it, yes. Another way is that it is not recognized for what it is.
SOCRATES: So the confrontee is "caught" between wanting or needing to continue the relationship and wanting or needing to dispel this confrontation and affirm the rightness of his experience.
MASSAGE THERAPIST: Yes. So he may walk away from her, leave her presence for awhile, argue with her, etc. These behaviors may continue until the confronter has had enough. Her confrontation serves the purpose of realizing her full experiential being in relation to the confrontee resulting in temporary satisfaction, but the satisfaction is unilateral, not mutual, and transitory, not permanent. The unacceptable behavior arises again and again, and more confrontations are made, resulting in temporary, unilateral satisfaction. The **effective level of satisfaction** has not yet been reached. And it may take the confrontee's dissolving the relationship before the effective level of satisfaction is reached. That is, it may take the dissolution of the relationship before the confrontee realizes the full composition of the affect that constitutes his experience, to grapple with this realization, and to achieve a new level of identity-experience.
SOCRATES: But whether this realization comes within the relationship or after the relationship dissolves, it is likely to occur.
MASSAGE THERAPIST: I'd say it is much more likely to occur in relationships of equal power than in relationships of unequal power, but whether it is more likely to occur or not to occur between equal power interactors, I cannot say. That seems to depend upon who each member is in these situations and how their situations effect each of them. Some people engage in a series of marriages, for instance, in which behavior patterns are repeated *ad nauseum*.
SOCRATES: The characters change but the program stays the same.
MASSAGE THERAPIST: Exactly.

SOCRATES: But in unequal power situations, only "some" of the characters change. Those in positions of power who use their power to rid themselves of those who assertively confront them, and hence challenge their identities and/or experienced absolutes, remain relatively unscathed. Not only are they not necessarily in a position to grapple with the confrontation, but they actively misunderstand and distort the assertive state-of-affairs and act "consistently" with their misunderstandings to rid themselves of the problem, e.g. by firing the "insubordinate" employee.

MASSAGE THERAPIST: In relationships of equal power, or near-equal power, e.g. a "democratic" marriage, where both husband and wife engage in assertive confrontations, grapple with these confrontations, and reach mutually agreeable solutions or resolutions, some objective state-of-affairs is determined.

MASSAGE THERAPIST: Optimally, yes.

SOCRATES: Not every mutually agreeable determination results in an objective state-of-affairs.

MASSAGE THERAPIST: No. There are instances where both interactors distort the state-of-affairs and "accept" mutually acceptable distortions.

SOCRATES: They agree to "live a lie".

MASSAGE THERAPIST: Probably without even recognizing the "lie" aspect of it. Rather, they will tend to evaluate their resolution-experience as right and fulfilling (satisfying), but such evaluation-experiences are themselves complex, i.e. a mixture of experiential components that are only partially recognized for what they are.

SOCRATES: Then those who reach mutually acceptable resolutions that reflect objective experiential states-of-affair must, it seems to me, recognize all aspects of their experience, i.e. all experiential components, for what they are.

MASSAGE THERAPIST: At least functionally, yes.

SOCRATES: Functionally?

MASSAGE THERAPIST: Their resolutions might contain some unsure, unclear, or doubtful aspects, but these aspects are not significant enough to prevent the resolution from obtaining and being satisfying. The resolution is acceptable and forthcoming behavior will attest to that acceptability, i.e. it will be consistent with it.

SOCRATES: But if the resolution-experiences are only functionally acceptable, then could you still maintain that the interactors' experience is an actual determination of the experiential state-of-affairs?

17. Phases of Determinations of Experiential States-of-affair

MASSAGE THERAPIST: I think so, yes. I believe I can legitimately divide **determinations of experiential states-of-affair** into three phases. Phase one is the **pre-functionally acceptable phase** where evaluation-experiences are intra- and inter-experientially consistent enough to prompt the continuing experiences to be based on their acceptance. Phase two is the **acceptable phase** where evaluation-experiences are intra- and inter-experientially consistent and consist of no discernible conflict and, continuing experience is based on the *assumed* or *nearly assumed rightness* of the experience. Phase three is the **post-functionally acceptable phase** where evaluation-experiences are, like at the pre-functional phase, consistent enough to prompt the continuing experiences to be based on their acceptance but not consistent enough to be assumed or intuited. At this phase the rightness of the evaluation-experiences is lessening in strength, doubt is "seeping in", boredom may be componentialized more often, and strong satisfaction is weakening.

SOCRATES: So long as the determinations fall within one of these phases of acceptability, they will correspond to or "match" the experiential state-of-affairs.

MASSAGE THERAPIST: Yes.

SOCRATES: But how would you deal with situations where "functional acceptability" is achieved, only to be overridden by the power of desire? Let's say that a married man is attracted to a woman who is overt in her sexual interest in him. She let's him know through body behavior and even verbally that she wants a sexual encounter with him. During one of their interactions she kisses him. He tenses a bit and pulls away slightly. He is both attracted and repelled simultaneously. He realizes that he shouldn't continue this, and what he has done in kissing her or allowing her to kiss him is going too far. He experiences his judgment-experiences in reference to his behavior of kissing the woman *and* his course of action of discontinuing the intimacy with the woman as *functionally right*. He may experience a slight confusion or ambivalence over his determination, but it is not enough to alter his experience. But the woman doesn't "read the signs" of his withdrawal, or she doesn't really care if he is having an "attack of conscience"; she wants him. So she kisses him again, this time with more passion than before, adding to it various other erotic behaviors. So much for the "functional rightness" of his prior determinations. Our man succumbs to the lustful passion

MASSAGE THERAPIST: An interesting scenario, Socrates, but I need some explication before I can comment upon it. First off, what do you understand to be the objective experiential state-of-affairs, and what is the judgment-experience that "matches" or corresponds to this state-of-affairs?

SOCRATES: Well, the experiential state-of-affairs is the actual componential structure and dynamics of the kissing-experience, and the judgment-experience is the experiential determination of the rightness:wrongness of the act.

MASSAGE THERAPIST: By rightness:wrongness do you mean moral or experiential?

SOCRATES: Moral.

MASSAGE THERAPIST: Problem. If rightness:wrongness is experiential, and the moral is subsumed under or constitutive of the experiential, then we're thinking similarly. But if not, then we're not thinking similarly.

SOCRATES: Could you elaborate, please?

MASSAGE THERAPIST: Yes. When I use the term rightness:wrongness, I refer to the evaluative aspect of a given set of components of consciousness or between sets of components and not necessarily to the morality of a given act. The componential structure of the individual (analyzed) experiences is consistent in that each component supports the other (intra-experientially consistent); and the relationship between individual experiences or sets of components of consciousness is consistent (inter-experientially consistent), i.e. there is no significant conflict or contradiction between experiences. If inconsistency, for whatever reason, does arise, it is relatively quickly *worked through* (as opposed to avoided, overgeneralized, misapplied, etc.) Whether or not a given act or event is moral depends upon 1) the componential content of the experience itself, and/or 2) the **set structure** of the continuous experience. For instance, if the man in your example experiences the kissing-experience thus:

cognition: this is nice
affect   : pleasure
behavior : kissing woman
sense   : woman, environment
environ : room
"I"   : ownership

Then his experience is right.
SOCRATES: Whoa! Perhaps this is why I said rightness:wrongness was moral in nature. The man is married, and you're saying that his kissing another woman is right?
MASSAGE THERAPIST: His kissing-experience is right in that his experience consists of a cognition of "this is nice", which is consistent with his affect of pleasure, his behavior of kissing, his sensation, etc. The man's experience admits of no significant doubt as to the rightness of his behavior - *at the moment*. Now, let's say that a thought enters his mind, e.g. "is this wrong". This is accompanied by the affect of trepidation (a fear of doing wrong, morally in this example), etc. What is happening here is the surfacing of an inter-experiential contradiction or conflict.
SOCRATES: An attack of conscience.
MASSAGE THERAPIST: That is a phrase I'd like to see eliminated from moral vocabulary. It smacks of Absolutism (absolutes beyond experience), i.e. a meta-experiential construct. It implies that there exists a moral principle that transcends experience and subjects experience to it. As if the guilt aligns with the act of breaking a superhuman moral code and conscience is the human faculty that aligns with the transcendent moral code.
SOCRATES: What would you prefer I say?
MASSAGE THERAPIST: The guilt-experience occurs because of *who the man is in this situation*. He values the principle of fidelity. His identity is in part constituted by this value. He recognizes kissing someone other than his wife in this fashion as a breach of fidelity (he need not do so). He feels guilt in relation to this cognized breach.
SOCRATES: So he has broken his own moral code.
MASSAGE THERAPIST: Ultimately, yes.
SOCRATES: And if he doesn't value fidelity? If he considers his act perfectly moral?
MASSAGE THERAPIST: Then he, in relation to himself, has not committed an immoral act. Or he has committed an immoral act but doesn't realize it. And by this I do not mean that he has broken a transcendent moral law and isn't aware of it, but that he has evaluated his experience inaccurately. In our example his evaluation-experience of the experiential state-of-affairs of the kissing-experience is inaccurate.
SOCRATES: So there would be an aspect of the kissing-experience that he is not fully aware of or clear about.
MASSAGE THERAPIST: Yes.

SOCRATES: Like a confusion or doubt that is rendered by a mixture of pleasure and, let's say, guilt.

MASSAGE THERAPIST: Yes. His pleasure may in fact be "tainted", and he does not focalize this "taintedness"; nor does he understand that "taintedness" to be part of the relationship between pleasure and guilt.

SOCRATES: So he could commit an immoral act and yet claim that it is moral.

MASSAGE THERAPIST: As we said before, yes.

SOCRATES: This brings up a problem. If this man can commit an immoral act and not recognize the experiential components that comprise that act (experience), can he claim functional acceptance? That is, he may be slightly bothered by his kissing the woman, but the bothersomeness is so slight and unclear that he can disregard it and claim that his experience is functionally right and, hence, moral.

MASSAGE THERAPIST: That is an interesting point, Socrates. You are pushing me to distinguish between functional rightness (or functional acceptance) and the objectivity of experiential states-of-affair.

SOCRATES: Yes. How can the functional rightness of a judgment-experience be objectively accurate if the components that constitute the actual-experience to which the judgment-experience refers admit of ill-analyzed or ill-recognized aspects?

MASSAGE THERAPIST: Let me clarify the problem first and then I'll try to address it within the experientialist perspective so far developed. The **actual-experience** (in our example the kissing-experience) consists of objective experiential components. In some instances these components will not be recognized for what they are. Judgment-experiences, of the experiencer or others, are also composed of objective experiential components, and these components refer directly to the actual-experience. Each type of experience is inherently evaluative, right:wrong, or acceptable:non-acceptable. Each type is either intuitively or functionally right:wrong. You're saying to me: If an actual-experience consists of a complex combination of components (e.g. a mixture), and this complexity is, basically, not recognized for what it is, i.e. it is understood by the experiencer as simple and straightforward, then the experience that serves as judgment of the actual-experience and is functionally right, is actually *not* functionally right. The functional rightness of the judgment-experience is illusory.

SOCRATES: Yes, I believe you've stated the problem accurately.

MASSAGE THERAPIST: It seems I've also addressed the problem, too. Analytically, let's say that the actual experience is rendered thus:

cognition: we are kissing (understood)
affect   : exhilaration
behavior : kissing, adrenaline pump
sense   : woman's lips
environ : room
"I"   : ownership
And:
cognition: I shouldn't be doing this
affect   : duty
behavior : self-conscious kissing
sense   : woman's lips
environ : room
"I"   : ownership

These are the two experiences that are being mixed, rendering this complex actual-experience:
cognition: this is nice
affect   : uncomfortable pleasure
behavior : kissing
sense   : woman's lips
environ : room
"I"   : ownership

Subsequently we reflect upon this experience and judge it. This judgment-experience can be rendered thus:
cognition: this (kissing) is right, good
affect   : uneasy confidence
behavior : somewhat reserved kissing behavior
sense   : woman's lips, etc.
environ : room
"I"   : ownership

The two experiences that combine to form the complex actual-experience exist as objective, experiential sets of components of consciousness. Each set (experience) is characterized by rightness: wrongness. The first experience (i.e. exhilaration-experience) is intra-experientially consistent. The cognition, affect, sensation, and the environment of the exhilaration-experience support the behavior. Whereas the cognition and affect of the duty-experience support the behavior only inasmuch as the "self-conscious" element alters the "quality of the behavior" of the exhilaration-experience. That is, the kissing behavior is consistent with the idea and feeling of "not" behaving in this manner only inasmuch as the behavior is "self-conscious" or lessened in intensity or fullness. Evaluatively, the duty-experience is right, i.e. it is wrong for him to be kissing the woman. But these two experiences contradict or conflict with each other. Kissing this woman is both right and wrong. How is this conflict "dealt with" or "handled"; or, more accurately, how is this conflict "resolved"? Because of who this person is in this situation, the conflict "resolves" into a complex, intra-experientially inconsistent actual-experience, i.e. the uncomfortable pleasure-experience. In this experience the cognition conflicts with the uncomfortable aspect of the pleasure. The behavior also conflicts with the uncomfortable aspect of the affect. The sensation may support the uncomfortable aspect of the affect in that it is "tainted", "shallow", not full, and the environment is still conducive to the existence of the other components. The evaluative aspect of this actual-experience is one part of the problem that you've posed.

SOCRATES: Yes. What is the evaluative experiential state-of-affairs of the actual-experience? Is it right or wrong?

MASSAGE THERAPIST: I'd have to maintain that it is more "wrong" on the right:wrong evaluative scale. I will argue in this fashion: The duty-experience exists as such in focal consciousness but only momentarily. It quickly shifts to peripheral consciousness. But the shift is not "clean" or "simple", as would be a shift from looking at a chair to a picture on the wall behind the chair, where the chair "simply" recedes into the periphery of consciousness and is "clearly" replaced by the picture in focal consciousness. When duty shifts out of focal consciousness it "leaves a trail of distortion", i.e. it distorts the components of focal consciousness. This distortion registers experientially as the uncomfortable aspect of affect and the uncommitted or superficial aspect of behavior and sensation. This distortion of experiential components is equivalent to the wrongness of the experience. This wrongness exists as an experiential state-of-affairs, and it exists as an aspect of focal consciousness as well as peripheral consciousness. In our example it exists as the distortion of pleasure and peripherally as it is (duty) in relation to the affect of pleasure.

SOCRATES: And the judgment-experience?

MASSAGE THERAPIST: The judgment-experience consists of a cognitive judgment claiming the moral rightness of the act, but such a judgment is not supported by other components of consciousness. The "uneasy" aspect of the confidence felt, the reserved nature of the kissing behavior, and the somewhat dulled sensation of the woman's lips, etc. are all unsupportive of the cognition.

SOCRATES: So the judgment-experience is similar to the actual-experience in that it is complex or consists of unrecognized, mixed components.
MASSAGE THERAPIST: Yes.
SOCRATES: And, therefore, the experiential state-of-affairs of the actual-experience is not wholly determined by the judgment-experience's experiential state-of-affairs, and the man in our example is virtually "living a lie" or "deceiving himself".
MASSAGE THERAPIST: I'd say so, yes.
SOCRATES: That's all well and good, but I'm really interested in those situations when the person is overcome by desire and there exists virtually no distortions in experience. For instance, the man may be ambivalent about his sexual behavior toward the woman until, let's say, she starts having oral sex with him in an intensely erotic fashion. At this point he casts his ambivalence aside and surrenders to the power of his erotic passion.
MASSAGE THERAPIST: In such a situation we very well may not find any intra-experiential inconsistency. His ambivalence is replaced, at least momentarily, by the consistent set of components constituting his erotic-experience. This experience, being intra-experientially consistent, is, therefore, experientially right.
SOCRATES: Of what would such an experience consist?
MASSAGE THERAPIST: It could be analyzed thus:
cognition: I am yours, you are mine
affect : intense erotic pleasure
behavior : oral sex activity
sense : oral contact with penis, other external contacts, physiological sensations
environ : room
"I" : ownership
SOCRATES: Yes. And here is the problem: This erotic-experience is componentially consistent; componential consistency is equivalent to experiential rightness; therefore, the act in which he is engaged is at least experientially right. It may even be held to be intuitively right in that it is self-justifying and self-grounded. He need not consult any component of consciousness to evaluate whether or not he is acting rightly.
MASSAGE THERAPIST: Yes, I would have to agree with you.
SOCRATES: But this man happens to value fidelity, and his behavior, even from his own point of view, certainly comes under the category of

infidelity. So my question is: How can his behavior be a component of an experience that is experientially right while simultaneously being morally wrong or contrary to the experiencer's own values?

MASSAGE THERAPIST: An intriguing question, Socrates. You are certainly earning your pay today.

SOCRATES: You're not paying me, my friend.

MASSAGE THERAPIST: So I'm not.

SOCRATES: Stop avoiding the question.

18. Levels of Experiential Consistency

MASSAGE THERAPIST (laughs): Ok. As I maintained before, there are *two individual levels of experiential consistency*: 1) **intra-experiential consistency** and 2) **inter-experiential consistency**. An experience can be intra-experientially consistent only to be followed by an experience or group of experiences that conflicts with that experience. The same holds for experiences that precede the actual-experience in question. Therefore, the man could experience ambivalence prior to the erotic-experience and after the erotic-experience while experiencing no such ambivalence (or only a *functionally insignificant amount* of ambivalence) during the erotic-experience. The morality of the experience in question is not an overriding, transcendent value that can be applied to the experience simply because of the nature of the experience; rather, it is the product of the combination of experiences that pertain to the experience. Such a combination of experiences (or set-of-experiences) may consist of intra-experientially consistent experiences, compound, complex, or compound-complex experiences. Each experience possesses its own "weight", "power", or "strength", which is determined by who we are in this situation. In our example the man's **set-of-experiences** consists of those that precede and are related to the erotic-experience, the erotic-experience itself, and those that follow and are related to the erotic-experience. The morality of this set-of-experiences is constitutive of the experiences themselves inasmuch as the experiences address moral issues.

SOCRATES: Are you talking in circles?

MASSAGE THERAPIST: No. All I'm saying is that many experiences, though subject to experiential evaluation or experiential right:wrong, are not moral experiences, e.g. sensing a mundane physical object, computing a math problem, feeling happy about going out to dinner, etc. Inasmuch as the experiences address moral issues or are examples of moral issues, they are *morally evaluative*. The *moral right:wrong experience* is subsumed under the *experiential right:wrong experience*. Therefore, what is morally right or wrong is necessarily experientially right:wrong. But what is experientially right:wrong need not and often times is not morally right or wrong.

SOCRATES: So the man's experience in our example is "topically" moral, and the experiential right:wrong is the evaluative, dynamic aspect of the actual-experience (which ever one we choose to discuss) as well as of the judgment-experiences that refer to it.

MASSAGE THERAPIST: Yes. Let's use the erotic-experience (e.g. oral sex) as the actual-experience. This experience is topically moral. (Let's accept those issues that are currently generally accepted as moral issues within our society.) If this experience is experientially right (intra-experientially consistent), then it is necessarily morally right, because, as I have just contended and will support forthwith, experiential rightness subsumes moral rightness. But if this actual-experience is contradicted by experiences that situate or contextualize it, then its experiential rightness is contradicted, and, therefore, so is its moral rightness. Using our example, the experiences prior to the erotic-experience consisted of ambivalence, mixed feelings, confused thoughts, fluctuating sensations and behavioral intensities, etc. These experiences could be compound, where the ambivalence is obvious, or complex, where the ambivalence is covert, or some combination thereof. As we said before, the evaluative aspects of these experiences were collectively placed on the "wrong" side of the right:wrong scale. But simply because our man's experience is predominantly one of wrongness, that doesn't mean it will remain that way. His experience entails the person with whom he is engaged. Her body and behavior constitute much of his sensual component of consciousness (so too does his own body, behavior, and sensations). When she "escalates" the erotic intensity, his experience changes. At some point in this interaction, his experiences of ambivalence, etc. are replaced by those of intense erotic desire. The inconsistency of his componential situation is replaced by a consistent componential structure, at least momentarily, and his erotic-experience is experientially, and hence morally, right.

SOCRATES: At the moment.

MASSAGE THERAPIST: Yes. But when the guilt-experiences pour in afterwards, they contradict the experiential rightness of the erotic-experience. The judgment-experiences are experientially right in their moral condemnation of the prior erotic-experience (and even the other sexual experiences that preceded the erotic-experience); and if the moral condemnation persists and remains relatively stable in its rightness:wrongness status, then the *experience-in-general* or *set-of-experiences* is determined to be immoral.

SOCRATES: It's like a scale where right-experiences pile up on one side of the scale and wrong-experiences pile up on the other. It's a matter of which side outweighs the other as to whether or not the experience (or as I like to say, "act") was or is immoral?

MASSAGE THERAPIST: Not quite. Though **quantity of experiences** does figure into moral determinations, it is not the sole nor even the most important factor involved. For instance, a man who does not value fidelity and who disingenuously pledges fidelity to his wife, may engage in numerous affairs without any significant guilt or compunction. He is "piling up" a lot of "right" experiences. And then his wife finds out and is terribly hurt. He then realizes how his sexual activities and subsequent cover-ups have caused great pain to someone he has at least overtly committed himself to and actually loves. The pain of realization is intense; the cognition of wrongness of the acts is clear and certain. This single (or near single) experience is sufficient for him to determine the morality of the act. And subsequent confirmation-experiences serve to support this determination even more, though such support is hardly necessary to make the determination.

SOCRATES: So it is the **quality of experience** that determines the moral rightness or wrongness of an experience (act, event, etc.)?

MASSAGE THERAPIST: Yes, primarily. But the quantity of experience is also important in such determinations. For instance, in our example, the man's erotic-experience is right or comparatively consistent, and, let's say, he experiences rightness in relation to his subsequent erotic experience up to and for a time after intercourse with the woman. Subsequently, he begins to experience guilt pangs over his act. He explains away the pangs and busies himself with other things. But the pangs will not go away. The pangs may not increase significantly, but the sheer number of them has a significant effect upon the man.

SOCRATES: Somewhat like children. Their behavior might not intensify over time, but the sheer number of like behaviors can significantly get on a parent's "nerves".

MASSAGE THERAPIST: Yes, I'd say that's a good analogy.

SOCRATES: Though quantity of experience could be an important factor in the determination of the morality of an experience, act, event, etc., it is the quality of experience that is critical.

MASSAGE THERAPIST: Yes.

SOCRATES: And of what does the quality consist? How do we distinguish one type of quality from another, or is quality "homogeneous", a "quantum", a "given wholeness"?

MASSAGE THERAPIST: Quality is a function of sets of components of consciousness *in relation* to other sets of components of consciousness. I've argued so far that each set of components of consciousness (i.e. experience) is inherently evaluative (i.e. experientially right:wrong). I've also used the phrase "strength of experience" to refer to a characteristic of experience. Now I'd like to associate the **strength of experience** with the **evaluative aspect of experience** and to further describe this aspect as necessarily related to other sets of components of consciousness. How strong an experience is is intimately related to the experience's componential structure, but it is not determined by it. In moral experiences, consistent componential and inter-experiential structures can determine experiential and moral rightness:wrongness, and this determination will "rule out" or "override" other componential structures and, hence, other moral determinations. The "strength" of the moral determination is manifested in its relationship to other determinations, i.e. the strongest determination persists with *functional consistency over time*. That is, there may occur "set backs", doubts, or insecurities as to the rightness:wrongness of the determination, but overall the determination (evaluative experience) will maintain its domination. Therefore, quality of experience is equivalent, in moral issues, to the strength of experience.

19. The Process of Morality

SOCRATES: One obvious problem arises from what you are maintaining so far. The relativistic quality of your argument is so glaring to me that I have to address it outright. The man in our example is married; he accepts fidelity as a value; he transgresses his own value (and the social moral law/code) by engaging in adulterous sex; and yet his erotic sexuality is morally right?! Are you saying that his sexual activity is morally right at one time and wrong at all the other times throughout the set-of-experience? How can this be?

MASSAGE THERAPIST: I think your perplexity stems from the Absolutist framework that you keep slipping into. The sexual "act" or "behavior" is, first of all, a component of experience. It is not a separate "thing" or "phenomenon" that we can somehow abstract from its experiential grounding and attach a moral determination to. This is Absolutist thinking. Each "act" or "behavior" that we analyze experientially is necessarily related to an affect, cognition, sensation, and physical environment. So each experience will consist of its own set of components of consciousness. It is the components of consciousness as owned [by us] which are related to each other and "arranged" into sets of components (experiences) that are related to each other that determine morality. Morality is an evaluative *process* which "rests" for lengths of time sufficient to allow it to be determined or objectivized, e.g. personally valued, socially codified, etc. We determine moral issues through experience, i.e. our experience determines the characteristics of our experience.

SOCRATES: Are you saying that experiences that are morally related to each other are "arranged" into a set of experiences, and that individual experiences that constitute the set can consist of componential structures that contradict each other, while proceeding to some relatively stable moral determination?

MASSAGE THERAPIST: Yes! You've summarized what I'm trying to say very well, Socrates!

SOCRATES: So within the experiential point of view, moral experiences can contradict each other without causing any serious logical problem.

MASSAGE THERAPIST: Yes. One or several morally right experiences within a set of related experiences does not necessarily determine the morality of the *entire set* or the *set-in-general*.

SOCRATES: But how can the erotic-experience, i.e. the most immoral aspect of this sequence of experiences, be moral?

MASSAGE THERAPIST: It is the most immoral aspect of the set-of-experiences only if it is based within an Absolutist framework. If you assume a transcendent morality, understand moral behavior as *acts of will*, and judge physical pleasure to be sinful or bad, then the erotic-experience is judged as immoral. But if you reject a transcendent morality as a meta-experiential construct, accept the a-causality of volitional experience (and, hence, volitional behavior), and accept that sexual pleasure is desirable based on overwhelming experiential evidence, then you can see how the intensely erotic experience(s) within a set of experiences can be considered moral even when the experience in general is immoral.

SOCRATES: My friend, I realize that you have already explained your use of meta-experiential construct, a-causality, and will, and the "naturalness" of attraction, but I really need to hear how you apply these ideas to morality as we're discussing it now, because I'm having a devil of a time allowing you even an ounce of credibility when your point of view seems so counter-intuitive to me.

MASSAGE THERAPIST: I'll gladly oblige, but I'll be as succinct as possible.

SOCRATES: Fine.

MASSAGE THERAPIST: Any moral code that is propounded, understood, and accepted as a code that transcends experience is a meta-experiential construct, i.e. it has no basis in experience and, hence, is inconsequential in regard to human affairs. The Ten Commandments of the Judeo-Christian tradition, *as traditionally conceived*, is an example of such a construct. Like I explained the other week (Blahnik, 1997), scientific laws of nature, rational laws of logic, and religious conceptions of God are all meta-experiential constructs inasmuch as they claim to be realities beyond experience that may actually create and determine experience itself without the explicit realization that such realities are aspects of experience itself. Scientific laws as **experiential constructs** addressing empirical experiences, laws of logic as experiential constructs addressing rational experiences, and God as an experiential construct addressing religious (and moral) experiences are all firmly grounded in experience, but it is experience that determines their nature and not the reverse; and it is experience that determines whether or not and how they determine experience itself. They can be misunderstood to be Absolute determiners of experience, claiming that "this" is right and "that" is wrong, despite what experience may dictate. If the man in our example experiences his intensely erotic-experience as right at the time his experience occurs, then within the *traditional moral framework*, he is simply wrong, because the experience contradicts the moral law against adultery. But experience dictates otherwise, at least in this example. If we were to isolate the man's experience to include only those intensely erotic experiences, and eliminate all the other experiences, we would be left with a perfectly consistent set of intra-experiential components and a perfectly or near-perfectly consistent set of experiences. There would be virtually no factors constituting the experiences that inhibit the experiences from obtaining. The man's experience may consist of:

cognition: I am yours; you are mine
affect   : intense erotic pleasure
behavior: oral sexual activity
sense   : oral contact with penis, etc.
environ : room
"I"   : ownership

Or:

cognition: I am yours; you are mine
affect   : intense erotic pleasure
behavior: sexual intercourse
sense   : penile-vaginal sensations, etc.
environ : room
"I"   : ownership

In neither of these experiences is there any inhibiting factor, i.e. no thought, feeling, sensation, or aspect of the environment that conflicts with the behavior occurring. There is no thought of wife or family, a thought which may be accompanied by the feeling of guilt and the behavior and sensation of greatly decreased intensity. There is no thought of "is this wrong". There is no feeling of guilt and no mixture of feelings. There are no significantly uncomfortable sensations, and there is nothing happening in the environment that disturbs the event. I contend that if such a componential structure occurs, it is experientially right, by definition. If the experience is characterized as fully within the category of morality, then it is morally right. Such an experience may help explain why people engage in intensely erotic acts even when they would consider these acts immoral.

SOCRATES: Because they raise themselves above their own immorality, if only for a moment? Oh, come on, my friend. I've heard some ridiculous things in my time, but this sounds like a very misguided rationalization or excuse for immorality.

MASSAGE THERAPIST: Not at all. The entire experience or the experience in general, at least in our example, is morally wrong because the **determining experiences** are qualitatively ones of wrongness. But when our man is "one with himself" by being "one with another", when all doubts, conflicts, mixed emotions, cognitive confusions, and self-recriminations are dispelled, i.e. when his behavior is in perfect (or near-perfect) accord with his cognition, affect, sensations, and the physical environment, his immediate experience is experientially and, hence, morally right. It is one experiential being desiring another experiential being without doubt, hesitation, or distortion. But this momentary rightness does not exonerate, excuse, or justify his overall behavior; it does lend an element of rightness to the experience in general, but the experience in general may be morally wrong.

SOCRATES: I understand what you're saying, but I have great difficulty accepting it intuitively; it contradicts my sense of logic which dictates that an act is either right or wrong. If this man's sexual behavior in relation to this woman is immoral, even if we accept your method of determining morality (as so far developed), and the erotic-experiences are examples of his sexual behavior, then it follows that the erotic-experiences are immoral as well.

MASSAGE THERAPIST: As I argued last week, logic is a type of experience; it "conditions" experience only inasmuch as experience conditions itself. Your experience of syllogistic logic as applied to this situation is only one logical way of experiencing this situation. Now, if you look at it using a part-whole or subset-set logic, you might experience a different intuitive slant on the situation. Analogously, the body may be riddled with cancer, while the heart is functioning perfectly. The part of the whole is "right", whereas the whole in general is "wrong". The whole is diseased while the part is functionally healthy. So too with our example: the experience as a whole (i.e. set-of-experiences) is "diseased" or immoral, whereas the intense erotic experience is functionally healthy or right. I maintain that not only is this logic applicable to our example, it is more accurate in its application than is your syllogistic logic. Let me explain.

SOCRATES: Please do.

MASSAGE THERAPIST: Your use of the word "act" must be "translated" into the experiential framework. Experientially, an "act" is either a behavioral component of experience or a set or series of interrelated experiences. So if you mean by "act" the series of sexual behaviors that starts with the first kiss (or possibly before that) and ends in the "after play" after sexual intercourse (let's say), then your understanding of "act" corresponds better with the *set-of-experiences* idea then it does to the *component of experience* idea.

SOCRATES: Yes.

MASSAGE THERAPIST: A set-of-experiences is by definition an interrelated combination of individual experiences. These experiences may be non-reflective or self-reflective (or simply "reflective", but we need not concern ourselves with this type of experience here). They may be focally cognitive, affective, behavioral, or sense-physical. They are always constituted by cognition, affect, behavior, sensation, the physical environment, and the "I", and they are always evaluative Also, when they are in a moral context, they are moral. The experiences (up to this point) are either simple in their structure (i.e. all components are consistent with each other), or they are complex (mixed components). Some experiences are primarily simple but complicated due to their compound relationship to other experiences. We'll discuss this later. If they are simple, they are evaluatively right, just like the heart, if considered individually, is functionally healthy. If they are complex, then they are evaluatively wrong. Experientially, individual experiences are not isolable, except for analytic purposes; they are inextricably connected to other individual experiences. Sometimes the relationship between individual experiences is contradictory. These experiences are referred to as compound experiences, each possessing its own evaluative aspect and strength. If we combine all the single, compound, and complex experiences (and combinations thereof) into a topically related whole, then we have a set-of-experiences which, as a whole, is evaluative, or experientially right:wrong. My claim is that the man's set-of-experiences is experientially wrong, and when it is in conjunction with a moral issue or topic, it is immoral. If your "act" can be divided into "sub-acts" that can be morally evaluated individually, as I think you will allow, then your act is closer to the heterogeneous set-of-experiences I'm propounding then to your own homogeneous "act".

20. Acts vs. Experiences and Sets-of-Experiences

SOCRATES: Let's say that I divide my "act" into the "sub-acts" of 1) kissing, 2) refraining from kissing, 3) passionate kissing, 4) oral sex, 5) intercourse, and 6) after play (as you called it). You're saying that if I can evaluate all of these sub-acts morally and, if I understand you correctly, render different judgments of them, then my use of "act" will be similar to your use of "set-of-experiences".
MASSAGE THERAPIST: Yes.
SOCRATES: But I see all of these sub-acts as immoral. The man is married; he values fidelity; he defines kissing (in this manner), oral sex, and sexual intercourse as sexual behavior; he understands fidelity to exclude sexual behavior with a woman other than his wife. Therefore, any sub-act within the act is morally wrong.

MASSAGE THERAPIST: Is the kissing sub-act on the same moral level as the intercourse sub-act? Are they equally immoral, or is one more immoral than the other?
SOCRATES: Intuitively, I'd say they are all immoral, but the oral sex and intercourse seem to be more immoral than the kissing.
MASSAGE THERAPIST: Why is that?
SOCRATES: Because kissing is the sharing of part of one's sexual self, whereas intercourse usually involves the sharing of a much larger part of one's sexual self.
MASSAGE THERAPIST: The greater the "quantity" of one's sexual self shared immorally, the more immoral the sub-act?
SOCRATES: Generally, yes. But even more important is the depth of sharing involved. The closer one gets to sharing the "core of one's sexual self", the more sexual is the act, and the more immoral it is if the act is of a moral nature.
MASSAGE THERAPIST: I need elaboration on a few ideas you've mentioned. What's a "sexual self"? What constitutes a "quantity of the core of that self"? And finally, why is the sharing of that self immoral in our example?
SOCRATES: I'd define the sexual self as that aspect of our identity or, as you like to say, "who we are" that entails sexual interest, excitement, arousal, climax or orgasm, and "after play". I consider all other sexual thoughts, feelings, actions, and sensations to fall somewhere within this description. A "quantity of the sexual self" includes any action, feeling, and/or sensation experienced in relation to oneself, shared with another (or even with oneself). The "core of one's sexual self" refers to the most vulnerable aspect of one's sexual self, i.e. that aspect of one's thoughts, actions, feelings, and/or sensations that, if shared, opens oneself up to hurtful rejection.
MASSAGE THERAPIST: So if our married man experiences sexual interest in a woman other than his wife, as he is looking at her, he is acting immorally.
SOCRATES: Inasmuch as his interest is sexual, yes.
MASSAGE THERAPIST: Curious. How does sexual interest differ from the attraction we already accepted as "natural" and not immoral?
SOCRATES: I'm not sure I like being on this end of the questioning, my friend.
MASSAGE THERAPIST (laughs): It gets a little uncomfortable at times, doesn't it?

SOCRATES: Yes, it does. Let me make this distinction. Sexual interest involves an openness toward the next phase of sexual interaction, i.e. excitement. Such an openness may involve the pursuit of interaction with the person, whereas sexual attraction does not necessarily involve this openness to pursuit. That is, our man could be attracted to the woman, look at her, etc. but have no intention of going any further than that, no intention or interest in pursuing any sort of personal contact with her. This would be "natural" *and* moral. It is expressing his male genetic constitution. Whereas an openness to pursuing personal interaction that is sexual in nature satisfies my definition of a criterion of the sexual self.

MASSAGE THERAPIST: In truth, Socrates, I like that distinction. One says "I'm attracted to you because of the way you appear to me" and stays there, whereas the other one says "I'm attracted to you because of the way you appear to me, and I want to act upon that attraction by furthering my personal contact with you." This is what you mean?

SOCRATES: Yes. And it is this "openness to pursue personal contact" based upon sexual attraction that "opens the door to immoral behavior".

MASSAGE THERAPIST: One need not intend to have sexual intercourse with the other.

SOCRATES: No. Just an interest in or openness to pursuing personal contact.

MASSAGE THERAPIST: So the initial attraction is sexual but not immoral.

SOCRATES: Yes. Sexual but "natural", genetic.

MASSAGE THERAPIST: I think I understand. Now, let me respond from the experientialist framework I've developed so far. If the man is sexually attracted to the woman and has no interest in pursuing further personal contact with her, his experience would be represented something like:

cognition: she's very attractive
affect   : sexual attraction
behavior: looking at her for a length of time
sense   : woman
environ : classroom (let's say they are college students)
"I"   : ownership

His experience would then be replaced by, let's say, something the professor is saying. Here we have a "natural appreciation of sexuality". Whereas if the first experience were replaced by something like:
cognition: "look at me"
affect : sexual interest
behavior : staring at her
sense : woman
environ : classroom
"I" : ownership
Then our man is "open to pursuing personal (sexual) contact with her, even though this sexuality is unilateral at the moment.
SOCRATES: I'd have to say, yes. His intent is primarily sexual, and he's open to further sexual contact.
MASSAGE THERAPIST: Then he pursues his interest, discovers mutual interest, furthers contact which leads to the kiss, and we're off to the races.
SOCRATES: A crude way of putting it, but yes.
MASSAGE THERAPIST: And each "step" in this process of sexual pursuit represents an aspect or part of his sexual self.
SOCRATES: Yes.
MASSAGE THERAPIST: And the closer he comes to sharing those aspects of his sexuality that are vulnerable to rejection, the closer he reaches his sexual core.
SOCRATES: Yes.
MASSAGE THERAPIST: And this is consistent, then, with the idea that an intense erotic-experience in which one "surrenders oneself sexually" to another is the most vulnerable aspect of one's sexual self. The giving of one's core sexual self, therefore, represents the most immoral aspect of our man's immoral act.
SOCRATES: That seems to follow, yes.
MASSAGE THERAPIST: Now, from the experiential point of view: If the man values fidelity and defines it as we've already defined it, his experiences are likely to be compound and/or complex; his sexual attraction, interest, pursuit, etc. will contradict his duty and guilt and often render his experience as doubtful, confused, and anxiety-ridden. During this period he experiences little consistency between experiences and a significant amount of inconsistency between components of individual experiences. Within a moral situation this translates into a quantitatively and qualitatively immoral set-of-experiences. But it is not his actions that are immoral, as you maintain. Experientially, morality is

a function of experience; it is not a transcendent quality of behavior (or thought, affect, sensation, or the physical environment). The man's behavior is no more immoral than the room he is in or the bed upon which he "surrenders his sexual self". Rather, the man's behavior (action) is a component of experience, experience that is sometimes consistent and continuous, sometimes inconsistent and discontinuous, and sometimes (as in our example) consistent and discontinuous (which I'll explain in a minute). Your "act", therefore, is not something to evaluate morally. As an individual behavior it carries with it its own evaluative aspect. Its evaluativeness is an inherent aspect of the experience of which it is a constituent. It is not *evaluated*; rather, it is *evaluative*. "We" do not evaluate it; it already possesses its own evaluativeness. Therefore, when the man is looking at the woman and thinking "look at me", his experience is evaluative. If the components of his experience are consistent, then the experience is right, *for the moment*. It can be rendered analytically thus:

cognition: you are incredibly sexy
affect : strong sexual attraction
behavior : staring
sense : woman, especially parts of her body
environ : room
"I" : ownership

Here the strong attraction is consistent with the thought, which is consistent with the staring behavior, etc. The components are consistent; hence, the experience is right. Now suddenly he reflects upon himself staring at this woman sexually. His self-reflective experience may be rendered thus:

cognition: my sexual staring as morally wrong (understood)
affect : guilt
behavior : looking away
sense : other sensual elements in room
environ : room
"I" : ownership

Here also the components of his experience are consistent. The guilt supports his self-reflective judgment; the behavior supports both affect and cognition, etc. The experience is evaluatively right. Since I'm claiming that moral rightness is a function of experiential rightness, and that componential consistency is equivalent to experiential rightness, then both of these experiences are morally right! Both behaviors, therefore, as components of morally right experiences, are also morally right! [Note: I'm referring to componentially consistent behavior; a behavioral component need not be consistent with other components and, hence, need not be morally right, even within an individual experience.]

SOCRATES: But these experiences contradict each other.

MASSAGE THERAPIST: Inter-experientially, yes. But intra-experientially there is no contradiction. The second experience is in part peripherally composed of 1) an **identification-memory** (a peripheral cognition which links oneself with one's past experience) and 2) a rejection of the moral rightness of the past experience. But a rejection of a previous right-experience is not contradictory "in itself"; this experience has its own consistency; it is, if you will, a *positive negation of the rightness of an experience*. It is *between experiences* where the contradiction lies. This argues for a **consistent-discontinuous-consistent** model of experience where two consistent experiences are linked discontinuously. The consistency between experiences is broken but the experiences are still linked, forming a discontinuous overall pattern or bond.

SOCRATES: What you're saying, if I understand you correctly, is that there are levels of experience in the process of determining morality: 1) the intra-experiential level, and 2) the inter-experiential level. Intra-experientially consistent experiences that are evaluatively right can be linked to other intra-experientially consistent experiences that are also evaluatively right but consisting of a content that is opposite, in some fundamental way, of the experience that it is linked to.

MASSAGE THERAPIST: Yes.

SOCRATES: Can you elaborate more on the relationship between these two levels of experience and how they determine the moral rightness:wrongness of a given situation?

MASSAGE THERAPIST: Yes. Our man's experience shifts from a non-reflective, intra-experientially consistent attraction-experience to a self-relfective, intra-experientially consistent guilt-experience. Each experience possesses its own evaluative strength. If the second experience were consistent with the first, it would be a confirming-experience, i.e. it would confirm the rightness of the first experience and the evaluative strength of the set-of-experiences would increase. Two experiences that are *topically linked* but contradictory form a **discontinuous inter-experiential bond** consisting of two **intra-experientially consistent experiences**, each possessing its own individual strength. Two experiences that are topically linked and consistent with each other form a **continuous inter-experiential bond**, each experience possessing its own evaluative-aspect as well as its own strength. The **evaluative-aspect of an experience** is equivalent to its componential structure. Simple and consistent componential structure is equivalent to experiential rightness. **Intuitive experience** is the "purest" form of experiential rightness. **Functionally acceptable experience** is the "next best thing" to intuitive experience. Componentially simple, consistent, and intuitive experiences that are consistently linked to each other form the basic **process unit of experience** determining the morality of a situation. The individual experiences constituting the bond are the basic **content units of experience** determining the morality of a situation. The **strength of an experience** is in part determined by the evaluative-aspect of the experience in that componentially simple, consistent, and intuitive experiences are generally, if not always, stronger than componentially complex, inconsistent, and contingent experiences. The strength of an experience is also determined by the **integrity of the experience**, or the maintaining of its componential structure through time, the **persistence of the experience**, or the recurrent aspect of the experience, and the **motivational power of the experience,** or its capacity to prompt other experiences, sets-of-experiences, groups of experiences, etc. An experience with strong motivational power will tend to exhibit a good deal of integrity and persistence, but it need not always do so. For instance, our man's erotic-experiences are preceded by very strong motivational-experiences, strong enough to prompt the replacement of all duty, guilt, doubt, and confusion with clarity, certainty, and sexual desire. But the integrity of this experience may be short-lived and its persistence weak. The man may be overwhelmed with remorse afterward, confess to his wife, work through any problems he is having in his marriage, and never experience such an experience (with another woman) again. Contrariwise, the experience may possess considerable integrity where the man engages in unbounded passion and seeks ways to extend or prolong that passion as it is occurring as well as engage in such experiences as often as possible. Now, applying these ideas to our example: prior to his "surrendering to sexual desire" or experiencing clear and certain sexual desire, his experience is ambivalent. His duty-experience (i.e. "I shouldn't do this") may be simple and evaluatively right or complex and some combination or ratio of right:wrong. That is, his duty-experience may be obviously ambivalent when contiguous to his desire-experience, and his behavior may be visibly vacillating between doing and restraining; or his cognition may be confused, his feelings mixed, and his behavior superficial. His desire-experience may also be simple, (e.g. his initial attraction-experience is simple, non-reflective sexual attraction) or complex (e.g. his duty may mix with his desire producing anxiety or, cognitively, his "shouldn't" thought mixes with his "should" thought provoking confusion). Now let's say that the duty-experiences are evaluatively equivalent to the desire-experiences, each constituted, roughly of equal "amounts" of simplicity:complexity and roughly equal strengths. Such a situation may sustain itself for awhile, maintaining a balanced intensity, and eventually become satiated and terminate; the two will stop their sexual interaction and move in different directions, or the interaction could intensify, prompting oral sex and intercourse. The direction of the interaction is a function of experience.

SOCRATES: He simply doesn't choose or decide to intensify the interaction.

MASSAGE THERAPIST: No. He cannot extract himself from his conflicting experience and "rationally" decide to intensify or increase the motivational power of the duty or sexual desire he feels. He can only experience other duty or desire experiences as possessing a certain level of intensity in relation to each other. So when the woman, whose experience interacts with and includes aspects of the man's experience, intensifies the sexual interaction by, let's say, removing the man's clothing, and kissing and caressing his body as she moves toward his genitals, the man experiences new sets of components of consciousness. Let's say that as the sexual interaction intensifies, his experience consists of:

cognition: she wants me
affect : sexual desire
behavior : watching her act
sense : bodily excitation, sensing woman's body, and his own body
environ : room
"I" : ownership

And:
cognition: "I can't do this"
affect : superficial duty
behavior : slight resistance
sense : bodily excitation, etc., slightly altered
environ : room
"I" : ownership

At this point he experiences a superficial duty, which has replaced a stronger, more integrated duty. He does not choose this replacement; it occurs given who he is in this situation and as a response to the woman's intensified sexual behavior. When she intensifies her sexual behavior, his experience is one of increased desire. He does not choose for this to happen either. Rather, "he" is such that, given this situation, he cognizes the woman's behavior as "wanting him", which co-exists with increased sexual desire, "cooperative" behavior, etc. He doesn't choose to think that the woman wants him, as if he had a "menu of thoughts" from which to select and apply to his situation; he simply thinks it. Nor does he choose to feel increased sexual desire; this is a consistent co-existent with the thought. Nor does he choose to act "cooperatively", as if he had a "menu of behaviors" from which to select and apply to this situation; he simply acts consistently with how he thinks and feels. Lastly, he does not choose for his sensations to be as powerful or intense as they are; they simply are that intense; they are consistent with the other components of consciousness and are expressions of who he is in this situation.

SOCRATES: In other words the strength of the man's desire-experiences is not the product of free will or rational choice. Nor can he apply free will or reason to the experiences in order to influence or control them.

21. Reason, Will, and the Process of Morality

MASSAGE THERAPIST: As I said before but need to further develop within the context of this example, free will and reason are not faculties; they are not human capacities that can be manipulated, developed, or perfected by an independent self. Viewed as such, they are meta-experiential constructs. I've discussed free will to some existent already, so I will limit my discussion of it here. But I've only touched on reason up till now, so I will develop this idea at some length and then show its connection to the **process of morality**. If our man never conceives a duty-thought, never feels duty in relation to his situation, never experiences the sensuously dulling effect of self-reflection or guilt, and never engages in superficial or uncommitted behavior throughout the course of this sexual situation, then there is no experiential evidence of reason "being employed". This behavior within this situation is as much a "matter of course" as is the behavior of reading a good book. He wants to have sex just like he wants to read a good book. He entertains no alternative courses of action. But when he conceives the cognition, "I shouldn't be doing this", he, in effect, is conceiving an alternative course of action, i.e. to stop doing what he is doing. At this point the traditional "free willist" and "reasonist" will argue thus: the man has a choice to continue kissing the woman or to stop kissing her altogether. He "considers" his courses of action and "judges" which course of action is proper, moral, or right. This considering, or reflective process of weighing the rightness of one course of action in relation to another, is, essentially, the implementation of the faculty of reason, at least in regard to moral issues. The more one is able to reflect in this way, the more developed is one's faculty of reason, the less one is subject to the power of one's desires.

SOCRATES: Yes, this is how I tend to understand reason in relation to moral issues.

MASSAGE THERAPIST: The experientialist perspective that we're developing here rejects the notion of a "faculty of reason". Experientially, reason is a concept that refers to specific sets of experiences. It is composed of these experiences; hence, it is composed of sets of components of consciousness. If our man never experienced any possible course of action other than the one he engages in, he would not be attributed the faculty of reason; he would be virtually no different from an animal that was driven by instinct. But once he conceives an alternative course of action, one different from the one he is engaged in, he is said to be capable of reasoning. Which course of action should he take: continue or stop (our example). Experientially, I've already argued that the "I" cannot possibly remove itself from experience in order to "decide" which course of action to take. The very process of deciding *is* the interaction between individual and sets of components of consciousness as owned and not the result of the use of a faculty of reason. Analytically, it breaks down like this:

cognition: we are kissing
affect   : exhilaration
behavior : kissing, adrenaline pump
sense   : woman's lips
environ : room
"I"   : ownership

This is a self-reflective experience where the "we", which includes the "I", is cognitivized (or componentialized) and inextricably related to (and focally co-constitutive of) the act of kissing. The cognitive constituents are: "we" (which includes the "I") and "are kissing" (which is an understanding of the behavior being performed in relation to another). At this point there exists no alternative course of action in consciousness, just the action that is occurring. The affect of exhilaration fully supports the cognition; it is thrilling to this man that this is happening. His kissing behavior is what is occurring; he is not judging it as wrong or possibly wrong at this moment; he is merely performing it. He senses the woman's lips, her odor, other areas of her body, and the environment situating her (and him). All components are consistent with each other. The experience is evaluatively right (intuitively or functionally) and its strength has yet to be determined.

SOCRATES: Why has its strength yet to be determined?

MASSAGE THERAPIST: Because we don't know 1) how long it will sustain its componential structure (integrity), 2) whether or not it will recur at some point, or 3) whether or not it will prompt another experience (motivational power).

SOCRATES: So the strength of an experience, though a constituent of the experience, is inaccessible to analysis until it is "limited" or "changed" by another experience.

MASSAGE THERAPIST: I think that is accurate, yes. There is an inter-experiential aspect in determining the strength of an experience. Though the evaluative rightness:wrongness consists of intra-experiential consistency and is relatively isolable from other experiences, the strength of the experience requires other experiences to determine what it is. This is consistent with what I argued before about the empirical indeterminacy of thresholds of action. Just as we cannot determine the threshold for action or the componential structure of a **prompting experience** until after the fact, i.e. after the experience changes, so too can we not determine the strength of an experience until the experience changes, and even then, because of the persistence criterion, we may not be able to satisfactorily determine the experience's strength. It is this inter-experiential characteristic of experience, along with the intra-experiential componential structure, that ultimately determines the morality of a given set-of-experiences or "moral issue".

SOCRATES: Please continue. How does it do that?

MASSAGE THERAPIST: Though the initial-experience (i.e. the exhilaration-experience) is evaluatively right, its morality has not yet been determined. The experience itself is morally right because 1) it is a moral issue and 2) it is experientially right and morality is a function of experience, but the set-of-experiences, which corresponds to the "moral issue" in question, is morally undetermined.

SOCRATES: A "moral issue" is different from a moral experience in that it is a "combination of moral experiences", where each experience that composes that combination, or set-of-experiences, possesses its own strength but only in relation to the other issue-related or topically-related experiences.
MASSAGE THERAPIST: Succinctly put.
SOCRATES: And, as you've already mentioned, the number of the right vs. wrong experiences alone does not determine the morality of the issue; rather, the quantity plus the quality of the experiences, giving more sway to the quality, will determine this. And the quality includes the evaluative-aspect as well as the strength of the experience.
MASSAGE THERAPIST: Accurate once again.
SOCRATES: Go on with the analysis.
MASSAGE THERAPIST: The strength of our man's experience is in part determined by the contiguous-experience replacing or "ultimately" influencing or distorting the initial-experience. In our example the initial-experience is followed by:
cognition: I shouldn't be doing this
affect   : duty
behavior : superficial kissing
sense   : woman's lips (dulled)
environ : room
"I"   : ownership
This is a self-reflective experience where the "I" is componentialized and focalized along with the cognition "shouldn't be doing this"; the guilt felt (if any) is associated with the cognition (recognition) of having done (doing) something morally wrong, the duty with an alternative course of action yet to occur. They combine to support the cognition or judgment. The behavior is consistent with the affect(s) and cognition in that it is superficial rather than committed as it was just previously; it has become tentative, hesitant. Such a superficiality can often be recognized by the partner as a "distancing", a "pulling away", a loss of intensity or interest. But it is also inconsistent because it is being judged as wrong while continuing to exist. The degree to which the consistency and inconsistency balance each other is the degree to which the experience is intra-experientially consistent. The man is not ready to stop what he is doing; nor is he ready to surrender himself to his passion; so he is superficial. The dulled sensation of the woman's lips, body, etc. also supports the other components, yet conflicts with them simultaneously in a way similar to that of the behavioral component. In

other words this experience is primarily simple and at least functionally right. This experience also possesses a strength of its own, i.e. an integrity, persistence, and motivational power. But it contradicts or conflicts with the initial-experience. The initial-experience affirms, relatively, the entire behavioral component; the contiguous-experience affirms only a part of it. But the contiguous-experience exists in conjunction with the initial-experience. The initial experience doesn't appear when the contiguous-experience occurs. Rather, it recedes into the periphery of consciousness, exerting its influence upon the contiguous-experience. Desire still exists and, depending upon the strength of the contiguous experience, may vacillate in and out of focal consciousness. If the desire-experience (generalized exhilaration-experience) becomes focal, it may very well be influenced by the duty-experience, thus complicating the basically simple structure of the initial desire-experience.

SOCRATES: May I assume that the strength of the desire-experience is about equal to that of the duty-experience; hence, the ambivalence?

MASSAGE THERAPIST: Yes. If the duty-experience was very strong, it would prompt the immediate cessation of the kissing behavior (unless an overriding experience intervened, e.g. stopping the act would be extremely embarrassing). But since it is comparatively equal in strength, it prompts the superficial behavior instead. Importantly, at this point, which is the point where the supposed faculty of reason is activated, our man cannot extract himself from his experience in order to evaluate which course of action (go full bore or stop) he should take. He cannot magically relieve himself of his desire and duty, take a third-person perspective on them, coolly and rationally judge them, then magically jump back into his experience and act in accordance with his judgment. Any judgment he makes is itself an experience.

SOCRATES: How so?

MASSAGE THERAPIST: Let's say that his duty-experience is very strong and it prompts the cessation of his kissing behavior. The reasonist would say, "Ah, the voice of reason! He's employing his faculty of reason to make a moral decision." Experientially, the question arises: What decision? If there is only one course of action available in consciousness, then what kind of decision is being made? (We're disregarding our man's experience prior to what we've referred to as the initial-experience, so any ambivalence he may have felt is, for the purposes of our example, non-existent.) When his desire-experience occurs, he is not deciding anything; he is just thinking, feeling, acting, and sensing desirously. If he were to die instantly, there would be no question of which course of action to take; there's only one course of action. Now, if the duty-experience occurs and is very strong, prompting the total cessation of the kissing behavior, virtually completely replacing the desire-experience, then again there is only one course of action in consciousness, i.e. the cessation of kissing behavior. Our man doesn't waiver or consider whether or not he should continue or stop; he stops. No doubts, no complications, only simple, intuitive, right, strong experience replacing a simple, intuitive, right, relatively weak experience. The man doesn't magically remove himself from his desire-experience, assume a third-person perspective, and think, "I don't think this kissing is morally right, therefore, I'll experience a strong duty-experience to overcome it" and then jump back into his experience and experience the duty-experience. And this is exactly what reasonists and free willists expect us to believe. The duty-experience occurs not because the man employs his reason to realize his wrongdoing and rectify it but because of who he is in this situation. He carries with him into this experiential situation all the values, identity-forming absolutes, pre-dispositions and predilections, human limitations and needs that make him who he is. He experiences a duty-experience at this point because he is a person who values fidelity, equates sexual kissing with infidelity, and can realize what he's doing shortly after he "gets caught up in the doing of it". He doesn't choose to be self-reflective at that moment; he *is* self-reflective. He doesn't choose to feel duty (vs. something else); he feels it. He doesn't choose for the duty-experience to be strong or weak; it is strong or weak.

SOCRATES: At this point I can accept what you're saying about reason not being employed as a faculty, though I have some problems that I'll bring up later. Right now I'd like to know how reason is "not used" if our man actually conceives of an alternative course of action, i.e. stopping his kissing behavior, as opposed to giving into his desire, while his experiential state-of-affairs is somewhere in between these two alternatives. For is not the process of deciding on alternative courses of action the actual functioning of reason in moral situations?

MASSAGE THERAPIST: That is what has been referred to as reason, yes. And I have no problem with referring to this process of "reason" or "reasoning". Used this way, reason is a concept referring to an experiential process and not a faculty used by human beings. To use "reason" as a concept to refer to a faculty is to create a meta-experiential construct, i.e. in this case a cognitive entity that transcends

or conditions its own cognitivity without recognizing that it is doing so. The experiential process we call reasoning looks something like this analytically:
cognition: I shouldn't do this (I should stop)
affect　　: duty
behavior: superficial kissing
sense　　: woman's lips (dulled)
environ : room
"I"　　　: ownership
Which changes to (let's say):
cognition: she wants me
affect　　: sexual desire
behavior: surrendering behavior
sense　　: woman's hands pulling his head closer to her face
environ : room
"I"　　　: ownership
Here the woman's behavior prompts a change in experience, i.e. an increase in sexual desire, a new cognition replacing the old duty-cognition, etc. Our man doesn't choose to think, "She wants me", feel a surge of sexual desire, behave in a surrendering manner, or enjoy the sensations of the woman's hands on his head; he simply thinks, feels, behaves, and senses in this manner. Now another experience occurs (let's say):
cognition: image of wife
affect　　: very mild guilt
behavior: very slightly superficialized
sense　　: woman's hands on his head, very slightly dulled
environ : room
"I"　　　: ownership
Here a duty-experience registers in consciousness, but it is significantly decreased in strength. It registers as a "flash", then disappears, only to be replaced by a desire-experience; perhaps he pulls her head closer to him as passion escalates. What has happened here is the registering of various conflicting experiences, each possessing its own strength and evaluative-aspect. The strength of the second duty-experience (image of wife) is short-lived and relatively weak. Our man does not choose for it to be so; it simply is so. Nor does our man choose to entertain the image of his wife; he simply does so. It is this process of conflicting experiences prompting other conflicting experiences that continuously change in strength in relation to each other, resulting in one, the other,

or an intermediate course of action that experientialists refer to as reason, at least in moral situations.

SOCRATES: It seems to me, as it did in your description of free will, that reason is outside of human control. It is an experiential force in which we get "caught up in" as we would a whirlwind or rushing rapids. The experiential process directs us and we have virtually nothing to say about it. There is no "I" that decides; experience "decides" for us.

MASSAGE THERAPIST: I agree with some of what you are saying, but I have some difficulty with the way you're saying it. Reason does reduce to a process of conflicting experiences that resolves itself whether we try to direct or control it or not. For our directing or controlling experience is nothing other than our experience of directing or controlling our experience. It is, in effect, experience (direct, control) conflicting with experience (desire, habit, etc.) But not all conflicting experiences are "whirlwind-ish". Many are clear and distinct, "cut-and-dry". Most are between these two poles. The point is, reasoning, whether it is a cold, calculating or impassioned, heart-rending process, is, at base, a collection of related conflicting sets-of-experiences that, through their interaction, resolve into some sort of experience that, optimally, is evaluatively right and strong, i.e. an experience that will prompt other experiences that help form a group of experiences that form an experiential basis for one's identity.

SOCRATES: And it is this strong, evaluatively right experience that serves the function for determining what is moral and what is not?

MASSAGE THERAPIST: Yes. This experience may register in consciousness as a functionally or intuitively right experience, but regardless of where on the **functional-intuitive scale** it falls, it is definitely experienced as right. Applying this idea to our example: If the man's duty and guilt experiences begin to outweigh his desire experiences, at least qualitatively, he will reach a point where a clear and distinct resolution will occur, i.e. a direction he must go in order for him to create or be who he is. This is the *moral point of no return*. His ambivalence is reduced to a non-functional level (i.e. insignificant), and whatever doubts or "set-backs" he may have in the future will be transient and rather weak. (They may be intense at times, but the intensity has no "staying power"; it does not maintain its integrity for any significant length of time). The bulk of experiences in relation to the **resolution-experience** is confirmation-experiences which serve to support and buttress the strength and rightness of the resolution-experience.

SOCRATES: And this resolution-experience is not something we can achieve through sheer will.

MASSAGE THERAPIST: No. If we conceive of a resolution, and then act to achieve it, then the conceived resolution is one experience, and the behavior to follow is another experience (or group of experiences), all not willed.

22. Levels of Experience

SOCRATES: One major question that I had when we first started out on this aspect of our discussion dealt with what I saw to be the relativity of your position. What if our man's erotic-experience is preceded and followed predominantly by consistent experiences? That is, he feels relatively no doubt or uncertainty as to the moral rightness of his act. In fact, he considers extra-marital affairs to be his right as a male, and though overtly decried by his culture, it is covertly accepted by his friends and cohorts. Does his intra-experiential consistency, which is now supported by his inter-experiential consistency and an interpersonal consistency in relation to his "immediate" culture, make the act morally right?

MASSAGE THERAPIST: This situation is very similar to the previous situation, only at a different **level of experience**. I want to answer your question, but I will give only an outline or framework for a much more detailed answer that will, no doubt, be a subject for a future discussion. So what I have to say now may sound quite didactic; I just want you to keep in mind that you can challenge all of what I say but not now, please. It will take us too far afield if I engage your challenges at this point.

SOCRATES: Fine. I'll simply ask for clarification if needed.

MASSAGE THERAPIST: Good. Let me divide experience into the following levels: 1) individual, 2) mutual, 3) group, 4) societal, and 5) inter-societal. The **individual level of experience** refers to one person's evaluative-experience, one person's intra-experiential and inter-experiential experiences. These experiences may align with or contradict the other levels of experience. They may prove superior to the other levels (e.g. Jesus, Buddha, Ghandi) or inferior (e.g. a son's acceptance of his father's demands on his behavior though he rejects the validity of those demands). The **mutual level of experience** refers to two people's evaluative-experiences involving each other as components of experience. These experiences may align with or contradict the other levels of experience. They may prove superior to levels 3-5 (e.g. a homosexual couple's right to marry) or inferior (e.g. a homosexual couple's behavioral compliance with others' demands to keep their affectionate expressions exclusively private or not expressed at all though the homosexuals reject the validity of the demands). But these experiences must be consistent with the individual level of experience. The **group level of experience** refers to the evaluative-experiences of three or more persons forming a specifiable group (e.g. family, association, company, friends, etc.) These experiences may prove superior to levels 4 and 5 (e.g. Jesus and disciples) or inferior (Jim Jones and followers), and they may align with or contradict levels 4 and 5, but they must be consistent with levels 2 and 1. That is, concerning any given issue *directly involving the experience of another within the group,* intra- and inter-experiential consistency must also obtain on the mutual and individual levels of experience. The **societal level of experience** refers to the evaluative-experiences of *groups of groups* (i.e. societies, states, and nations that govern the interrelated activities of the groups that constitute them). These experiences may prove superior to level 5 experiences (e.g. U.S. democracy over German totalitarianism) or inferior (e.g. the reverse of U.S./German example). They may also be consistent or inconsistent with level 5 experiences, but they must be consistent with level 4-1 experiences. The **inter-societal level of experience** refers to the evaluative-experiences of interrelated societies (e.g. international organizations). These experiences must be consistent with all other levels of experience. That is, concerning any given issue *directly involving the experience of a member of the inter-societal group,* consistency of experience must obtain between societies (nations, etc.) which constitute the inter-societal group, the groups which constitute the societies, the pairs that constitute the groups, and the individuals that constitute the pairs. Now, I already mentioned that a continuous experiential bond is the relationship between related experiences that are intra-experientially consistent. It is the basic process unit of experience. It is exactly this process that underlies the formation of morality. The "initial" experience in the formation of morality is the resolution-experience. It is initial only inasmuch as it is a decision-experience-of-no-return resulting from a struggle between conflicting experiences. We need not "start" here with the construction of morality, but starting here has its heuristic value.

SOCRATES: Children may learn and inculcate moral rules without going through a struggle and without resolution-experiences obtaining.

MASSAGE THERAPIST: Exactly. But since such a transmission of morality will eventually become subject to struggle and resolution, either within the child's lifetime or in subsequent generations, I'll get right to the process itself.

SOCRATES: Go ahead.

MASSAGE THERAPIST: Let's use your example of the man who sees infidelity as his masculine right even though the larger society within which he lives judges it as immoral and legislates against it. Using the levels of experience I just defined, his individual experience is that sexual experiences with women other than his wife are, for the most part, intra-experientially consistent. There are virtually no inhibiting factors that throw the experience into conflict with itself. So on the individual, intra-experiential level of experience, the criteria for morality (rightness in this instance) are met.

SOCRATES: The man's sexual experiences are morally right, for him, at least at this point.

MASSAGE THERAPIST: Intra-experientially, yes. He experiences them as morally right, or, more accurately so as to avoid the objection of relativism, the objective, experiential state-of-affairs is such that all components of his experience are consistent. Therefore, by definition, the experience is right. And since it is a moral issue we're dealing with, the experience is morally right.

SOCRATES: Even though it may be a part of a set-of-experiences that is morally wrong.

MASSAGE THERAPIST: Yes.

SOCRATES: This still sounds very strange to me but go on.

MASSAGE THERAPIST: At the mutual level of experience we'll run into our first serious problem. Let's say that the woman that our man is having an affair with is very accepting of her role; she has no emotional designs on the man, no wish for a long-term relationship or emotional commitment; she's in it for the sex, and she has no moral qualms over her behavior. Therefore, her experience will not entail the alteration of his intra-experientially consistent experience.

SOCRATES: She won't have an attack of conscience in the middle of foreplay.

MASSAGE THERAPIST: Exactly. So the mutual level of experience between the man and the woman is experientially consistent. His experience is compatible with her experience and vice-versa. But the mutual level of experience in relation to the man's wife may be another matter.

SOCRATES: But this issue is sex with a woman who happens not to be the man's wife. His wife doesn't figure directly into this situation. You did say that within a level of experience the members that constitute it are "directly involved in the experience".

MASSAGE THERAPIST: Oh, no. I see you've misunderstood. I wasn't clear enough with my definition. Let me elucidate. An experience is individual inasmuch as its components involve primarily oneself in relation to one's world. For instance, a woman could decide not to engage in a sexual relationship with a man because of her principle of fidelity. Her experience of such a decision would look something like this:

cognition: "I won't pursue this sexual relationship"
affect   : commitment
behavior: confident posture, normal physiology
sense   : environment, normal body sensation
environ : wherever
"I"   : ownership

Such an experience does not admit of a specific person other than herself. The man involved is involved *through relationship* and not componentially. It is the principle of fidelity in relation to her, as an individual, that is *directly involved in this experience.* This principle is equivalent to the components of experience that consist in part of an abstract cognition regarding a certain type of action or behavior in a certain type of situation and is not directly concerned with a certain person. Any person who fits this situation would do. Though her experience (i.e. decision) directly affects another person, it is an individual-level experience. It is individually right, individually moral. So the experience of the other person and her own group, society, or entire societal world (inter-societal experience) is not directly involved in her experience.

SOCRATES: If another "concrete" individual or "concrete" group of individuals is not a component of an individual's experience, then the individual's experience may satisfy the definition for an individual level of experience. And this level of experience need not be consistent with any other level of experience in order to be right, or in our case, moral. It is, or can prove to be, moral on its own.

MASSAGE THERAPIST: Yes. Theoretically, any person's experience could consist of such a strong rightness that it would continually recur over a significant length of time (confirming itself) even in the face of great opposition or rejection.

SOCRATES: Regardless of who opposed or rejected the **principle-experience**...if I may so name it..
MASSAGE THERAPIST: You may.
SOCRATES: ...the experience is still confirmed as right over time.
MASSAGE THERAPIST: Yes, and after, should the same principle be experienced by someone else surviving this individual. Therefore, a person like Jesus could experience great moral conviction (resolution-experience), suffer all sorts of opposition and rejection, even death, without losing faith in himself, without losing those confirmation-experiences necessary to support or buttress his resolution-experience.
SOCRATES: So Jesus' behavior, a component of his intuitively right experience (and his functionally right experience), can directly affect another person or persons without the experience losing its individual-experience status.
MASSAGE THERAPIST: Yes. It is not whether or not a person's behavior affects someone that is important here; it is whether or not the other person is a **primary component of experience** that is important.
SOCRATES: You've introduced a new idea here, i.e. primary component of experience. What distinguishes this component from regular or, as you've already defined them, focal and peripheral components?
MASSAGE THERAPIST: A primary component of experience refers to an experiential being that constitutes a part (focal or peripheral) of experience. If our man experiences the woman as an experiential being, i.e. as a person whose experience is valid in and of itself, then this experiential being is a component of his consciousness; his experience exists on a mutual level. Contrariwise, if his experience includes the woman as an object for his sexual satisfaction or a receptacle for his erotic desires, his experience is individual, even though she, or more accurately aspects of herself, may constitute his focal and/or peripheral consciousness. For her to be a primary component of experience, she as a thinking, feeling, behaving, and sensing being within an environment, must be constitutive of the man's experience. If only her body is primatized, to the near exclusion of other components of experience, then our man is not interacting with an experiential being, and the mutual level of experience is automatically unattainable. The best this man can do is achieve an individual level of experiential rightness and morality.

SOCRATES: If I were to make a decision that affected you directly, even after I had considered you an experiential being rather than an object, then am I acting on the mutual or individual level of experience?

MASSAGE THERAPIST: If I never agreed to the effect that your decision had upon me or to some methodological or organizational procedure as to the **scope of effect** of your decision (to be explained later), then you are acting on the individual level of experience. You have not yet met the requirement of experiencing me as an experiential being. Your "consideration" of me is your own internal reasoning or rationalization, as the case may be. If you never gain my **functional or intuitive acceptance** of your decision as it directly applies to me (i.e. alters my **course of experience**), then you are experiencing me as a component of experience (i.e. my behavior) and you are functioning on the individual level of experience.

SOCRATES: As your boss, then, let's say, any decision I make that requires you to act in a way you've never agreed to act is incompatible with my experiencing you as an experiential being.

MASSAGE THERAPIST: Yes.

SOCRATES: And it is an example of the individual level of experience.

MASSAGE THERAPIST: Yes.

SOCRATES: And how does this tie in with morality? If I experience you primarily as a component of experience and make decisions that affect you "unilaterally" or without your agreement, then am I acting immorally? Because if you are consistent with what you've said so far, then as long as my individual experience is componentially consistent and inter-experientially consistent, my experience is right, and hence my behavior is moral.

MASSAGE THERAPIST: Yes and no. Let's use our erotic example again to clarify. If our man "decides" that the woman wants some coercion or force in her sexual encounter with him based on her responses to his introducing some low level force into their eroticism, then he escalates the force of his eroticism. He does so *individually*, even though he is acting partly in response to her previous responses to his erotic behavior. His behavior is equivalent to an assertive confrontation inasmuch as he is behaviorally expressing (vs. verbally expressing) how he feels, thinks, and senses in relation to an experiential being. The "force" that characterizes his erotic behavior is therefore not a unilateral expression of power but an individual assertive expression of himself as an experiential being relating to another experiential being.

But when he escalates his forceful behavior to a certain point, the woman responds negatively. For whatever reason, she rejects this degree of forcefulness. If his experience consists of her-as-rejecting-his-forceful-erotic-behavior, and he stops or alters his forceful behavior or inquires as to her experience in relation to his behavior while suspending his course of action, then he is experiencing her as an experiential being. She is a primary component of his experience; that component is his cognition of "she-as-rejecting-my-forceful-erotic-behavior". Let's say he experiences his behavior as right; that is, based on her responses to his previous forceful erotic behavior, he concludes that he can escalate that force in relation to her. But he is not alone in this situation; the rightness of his experience, though a temporary whole, is not yet "complete" or "determined" in relation to the other person involved. It is here that the mutual level of experience is addressed or at least approached: the rightness of his experience is dependent upon another person; he alone cannot determine the rightness of his own experience and have his experience be mutual. And if the situation is a moral one, then he alone cannot determine the morality of his experience and have his experience be mutual.

SOCRATES: So the mutual level of behavior requires 1) another person and 2) that each person be experienced as an experiential being. And to be experienced as an experiential being means to be 1) a primary component of experience (one's own and another's), and 2) to respect another's experience as legitimate or valid.

MASSAGE THERAPIST: I'd like to refer to the experience of an experiential being as **interpersonal experiential consistency**. This refers to 1) the consistency between components of consciousness in immediate experience (intra-experiential consistency), 2) the consistency between one's own experience through time relating to this issue (inter-experiential consistency), and 3) the consistency of the experiential structure between two people in relation to this issue.

SOCRATES: Therefore, if our man's immediate experience in relation to this forcefulness issue is intra-experientially consistent, and the woman's immediate experience contradicts his (even though her contradictory-experience is, itself, intra-experientially consistent), then the experience is interpersonally inconsistent.

MASSAGE THERAPIST: Yes.

SOCRATES: Her own *experience in general* is inter-experientially inconsistent in that her previous experience, which involved some forceful eroticism, contradicts her current experience, which also involves forceful eroticism.

MASSAGE THERAPIST: Yes.

SOCRATES: It is the issue of forceful eroticism that links the "accepting-experiences" with the "rejecting-experiences" into a set-of-experiences. All of the experiences, whether accepting or rejecting, are valid to each person involved in the interaction. And this experiential validity is a necessary aspect of a primary component of experience.

MASSAGE THERAPIST: Yes.

SOCRATES: What, exactly, does "valid" mean here?

MASSAGE THERAPIST: It means experientially objectively real. In other words, experience consists of cognition, affect, behavior, sensation, and the physical world, as owned. An experiential being is experience-made-human. If our man's componential structure consists in part of the woman as experience-made-human, then he is interacting with an experiential being, and his individual morality is open to the possibility of "transcending" itself and moving onto the mutual level of experience. But if his componential situation admits of only one or several components of the woman's experience, e.g. her body, her behavior, or a combination of her body and behavior, to the exclusion of her thoughts, feelings, and sensations, then he is not open to transcending his individual level of experience.

SOCRATES: The man must be able to componentialize the woman's thoughts, feelings, and sensations before he can interact with an experiential being. He must be able to experience her thoughts, feelings, and sensations as primary, along with her physical body and behavior. And he must do so because they are objective realities and, hence, valid aspects of her experience.

MASSAGE THERAPIST: Yes.

SOCRATES: I can understand so far the criteria for interacting on the mutual level of experience involving two persons who are directly engaged in the interaction with each other, but I'm not very clear on how another person (i.e. wife), who is not present, can meet this criterion and be a primary component of the man's experience.

MASSAGE THERAPIST: An image or memory of the other person could serve as a primary component and be equally effective in determining the rightness of the experience.

SOCRATES: Could you give an example?

MASSAGE THERAPIST: Sure. An image of the man's wife as the cognitive component of an experience could co-exist with an affect of guilt, a behavior of halting erotic interaction, etc. and be strong enough to reverse the interaction and terminate the affair altogether. The wife need not be there at all to have this effect, though she does need to be a primary component of experience.

SOCRATES: Is the mutual level of experience, then, occurring between the man and his absent wife?

MASSAGE THERAPIST: Yes, inasmuch as the image of the wife is an image of an experiential being and not that of an object or "role-filler". That is, the image of the wife could be representative of the wife-as-conscience rather than wife-as-experiential being, i.e. her condemnation of his behavior. In such a case, the man's experience consists primarily of his wife's condemnation. If the image represented his wife-as-experiential being, then his experience would consist of her entire experiential involvement in this situation, i.e. how she thinks, feels, acts, and senses in relation to this situation. She would virtually be there not as a moral conscience but as a person whose experience is intimately and inextricably intertwined with this situation. If she is there as a moral conscience, then his experience in relation to her is individual rather than mutual. He experiences her as a "nay-sayer" or "a judge" and not as a full person. This type of experience often supplies a person with false justification for not telling the wife. He sees the wife as "unifaceted" rather than "multi-faceted", i.e. a condemning cognition (judge) rather than a thinking, feeling, behaving, and sensing being. Such an image does not admit of mutuality. If he were to experience the image of his wife as an experiential being, he would be disposed to telling her the truth, whether he feels good or bad in relation to what he is doing.

SOCRATES: Why would he have to be disposed to telling her the truth?

23. Truth as Objective Experiential Consistency

MASSAGE THERAPIST: Because the **truth**, even though difficult to convey or disclose, is *equal to intra- and inter-experiential consistency*. The truth is knowing and being ourselves in relation to others. If he doesn't disclose the truth, inconsistent experiences will increase in relation to his wife (e.g. he'll have to cover up more), which will further distance him from the mutual level of experience and deepen the split in his identity that already exists.

SOCRATES: So in order for our man to establish the rightness or morality of his sexual interaction with this woman, a rightness he may actually experience intra-experientially and inter-experientially, at least in a limited sense, he would have to be able and willing to maintain a predominantly inter-experientially consistent set-of-experiences by working through any inconsistencies in experience that arise because of his experience in relation to the woman. In other words, he would have to confront his wife with what he experiences to be the rightness of his act.

MASSAGE THERAPIST: Yes. Or the wrongness of his act. That is, the image of the wife during the act may be that of an experiential being which is associated with guilt. The man is guilty in relation to his wife. In order for him to reach or re-establish a mutual level of experience between him and his wife, he must disclose the truth and deal with the consequences. Otherwise, his experience in relation to her will be riddled with inconsistency.

SOCRATES: So in order for an experience to be mutual, it must consist of a component of consciousness that itself consists of another person or image of the person, etc. (primary component), and that component must be of an experiential being, not merely a component of experience.

MASSAGE THERAPIST: I'd say that sums it up quite well. If you can add to this notion, I welcome your in-put.

SOCRATES: I am a little confused about one thing: is the experiential being a component of experience or an actual person?

MASSAGE THERAPIST: Remember that experience, as I've defined it, consists in part of the physical world. Phenomenologists have already shown that "consciousness" is intimately and inextricably linked to some sort of object (of consciousness), whether that object be physical or mental or some combination thereof. I've already elaborated on the experiential position in relation to this phenomenological thesis in our previous discussion, so I'll limit my comments here to this: consciousness is not a "means by which we know or experience the world"; it *is* the world in relation to us. An experiential being is both a component of experience and a person, inasmuch as a person *is* a component of experience, *and* in that the person is a particular type of person, i.e. a whole person and not just a part (e.g. a body) for another person's use. A person who is experienced as a part of experience is not an experiential being. I may experience you as a mid-wife to my ideas only and not as a mid-wife who gets tired of being a mid-wife and would rather be a joker, a dancer, or a drinker of fine wine for awhile. The fact is, you are all of these things; all of these things constitute your experience. And if I do not respect the validity of all of these aspects of you, all of these components of consciousness as owned [by you], then I will experience you as less than an experiential being. I may not agree with your theories; I may get irritated over your behavior; I may think your feelings are unjustified or groundless; I may think your sensations to be exceedingly dulled or perverse, but if I am to experience you as an experiential being, I must affirm the validity of your experience, and as an experiential being your experience is always valid. To the extent that I reduce you to a component of experience, e.g. a physical body, an intellectual challenger, an empathic helper, etc. is the extent to which you are not an experiential being. In a sense, an experiential being is experience personified. It is all the components of consciousness as owned [by you or me or whomever] as manifested by one person.

SOCRATES: You may engage me as an intellectual challenger, but such an engagement must be on mutual terms, a mutual agreement. And the direction of that activity must also be mutually agreed upon, because the activity, though primarily intellectual or cognitive, is necessarily also affective, behavioral, sensual, and environmental.

MASSAGE THERAPIST: Yes, exactly. The extent to which you may want to utilize your intelligence in this fashion may differ from mine, and we need to coordinate our interaction accordingly, and respect each other's wishes in regard to it.

SOCRATES: Just as our man must respect the woman's wishes in regard to the extent to which she feels uncomfortable about the force used in erotic interaction.

MASSAGE THERAPIST: Yes. As experiential beings we consist of components of consciousness as owned. Certain components may be emphasized in our interaction, but all components must be taken into account.

SOCRATES: Therefore, when our man experiences the woman as fully agreeing with his erotic behavior in relation to her, and vice-versa, they are engaged in an activity on the mutual level of experience.

MASSAGE THERAPIST: Not quite, not necessarily anyway. The man's "experience of the woman's experience" may very well differ from the actual experiential state-of-affairs. He might experience her behavior as cooperative when it is in fact a mixture of cooperation and resistance. His experience, which includes an interpretation of her behavior, need not match her experiential state-of-affairs. And as

Truth as Objective Experiential Consistency

already shown, even her experience in relation to her own state-of-affairs (i.e. her evaluation-experience) may not match her state-of-affairs. It is the consistency between each other's experiential states-of-affair that determines the mutual level of experience. It is interpersonal experiential consistency that places experience on the mutual level. When such a consistency obtains, mutuality is reached between two experiential beings. Now in regard to the morality of this situation: an individual can unilaterally claim and eventually establish a morality (or the morality of an issue) if he (let's say) experiences a resolution-experience strong enough to prompt confirmation-experiences over time. This individual, living within a larger society, will inevitably come into contact with others who will not share his moral commitment. Their interaction with him will prompt conflict within their own experience as well as his. But if his confirmation-experiences outweigh his disconfirmation experiences (i.e. doubts, fears, etc.), he will maintain and strengthen his moral position and in all likelihood gain support from others. He will not only gain their intellectual support but their entire experiential support. That is, they will not only understand and agree with his moral point of view, but they will be able to act in relation to others in support of their newly inculcated moral view. Again, Jesus serves as a good example, at least in some ways. Jesus gained support from the apostles not simply because he was a convincing speaker but because he *was* what he spoke (if I may make this claim at all). He was not out to "win votes" or tell people what they wanted to hear; he was speaking as he was; his speech was a consistent expression of himself. Such a man gains supporters who are committed to the morality he is espousing on all componential levels of experience, i.e. intellectually, affectively, behaviorally, and sense-physically. And when such support or agreement is reached between people, experience exists on the mutual level. Jesus, an experiential being, expressed himself through words and action to other experiential beings (apostles), eventually prompting their total or near-total assent (experiential commitment). On the individual level of experience, Jesus' experience was intra- and inter-experientially consistent. Any conflict he experienced through his interaction with others was *worked through* or *grappled with* and eventually superseded by confirmation of his original resolution-experience, allowing for alterations of the experience as experience changed. Therefore, Jesus' experiential structure was constituted by numerous intra-experiential experiences and his set-of-experiences (regarding any given issue) was also consistent; hence, he was acting morally - on the individual level of experience. And when he interacted with the apostles, he did so primarily on the mutual level of experience inasmuch as he experienced them not as apostles or followers but as experiential beings who supported his leadership, a leadership that was a behavioral expression of who he was.

SOCRATES: Therefore, when one's experience is componentially and inter-experientially consistent, one is acting morally on the individual level of experience. But this does not mean that one is simultaneously acting morally on the *interpersonal or mutual level of experience.*

MASSAGE THERAPIST: Exactly. And this is where our man who considers it his right to have affairs runs into problems. Personally, his experience is consistent and right, but interpersonally he has to contend with his wife, family, groups, and society, and possibly the world of societies. He may very well find affair partners who are primary components of his experience and, hence, experiential beings in relation to him, and therefore be experientially right and moral on the mutual level of experience, but in other interpersonal situations he will not fare so well. If he is to maintain his morality of experience in relation to this issue, his experience must be primarily consistent in relation to this issue *in relation to others.* In this case the man must be willing and able to disclose his affair to those who fall within the *scope of effect* of his action. For instance, in order to maintain mutuality and, hence, morality on the mutual level of experience, the man must be willing and able to disclose to his wife that he is having or had an affair (engaged in sexual relations with another woman).

SOCRATES: But who would be willing to do such a thing?

MASSAGE THERAPIST: In our society, Socrates, a society composed of many religious groups that morally condemn infidelity and a government that legislates against it, if not directly then indirectly, the odds are extremely good that any morality or experiential rightness pertaining to a man's erotic interaction with someone other than his wife (and vice-versa for women) will be strongly contradicted on some interpersonal level of experience. On the mutual level his wife may object to infidelity. And even if the man's erotic experiences do admit of some intra-experientially consistent experiences and a set-of-experiences (within, let's say, his group of friends or cohorts) that is also consistent, he may find great difficulty in maintaining that consistency when faced with his wife.

SOCRATES: If she asks him about it, he'd lie.

MASSAGE THERAPIST: Or something similar, yes.

SOCRATES: So what? By that I mean, what difference does it make to him if he lies about it to his wife? If he personally believes his erotic activities to be moral, or at least amoral (even though society may disapprove), and he's able to maintain consistency of experience between him and his erotic interactor and between him and his friends or cohorts, "and" he considers his wife's questioning him on this issue to be absolutely none of her business, then why should there be a contradiction? "He" seemingly wouldn't experience any contradiction.

MASSAGE THERAPIST: The contradiction would exist on the interpersonal level of experience. If he had experienced his wife as an experiential being when he experienced his vows of fidelity to her in relation to the larger society, i.e. when he entered into an agreement to act in a certain way in relation to her, and has done nothing to alter that agreement through negotiation, then his sexual acts with other women, though individually and even mutually right or moral are simultaneously mutually and societally wrong or immoral. They are mutually right between him and his sexual partner but mutually wrong between him and his wife and between him and his society.

SOCRATES: Tell me, my friend. If the man vows fidelity to his wife, as one experiential being to another, is he not morally obligated to maintain that fidelity unless he re-negotiates his vow with his wife? Does not such a moral situation transcend change? Is not such a moral principle inviolable and always binding?

MASSAGE THERAPIST: In theory I may very well agree with you. I, too, affirm the principle which says that one's promise is binding; it is wrong to break an agreement, etc. But in practice I think we very often find it much more difficult to determine just what is promised and what is expected by those involved in the situation. For instance, how does each person involved in taking the vow of fidelity understand "fidelity"? What does it mean to each of them? What would constitute a breach of fidelity: Flirting? Kissing? A series of intimate discussions? Petting? Falling in love? Oral sex? Sexual intercourse? Let's say that this man thinks of fidelity primarily in sexual terms, i.e. no sexual contact with another person beyond, let's say, a little flirting; whereas the woman includes an emotional element in her understanding of fidelity, i.e. no falling in love with another person, in addition to the sexual element. Let's say that there is little explicit discussion of what their respective understandings of fidelity are prior to taking the vow, just lots of built-in assumptions.

SOCRATES: Sounds quite typical.

MASSAGE THERAPIST: Yes. So as their marriage develops, the man finds himself attracted to another woman. This does not mean he is any less attracted to his wife. He is attracted to both his wife and the other woman. But, as already determined, attraction alone does not constitute a breach of fidelity for these two. The man can "exhibit attraction behavior" toward the woman in the presence of his wife without being reproached by her. She may be a little "concerned" but not reproachful, a little "threatened" but not rejecting. Let's say that over the socially or professionally determined course of interaction between the man and the woman, his attraction to her increases. He's attracted not only to her physical appearance but also to her demeanor, intelligence, and aspects of her personality. He enjoys being around her. But, again, this enjoyment of another person does not detract from his enjoyment of his wife; he enjoys both. If his wife, for some reason, inquires about her, he might say, "Yes, she's attractive and I like her." This is still acceptable to the wife, i.e. not a breach of fidelity, though her concern may increase. This concern seems to dissipate, though, when in her husband's company, because he enjoys her company overall, and she his; but it may increase when he talks about the woman a bit "too much" or sometimes when he is at work, leaving her with time to think about him and the woman. Now, during the course of the work day, the man asks the woman to have lunch with him. She accepts. They disclose more information about themselves to each other, and he experiences an increased attraction and acceptance of her. He or someone else informs his wife that he went to lunch with the woman. This prompts serious concern for her and perhaps some "probing questions" for information about his feelings for her, etc., but this still does not merit the determination of infidelity. At some point the man falls in love with the woman. He accepts and affirms her as she is and allows himself to be vulnerable in relation to her by telling her that he loves her. He is physically attracted to her but not otherwise sexually involved with her.

SOCRATES: Then he "is" at some level sexually involved with her? His being physically attracted to her necessarily involves his being sexually attracted to her.

24. Physical Attraction as Sexual, Sensual, and Aesthetic

MASSAGE THERAPIST: Not necessarily. He could be physically attracted to her in an aesthetic or sensual sense rather than a sexual sense. A homosexual man need not experience any sexual attraction to a woman but could still be attracted to her form, her muscle tone, how she carries herself, etc. He could also be sensually attracted to her in experiencing pleasure in looking at her, smelling her, touching her, etc. without feeling sexually attracted to her. So, *physical attraction* could be categorized (at least) as: 1) sexual, 2) sensual, or 3) aesthetic. Analytically, a sexual attraction would consist of something like:

cognition: nice breasts
affect   : attraction/pleasure
behavior : looking
sense   : woman's breasts in relation to rest of body
environ : wherever
"I"   : ownership

A sensual attraction would consist of something like:

cognition: soft, supple skin
affect   : attraction/pleasure
behavior : touching other person's skin
environ : massage room
"I"   : ownership

An aesthetic attraction would consist of something like:

cognition: muscular body
affect   : attraction/pleasure
behavior : looking
sense   : other person's body musculature
environ : beach
"I"   : ownership

These experiences overlap in some areas but are different in other areas. The differences may not be immediately recognizable; they may become evident as the set-of-experiences develops. (I'll explain that in a moment). **Sexual attraction** is an experience of a body, areas of a body, or aspects related to a body that imply or "point toward" genital stimulation, arousal, and/or orgasm. One could be attracted to another's (or one's own) sexual areas (i.e. genitals), sexually-related areas (e.g. upper thighs, hips, derriere, breasts), or sexually-related aspects (e.g. clothing, body motion, areas of the body not so commonly recognized as sexual, like shoulders, calves, feet, hair, etc.) Sexual attraction can apply to virtually anything that can be sexualized or experienced as implying or pointing toward genital stimulation, arousal, and/or orgasm. **Sensual attraction** is an experience of a body, areas of a body, or aspects related to a body that consist of a sustained focal sense-physical component of consciousness constituted by the co-existing peripheral affect of pleasure. I want to limit sensual attraction to the human body because this will serve my purpose in distinguishing the sensual from the sexual and the aesthetic, not because non-human things cannot be experienced as sensual. Understood this way, sensual-attraction experiences subsume sexual-attraction experiences. A woman can be sensually attracted to a man's derriere but not be sexually attracted to it. She may gaze at it with pleasure but not experience any implication or pointing toward genital stimulation. But she cannot be sexually attracted to his derriere without being sensually attracted to it, unless we expand our definition of sensual attraction to include painful sexual experiences that are nevertheless attractive to us (e.g. masochistic experiences). For our purposes now, I'd like to use the more limited definition and require the attraction to be pleasurable. **Aesthetic attraction** is an experience of a body, areas of a body, and/or aspects related to a body and co-existing with the affect of aestheticness. Aestheticness is a particular type of pleasure; therefore, aesthetic experience is a particular type of sensual experience. A woman can be sensually attracted to a man's body without being aesthetically attracted to it. For instance, she may pleasurably touch his body without "feeling" its beauty. But if she does "feel its beauty", she must be sensually attracted to it. For in feeling its beauty, she feels pleasure; and in touching his body, she senses him. Therefore, aesthetic and sexual attraction are both subsets of sensual attraction. All consist of sensing a physical object (body) and some form of pleasure. Sexual pleasure is a particular type of sensual pleasure, i.e. an internal, physiological sensation of intense pleasure; aesthetic pleasure is a sublime psycho-spiritual pleasure. Sensual pleasure is any pleasure co-existing with or supporting the sense-physical component of experience.

SOCRATES: Let's take a male massage therapist and a female client. The massage therapist is physically attracted to the client. He thinks she is beautiful; her skin is soft and supple, her muscles firm and well developed; her thighs, hips, and breasts are firm and well proportioned. In massaging this woman will this man experience all these forms of attraction?

MASSAGE THERAPIST: If he is heterosexually oriented, physically capable of being sexually stimulated, and psychologically disposed to aesthetic experience, and she is at least functionally accepting of his massaging her, then I would say, yes, he will feel all three forms of attraction.

SOCRATES: If he feels sexual attraction toward the client, then according to your definition, his experience implies or points toward genital stimulation, arousal, and/or orgasm. It seems to me that if he doesn't do something about this sexual attraction, he's going to be one embarrassed massage therapist facing a possible law suit and loss of license.

MASSAGE THERAPIST: An interesting situation, no doubt.

SOCRATES: I have a number of questions in relation to this situation, and I'd like to see how your responses will fit in with your development of the levels of experience and morality: 1) If he feels sexually attracted to her, can he willfully transform that attraction into another form of attraction or rid himself of attraction altogether using some form of mental concentration, cognitive "re-programming", or attention diversion? 2) Morally, should he do this, or at least try to do this; and if he doesn't, is he morally and ethically culpable? 3) What is her part in this situation? Is she a completely passive experiential being? Is her experience individual or mutual or both? And 4) How do the ethics of the group fit in, i.e. his professional ethical code?

MASSAGE THERAPIST: 1) The massage therapist is a healthy heterosexual man; 2) the client, let's say, is a healthy heterosexual woman; 3) the massage therapist is sexually attracted to the client; 4) the massage therapist's job is to apply various strokes to various areas of the client's body; 5) these areas include upper thighs, lower back, derriere, upper pectoral area of the chest, i.e. areas generally recognized as sexually-related though not specifically sexual areas of the body. (Though it should be noted that massages need not involve all of these areas of the body; I'm speaking generally.) If these are the circumstances of the situation, then I'd say that sexual interest or attraction initially will in all likelihood continue, if not increase, throughout the massage, barring inhibiting factors that might decrease or eliminate sexual attraction altogether (e.g. anything the therapist might experience about the client as repulsive.) If this is so then the massage therapist will experience some degree of sexual stimulation that could range from sexual interest to orgasm. *Sexual interest* involves a componential structure that consists in part of the sexual areas of one's own body. A woman can look at a man's body and be sexually interested in it (as a whole or as parts relative to the whole) without noticing any physiological stimulation of her sexual organs, but she will notice, if she reflects upon it, that she is actually aware of her own sexuality in relation to the man. If the woman simply looks at the man's body, is physically attracted to it, but does not relate her own sexuality to it, then she is sensually attracted to the man. The man's body appeals to her and gives her pleasure in the act of sensing it. But once her experience consists of her own sexuality in relation to the man while being physically attracted to the man, then she is sexually attracted to him.

SOCRATES: If I look at a curvaceous woman walking past me, wearing a tight dress, her breasts and hips bouncing, and I think, "What a sexy body!", but do not relate this experience to my own sexuality, then my attraction is merely sensual and not sexual? This seems a bit ridiculous to me.

MASSAGE THERAPIST: As it should. I do not see how your experience in such a situation is devoid of your own sexuality. Even if you are homosexual, the very recognition of the woman's sexiness in addition to your physical attraction to her includes your own sexuality in relation to her. It is an example of a heterosexual sexual attraction experience. Such an experience may surprise or even shock a homosexual man. I'll use the male massage therapist to clarify my position. The massage therapist may be physically attracted to the client but not aware of any genital stimulation occurring in him; nor is he aware of *any disposition toward genital stimulation.* It is this *disposition* that constitutes his sexuality, sensuality, or aestheticness in relation to the client. If he reflects upon himself and finds no disposition toward genital stimulation, i.e. awareness of his own sexuality, and there is, in fact, no disposition constituting the experiential state-of-affairs, then we may conclude that the experience is not one of sexual attraction. The attraction may be sensual or aesthetic but not sexual.

SOCRATES: What, exactly, constitutes a "disposition toward genital stimulation"? How does such a thing register in experience?

MASSAGE THERAPIST: A sexual attraction experience, as shown before, would look like this:
cognition: nice body!
affect   : attraction/pleasure
behavior : looking, staring
sense   : woman's body
environ : wherever
"I"   : ownership

A self-reflective sexual attraction-experience would look like this:
cognition: I-as-interested-in-her (as-a-potential-sexual-partner)
affect   : sexual attraction

behavior : looking/staring
sense : woman's body
environ : wherever
"I" : ownership

Now the cognition may register as "I love those sexy breasts" as he looks at her cleavage, or "I-as-staring-at-her-curvaceous-hips" as he watches her walk away, but the interest in her as a potential sexual partner, even if that potentiality is automatically nullified by other experiences (related to time constraints, marital situation, etc.), is an inherent aspect of the experience. He wouldn't be interested in her primarily as a model for his painting or camera; in such a situation the attraction would be aesthetic. Nor would he be interested in her as a potential client, as might a massage therapist; in such a situation attraction would be sensual. His interest in her is as a potential sexual partner in relation to him. And as this interest grows, so too does his sexual involvement with her (i.e. stimulation and arousal of his genitals).

SOCRATES: I could understand this type of self-reflective experience occurring in relation to a man who is in a position to dispose himself sexually to another without compunction or doubt, when a sustained look at a woman's body means, "I want to go to bed with you", but many of these "sexual" looks do not mean that at all. They might mean, "You've got a sexy body" or "I'd like to touch that", but they don't go beyond that meaning. The thought of her as a potential sexual partner never enters the man's mind. The sexual attraction is transient; it starts and stops at the "looking stage" or the "imagination stage"; it would never convert into the stage of sexual intercourse.

MASSAGE THERAPIST: Why not?

SOCRATES: Because such acts are often not practically feasible or morally acceptable. A psychiatrist's sexual intercourse with a client is morally unacceptable no matter how sexually attracted she is to him.

MASSAGE THERAPIST: And if circumstances were conducive to sexual intercourse?

SOCRATES: If practical and moral issues did not inhibit increased sexual involvement?

MASSAGE THERAPIST: Yes.

SOCRATES: Well, the disposition of the man alone may be such that he merely wants to look at her, not touch her, and certainly not have intercourse with her. This type of situation doesn't imply or point toward genital stimulation, arousal, or intercourse at all. It stops at interest. But it is still sexual interest. It is a sexual look.

MASSAGE THERAPIST: So if a man looks at a woman's breasts, and is aware of himself looking at her breasts, and is aware of his physical attraction to the woman, his experience need not consist of any componential evidence of sexual interest that might escalate into arousal and "end" in orgasm.

SOCRATES: Exactly. His sexual interest is limited to looking at her breasts, or other parts of her body, or her body as a whole. And if this is so, then what is the difference between sexual interest and sensual interest? They seem to be identical, at least at this stage of development.

MASSAGE THERAPIST: I think you hit on a key point, Socrates. I mentioned before that sensual, sexual, and aesthetic attraction overlapped and might be difficult to differentiate until the set-of-experiences occurs that will determine just which attraction had occurred. If the man who looks at the woman's breasts finds himself fantasizing about them, only to reflect upon the genital area of his own body, then the original experience is probably a sexual experience, the original attraction a sexual attraction. And I say "probably" because there is a possibility for sensual experience to prompt a sexual experience (which will be discussed later). But if after looking at the woman's breasts the man wonders how the skin of her breast would feel or how the breasts would look unclothed, without reflection upon his own sexuality, his experience would (probably) be one of sensual attraction, even though breasts are generally accepted as a sexually-related area of the female body. In this situation, self-reflective experience does not consist of any component related to his sexual attraction or physiology. His interest is in the feel of her breasts or the sight of them. Such images do not necessarily co-exist with sexual excitation or arousal. They do not point toward excitation or arousal; rather, they are ends in themselves, pleasurable in themselves. Sensual pleasure does not consist of an **escalation of intensity** as does sexual pleasure. A sexual look is a part of a set-of-experiences that entails self-reflective sexual experience (awareness of one's own sexual parts) and the escalation of sexual intensity terminating in orgasm. Whereas a sensual look is a part of a set-of-experiences that entails self-reflective sensual experience (e.g. the feel of the skin, musculature, etc. or the sight of areas of the body, including sexual areas of the body) that are pleasurable in themselves and are not disposed to escalating intensity.

SOCRATES: Are you saying that a man can look at a woman's breasts, be attracted to them, imagine how they would feel, and even

touch them or stroke them, and all of these experiences would be sensual and not sexual?!
MASSAGE THERAPIST: Yes.
SOCRATES: Now I could see a homosexual man looking at a woman's breasts, being attracted to their voluptuous appearance (or whatever aspect attracts him), imagining how they would feel to his touch, and even touching them without experiencing any sexual stimulation, but I can't imagine that being the case for a healthy heterosexual man interacting with a woman to whom he is physically attracted.
MASSAGE THERAPIST: I can't either. But that still doesn't mean that his experience would be sexual vs. sensual. Though constituting a more complicated situation, such experiences could very well be understood as sensual and not sexual, or as primarily sensual and secondarily sexual, or immediately sensual and derivatively sexual, or **focally sensual** and **peripherally sexual**. Such is the case for the massage therapist who is sexually attracted to the client and who actually touches or strokes sexually-related areas of the client's body. Let's use a female massage therapist and a male client to exemplify. The massage therapist is sensuously and sexually attracted to the client. Her self-reflective experience entails some awareness of her own sexuality in relation to him, i.e. she may be aware of how tight her skirt is, how her breasts might appear to him, etc. Such experiences imply or point toward sexual stimulation though they are only at the sexual interest stage of development. She is simultaneously sensually attracted to the client, feeling pleasure in relation to looking at him, listening to his voice, shaking his hand, etc.
SOCRATES: Both attraction experiences are occurring throughout this interaction.
MASSAGE THERAPIST: Yes. In administering the massage, she applies various strokes to the man's upper thighs, lower back, and derriere. These experiences could consist of a number of different componential structures. For instance, in administering a friction stroke to the anterior (front) thigh (i.e. a smooth, gliding stroke affecting the skin and superficial musculature, nerves, and circulatory vessels), she starts her stroke just above his knee and runs her hand along his inner thigh, moves superiorly (toward his head) and angles the stroke across his thigh laterally (toward outer thigh) just as she approaches his pubic area. One possible *course of experience* that could occur, given the fact that she is overall sexually attracted to the man is this:

At the sight of the thigh:
cognition: nicely shaped, firm
affect : attraction/pleasure
behavior: looking at thigh, readying her stroke delivery
sense : client's thigh, a slight "nervousness"
environ : massage room
"I" : ownership
As she starts the stroke:
cognition: supple skin, firm muscles
affect : pleasure
behavior: applying stroke
sense : man's thigh and massage therapist's hand as it moves, slight decrease in "nervousness"
environ : massage room
"I" : ownership
As she approaches the client's pubic area:
cognition: I want to touch as much thigh surface without touching genitals
affect : pleasure/caution
behavior: moving stroke superiorly then laterally
sense : man's thigh, genital area (covered by sheet), slight sexual stimulation
environ : massage room
"I" : ownership

In this series of experiences her first cognition consists of sensual ideas (shape and firmness of his thigh), her affect is sensual pleasure, her sensations are multiple (she sees his thigh, feels a slight nervousness, hears the music playing (if she has music), etc.)

SOCRATES: Why does she feel nervousness?

MASSAGE THERAPIST: When someone is sexually attracted to someone else, the thought or act of touching him or her in areas close to his or her genitals may prompt some nervousness.

SOCRATES: The nervousness is basically sexual then.

MASSAGE THERAPIST: Yes.

SOCRATES: Is her pleasure related to her nervousness?

MASSAGE THERAPIST: Only inasmuch as they are both related to the sense-physical component of consciousness. Her nervousness is not pleasurable; nor is her pleasure nervous. Rather, her sense-physical experience is constituted by both nervousness and pleasure. The pleasure is sensual; the nervousness is sexual. We can also say, based on the development of the series of experiences, that the sensual pleasure outweighs the sexual nervousness in strength.

SOCRATES: How can we conclude that?

MASSAGE THERAPIST: Because the stroke is completed confidently. Strong sexual nervousness would tend to inhibit the confident completion of the stroke; she might shorten the stroke as she approaches the pubic area. But the pleasure she feels (mixed with her professional confidence) allows her to complete the stroke despite her nervousness. With the successful completion of her first stroke, her next stroke might be more sensually delivered, less tentative around the pubic area, and clearly more pleasurable.

SOCRATES: So there is sexuality involved right from the first stroke of the thigh.

MASSAGE THERAPIST: Certainly.

SOCRATES: Nevertheless, the stroke is sensual, not sexual.

MASSAGE THERAPIST: Yes. It contains a peripheral sexual component in that her sexuality is related to his; hence, the nervousness as she prepares to stroke his thigh, and hence the slight sexual stimulation as she completes the stroke near his genitals. But neither the nervousness, the adrenaline surge, nor the sexual stimulation is strong enough to alter the course of sensual experience. But we must remember that sensual attraction need not be the reason the stroke is completed. Throughout the course of the massage, the therapist's experience might very well shift to more of a mechanical mode and her stroking of the client's thigh, regardless of how attractive she might judge him to be, would be experienced by her as a mechanical task, applied to relieve him of any pain he might have in his thigh. In this case, her sensual attraction, as well as her sexual attraction, becomes peripheral to the focalization of stroking-to-relieve-pain. Any pleasure associated with this experience is incidental or the result of professional competence.

SOCRATES: How would her experience change if it were to shift mid-stroke, let's say, from primarily sensual to primarily sexual?

MASSAGE THERAPIST: Let's say that her typical massage involves three medial (inner) thigh friction strokes and three lateral (side) friction strokes. Though her experience consists of "some" sexual component (e.g. awareness of her proximity to his genitals), her experience is primarily sensual (though it could very well be primarily mechanical). As she performs her second medial stroke of his thigh, she notices a slight bulging of the sheet over his pubic area and a slight change in the

rhythm of his breathing. She realizes that her strokes are prompting sexual arousal, but the client makes no indication that she should stop. Her experience now consists of something like:
cognition: He's getting turned on
affect : concern (that she's causing him embarrassment)
behavior: slight hesitation
sense : sheets over man's pubic area, man's thigh
environ : massage room
"I" : ownership
Her experience immediately shifts to one of self-reflection:
cognition: I need to stop this stroke
affec : commitment, certainty
behavior: switching to lateral stroke of the thigh, decreasing its strength
environ : massage room
"I" : ownership

The first experience's cognition consists of a sexual component, i.e. his sexual arousal and the observation of the bulging sheet above his pubic area as well as the changing breathing pattern. Prior to this, the massage therapist didn't know if the client was sexually stimulated or not. The self-reflective experience ties her behavior directly to the client's arousal. Because of who she is in this situation, she feel commitment and certainty as to what she should do; there are no multiple courses of action, no ambiguity of meaning, no ambivalence of affect. Her reaction is to alter her course of massage.

SOCRATES: Here she seems to be judging that his sexual arousal is inappropriate for this situation not because she is acting immorally or sexually or that his partial erection is due to his own immoral or sexual thought but because she believes a continuation of her medial stroking may produce increased arousal and, hence, embarrassment for him (and her). She doesn't want to make him feel uncomfortable.

MASSAGE THERAPIST: I'd say that's accurate. In this situation the therapist's sensual-attraction experience is interrupted by a sense-physical experience of a sexual nature, i.e. bulging sheet, and change in breathing, which is cognized as sexual arousal. Her sensual pleasure dissipates quickly and is replaced by concern for his welfare. Any nervousness she may have experienced in relation to her looking at or stroking his thigh is virtually gone. The sexual component of her experience, in effect, disappears. Now let's contrast this experience with another. Let's say that the massage therapist witnesses the bulging

sheet and hears the change in breathing rhythm and her experience is thus:
cognition: he's getting turned on
affect : discomfort
behavior : definite hesitation
sense : sheet over man's pubic area
environ : massage room
"I" : ownership
Which shifts to:
cognition: I can't do this [I did wrong]
affect : anxiety [fear and guilt]
behavior : administering a very tentative finger-tip stroke to lateral portion of thigh
sense : lateral portion of thigh, her own upset stomach
environ : massage room
"I" : ownership

Here the massage therapist recognizes the client's sexual arousal, experiences herself as the direct agent of its production, judges herself as immoral, and alters her massage pattern accordingly. In this situation the sexual attraction-experience is rudely interrupted by an anxiety-experience that is a misconstruel of an experiential state-of-affairs. The state-of-affairs consisted of a sensual focus and a sexual periphery. The recognition of the sexual in the client's arousal prompts a misapplication of *agented cognition* to a peripheral state-of-affairs.

SOCRATES: In other words she feels guilty for no good reason.

MASSAGE THERAPIST: Right. The client's sexual arousal can be experienced in many different ways. The sexual-ness of the experience is focal, but that doesn't mean that the experiences that preceded it are primarily sexual nor that the experiences that follow will be primarily sexual. Let's say that the massage therapist's experience consists of:
cognition: he's getting turned on
affect : pleasure
behavior : moving toward administering the stroke
sense : sheet above client's pubic area, change in his breathing pattern
environ : massage room
"I" : ownership
And moves to:
cognition: he enjoys this
affect : pleasure

behavior : delivering medial stroke
sense : client's leg
environ : massage room
"I" : ownership

Here the massage therapist interprets the client's arousal and change of breathing pattern to be something pleasurable for him, not a source of embarrassment nor the result of an immoral act on her part, nor as a situationally inappropriate occurrence. In none of these experiences, from the massage therapist's point of view, is the experiential state-of-affairs constituted primarily by sexual attraction. Even if the pleasure that the massage therapist feels is partly sexual, the bulk of her pleasure is sensual. Her pleasure is derived from her actual sensual contact *and* the cognition of his pleasure. If she is accurate in her assessment of his experiential state-of-affairs, then she is primarily pleased sensually because he is primarily pleased sensually. Her sexual pleasure is peripheral and derivative; so is his.

SOCRATES: Are you saying that the client's sexual arousal is not primarily a sexual experience?

MASSAGE THERAPIST: As I've set up the experience, yes, it is not primarily a sexual experience. His experience, let's say, consists of an initial "feels good" as the therapist moves from just above his knee toward his genital area; then he notices a change in the pressure of her stroke as she approaches his genitals and crosses laterally, which he cognizes as an unsureness, a nervousness in relation to her proximity to his genitals. Her next stroke, though, is consistently firm. He cognizes that the stroke is strong and that the massage therapist is feeling comfortable with her sensuality, that she is deriving pleasure from massaging his thigh. This prompts the following experience:

cognition: this feels so good
affect : pleasure
behavior : passive body, alteration of breathing pattern, partial penile erection
sense : pressure against skin, muscles; sexual stimulation
environ : massage room
"I" : ownership

The client's experience is primarily sensual. His interpretation of the massage therapist's stroke is not that she is sexually stimulated by the stroking of his thigh, nor that her stroke implies an intention either to express her sexual stimulation or to prompt his own sexual stimulation; rather, he understands her stroke to be professionally competent, her affect to be one of sensual pleasure, her evaluation of her sensual pleasure as one of rightness (self-acceptance); and since her sexuality is a form of sensuality, and she is massaging an area of his body that is generally accepted as sexually-related, any sexual interest or stimulation she might feel is experienced as acceptable and right. For his part, he, let's say, is aware of some sexual stimulation amidst the sensually stimulating strokes, though the sexual stimulation is not sufficient to prompt embarrassment; it may prompt a slight degree of self-consciousness though. He feels sensual pleasure in relation to the stroke and a modicum of sexual pleasure. The self-consciousness is not sufficient to constitute a conflicting experience which would challenge the rightness of his sensual pleasure-experience. Therefore, the experience is experientially right, and if this is a moral situation at all, then it too is right. The same holds true for the massage therapist's experience.

SOCRATES: Let me understand what you're saying here. The massage therapist need not cognize the client's sexual arousal as an inappropriate event but rather as a quite natural response to sensual stimulation of a sexually related area of the body. The stimulation is sensual in its delivery; its end or purpose is sensual pleasure (or in a mechanical situation, pain reduction). The fact that it prompts a sexual response can be experienced by the massage therapist and the client in a variety of ways, ranging from strong embarrassment to strong satisfaction. As long as the experience of each party is intra- and inter-experientially consistent, it is morally right.

MASSAGE THERAPIST: Within and between themselves, yes.

SOCRATES: Let me push this to its "logical" or "natural" conclusion. If the client is stimulated enough to reach orgasm and feels comfortable in doing so, and the massage therapist is comfortable in witnessing the event, i.e. she considers the response to be wholly natural in some instances with some men, then are their respective experiences morally right?

MASSAGE THERAPIST: If the client's experience includes no intra-experiential or inter-experiential inconsistency or conflict, then the experience is one of rightness, and, if a moral situation, one of moral rightness, for her, at this time. If the massage therapist's experience is similarly structured, then her experience is also morally right. The interpersonal level of their experience is consistent; they have reached a mutual level of experiential and moral rightness. But in determining the moral rightness of this particular act, the set-of-experiences to which the moral judgment is to apply requires not only the present interaction between the client and the therapist, but also any other people who figure into the moral determination of the act. This event, though taking place in the privacy of the massage room, is not simply a private event between a consenting, agreeing, or approving pair of people. The ethics of the profession bear upon the activity that transpires between these two people, as well as the ethics of any larger organization of people, e.g. local, state, federal, and, if applicable, international governments. Most professional codes of ethics for massage therapy will prohibit "sexual conduct" or "sexual activities". The question is: what specifically constitutes "sexual conduct" or "sexual activity"? So far I've argued that the administration of a sensual stroke over a generally recognized sexually-related area of the body, even one that produces an intense sexual response (i.e. orgasm) is not a sexual activity. The activity is sensual (or mechanical); one response to part of the activity is sexual. The massage therapist who inadvertently prompts a client's orgasm has not participated in a "sexual activity". Even if she derives pleasure from the delivery of strokes that prompt the sexual response, the activity is sensual; the pleasure is an end in itself; it is not tied to sexual arousal and orgasm, i.e. it is not escalating.

SOCRATES: If the massage therapist understood the bulge under the sheet as evidence of the client's sexual arousal, and she, in turn, is sexually stimulated by his arousal, and then she proceeds to deliver her strokes as usual, or perhaps with more "vigor", is her experience and the activity not primarily sexual, even though she has no intention of escalating his or her own arousal? They're becoming aroused even though they never intended to become aroused.

MASSAGE THERAPIST: A good question, Socrates. It forces me to come up with criteria differentiating those experiences I've referred to as "primarily X" and "secondarily X", or "focally X" and "peripherally X". I'll offer the following distinction for your critical scrutiny: A single experience is primarily sexual when its focal component consists of another's body (or any sexualized object, or one's own body) in relation to one's own sexuality. "Sexuality" refers to the set-of-experiences which is structured thus: sexual interest - sexual stimulation - sexual arousal - orgasm. The sexual set-of-experiences is escalating. So when one's focal component of consciousness consists of a sexually-related part of another's body (e.g. derriere), the experience is primarily sexual if the component co-exists with sexual interest, stimulation, arousal, or orgasm. Understood as such, the massage therapist who is sexually attracted to a client will be a part of a primarily sexual experience when her focal consciousness consists of the client's body (or parts of it) that co-exist with her own sexual interest (sexual pleasure). This differs from a primarily sensual experience in that the focal component of the sensual experience consists of another's body, etc. co-existing with an interest or pleasure that is not escalating but static, or deepening. This interest is able to be "cultivated" or "refined", but it is not able to escalate and intensify in the manner of a sexual interest.

SOCRATES: I understand that sensual interest or attraction in relation to a sexual or sexually-related body part refers to an interest in seeing, touching, tasting, smelling, or hearing that body part, and that such an interest may be "deepened" or "cultivated" by experience, but if sexual interest co-exists with sensual interest, then how do we know when sexual interest "overtakes" sensual interest in experience?

MASSAGE THERAPIST: I know what you're asking, Socrates, and I am getting to an answer, though perhaps a bit slowly. Please be patient. I'll analyze the two co-existing experiences and attempt to show how they might "evolve" into a predominantly sexual experience. Let's say that a healthy heterosexual man looks at a woman wearing a bathing suit as she walks by him. His focus initially is full-body. His experience can be represented thus:

cognition: nice body
affect   : attraction/pleasure
behavior: looking at woman
sense   : woman's body, environment
environ : beach (let's say)
"I"   : ownership

Now his focus shifts to a particular part of her body:

cognition: shapely breasts
affect   : increased pleasure
behavior: looking at woman's breasts
sense   : woman's body, environment
environ : beach
"I"   : ownership

This is a fairly typical set of non-reflective sexual experiences. The man's sensations constitute his focal consciousness and his pleasure is of the escalating type. If there were no inhibiting factors to prevent or influence him not to act upon his attraction in relation to her, he would so act, because the physical attraction exists and is intensifying as time passes. The massage therapist's experience may be something like this:

cognition: attractive man (face and body)
affect   : attraction/pleasure
behavior: looking at and greeting man
sense   : woman's body, face, touch of hand (shake)
environ : massage office
"I"   : ownership

Which shifts to:
cognition: nice eyes, bright face
affect   : pleasure
behavior: looking at man's face
sense   : man's eyes, face, hearing voice
environ : massage office
"I"   : ownership

Which shifts to:
cognition: "Have a seat"
affect   : confidence
behavior: showing him where to sit
sense   : man, environment
environ : massage office
"I"   : ownership

Here the focal consciousness shifts from the environment (man's face, body) to another environment (man's face only) to a cognition (request for him to sit). The pleasure felt initially is sensual, i.e. his face and body please her. His eyes also please her, but her pleasure does not intensify; rather, it deepens. She is "drawn to" his overall body but "drawn into" his eyes. The sensory tends toward depth, whereas the sexual tends toward intensification. The sensory tends toward lingering with and being drawn into the sensible object, whereas the sexual tends toward escalating stages of intensity. The sensuous is the scuba diver who is keenly aware of the life and the objects that surround her, whereas the sexual is the sky diver who builds excitement and "explodes" into the air. Now, let's say that the massage therapist is administering a massage to this man to whom she is sexually attracted. She takes pleasure in administering her strokes, feeling the suppleness of his skin and the firmness of his muscles. As she delivers a stroke near his pubic area, he let's out a soft moan. She interprets or cognizes the moan as evidence of sexual pleasure. She cognizes herself as the producer of his sexual pleasure, even though her strokes are primarily sensual. It is here that her consciousness shifts from primarily sensual to primarily sexual. His sexual stimulation prompts her own sexual awareness in relation to him. Now her experience consists of:

cognition: he's sexually excited
affect   : sexual excitement
behavior: delivering a stronger stroke around pubic area
sense   : man's body, skin
environ : massage room
"I"   : ownership

The massage therapist's cognition shifts from her appreciation of the client's body, i.e. its shape, firmness, and suppleness to his sexual excitement; her affect shifts from sensual pleasure to sexual excitement or titillation. The pleasure, therefore, shifts from the "inward-traveling depth of sensation" to the "outward-traveling expanding excitement". She is "on the road to orgasm" (his and possibly hers) should she continue in this direction. When her experience is composed of components that escalate in intensity and, barring inhibiting factors, would eventually culminate in orgasm, then the act is primarily sexual and secondarily sensual. She is now less concerned with the suppleness of his skin or the firmness of his muscles; these things are of concern to her not as ends in themselves or as pleasurable for what they are but as means to sexual stimulation, arousal, and/or orgasm. Her stroke changes from a sensual appreciation of shape and texture to an eroticized, sexually-charged stroke that no longer luxuriates in the sensation of the object but hastens to increase the intensity of the excitement. A primarily sensual stroke would be analyzed thus:

cognition: firm, shapely legs
affect   : pleasure
behavior: stroking leg
sense   : client's leg, possibly a slight sexual stimulation
environ : massage room
"I"   : ownership

Whereas a primarily sexual stroke might look like this:

cognition: sexy legs
affect   : excitement (sexual pleasure)
behavior: strong stroke intensifying at it approaches pubic area
sense   : client's leg, strong sexual stimulation
environ : massage room
"I"   : ownership

Any sexual stimulation experienced within a sensual-experience is, I'd have to say, minimal; it is outweighed by the strength of sensual pleasure. But when sexuality shifts from peripheral to focal consciousness (another's sexuality or one's own) and is subject to intensification, I think it's safe to say that the act is primarily sexual.

SOCRATES: So even though the therapist may not intend to bring the client to orgasm, or even to further stimulate him sexually, her stroke is sexually energized in that her sexual stimulation overtakes her sensual pleasure in strength and her stroke, though not technically intentionally sexual, is, in fact, sexual.

MASSAGE THERAPIST: Yes. She has crossed the boundary between sensual pleasure and erotic excitation. The central focus of erotic excitation is the genitalia. Erotic stroking of the breasts or derriere, though pleasurable in itself, serves the overall purpose of stimulating the genitals and producing orgasm. Sensual stroking, on the other hand, serves no purpose other than the production of its own sensual pleasure (though it may produce positive physical and psychological responses in addition to or because of the sensual pleasure felt.)

SOCRATES: One possibly disturbing conclusion I think I can draw from your argument is that a stroke can be delivered to a sexual area of the body (i.e. genitalia) and not necessarily be sexual. Even more, a woman (let's say) who is sexually attracted to a man (let's say) can deliver a stroke to his genitals without the act being primarily sexual.

MASSAGE THERAPIST: Certainly.

SOCRATES: I'm sorry. I do not share your certitude here. How is this so?

MASSAGE THERAPIST: It happens sometimes with lovers. Lovers may not intend or desire to "have sex" with each other, i.e. generate sexual excitation to the point of orgasm. They may simply want to touch each other's body, luxuriate in each other's bodily forms, textures, smells, and/or tastes. They may be partially aroused in their mutual exchange, but sexual arousal is peripheral and static. Hence, the experience contains a sexual component but is overall a sensual experience.

SOCRATES: But I understand that the stroking of any kind, whether sensual, sexual, or mechanical, of the genitalia is prohibited by most codes of ethics in massage.

MASSAGE THERAPIST: Yes.

SOCRATES: Why? It seems to me that if human genitalia are an integral part of experiential beings and they can be touched mechanically or sensually, then they should, or at least could, be included in the activity of massage without transgressing morality.

MASSAGE THERAPIST: I agree with your reasoning, Socrates. If sexually-related areas of the body are included in massage and are stroked not only for reasons of pain reduction but pleasure production, and this pleasure is experienced by both client and massage therapist as primarily sensual, then it seems consistent to allow the sensual pleasure producing stroking of the genitals. But where do we draw the line between an acceptable and unacceptable sexual response to a sensually-delivered stroke? Two or three friction strokes applied to the genital area will resemble masturbation strokes, and the chances of prompting a sexual experience (the overtaking of sensual experience) is greatly increased. Whereas the application of *hypnotic strokes,* or what I would prefer to call *veneration strokes* (i.e. a very light finger tip or whole hand motion over the surface of the skin or draping) may very well be sensual without prompting a sexual experience. Do we as individuals determine for ourselves what degree of sexual response is acceptable and unacceptable? Is it mutually determined between therapist and client? Is it determined by an ethics board? These are good questions for further research and discussion.

SOCRATES: Such a "veneration" stroke might be construed as a sensual affirmation of the entire body of the experiential being, including his or her sexuality.

MASSAGE THERAPIST: Yes. I think a strong case can be made for that.

SOCRATES: So in answer to my question of whether or not a massage therapist should stop or alter her strokes if the client shows signs of sexual arousal, and whether or not her choosing not to alter her strokes is immoral, you would say that if the client's sexual arousal prompted her own sexual arousal which energized her strokes, and if she were to continue her normal stroking pattern, she would be engaging in a sexual act with the client which, even though their respective experiences are evaluatively right and, hence, moral, is an infraction against the ethical code of the profession. If this is so, then my question is: Is this act moral or not?

25. Sensuality, Sexuality, Morality, and Levels of Experience

MASSAGE THERAPIST: Despite each person's experience being intra- and inter-experientially right and moral at this time, each set-of-experiences is subject to the group level of experience. A massage therapist and client could conceivably engage in sexual acts ranging from "unintentional" sexual stroking to intercourse without ever having to deal with the group level of experience in relation to morality and ethics. The therapist and client's experience would be intra- and inter-experientially consistent, at least functionally. They would experience nothing significant in the way of guilt, remorse, or even fear of being caught. Hence, they would go to their graves believing that they acted morally and ethically throughout. But this still does not relieve them of their connection to the group level of experience. If the group level determines, for the profession in which the therapist works, an ethical code of conduct against which the therapist acts, then the therapist, whether she/he recognizes it or not, is subject to the group's judgment. Politically the group may be endowed with the power to define what conduct is ethical and unethical, and to enforce its definition through certain punishments or professional penalties. If the sexual actions are made known to the professional ethics group, then it is within their power to determine the ethical status of the conduct and act accordingly within their professional parameters. So if there is a conflict of experience where the therapist maintains that he/she is acting morally and the professional group maintains that he/she is acting unethically, then the power of the group will come to bear upon the professional.

SOCRATES: So the group does not ultimately determine the morality of a given act?

MASSAGE THERAPIST: No. The group has the political power to define "morality" in relation to its profession and enforce its definition, but only experience itself can determine the morality of a given act or experience.

SOCRATES: In our example, we have at least three levels of experience involved in the determination of morality: the individual, the mutual, and the group level. In addition, the group level appears to be multiple. That is, there is the political group referred to, let's say, as the board of ethics or the ethics board, and the less specific group of professional peers. The therapist has to "answer to" both groups, does he not?

MASSAGE THERAPIST: Yes. If a peer or colleague was informed about the sexual conduct of the therapist, he/she might experience a duty to inform the ethics board. In other words the experience of the peer in relation to the conduct of the therapist would be interpersonally inconsistent with that of the therapist (and the client). And for the peer to maintain his/her own experiential consistency, he/she would inform the board. The board's collective experience and ultimate determination would thus represent the judgment of the board. The board's determination is an experiential as well as a political determination of morality (ethics). Inasmuch as the board members' experience is intra- and inter-experientially consistent in relation to a given moral issue, the board's determination is morally right, for it, at this time. But so too is the determination of the therapist (and client). When the individual (and mutual) levels of experience conflict with the group levels of experience, the political determination of morality rests with the empowered group, but the experiential determination rests upon experience itself. On the level of experience itself, all individuals, whether alone, in pairs, in groups, in societies, or in the world of societies, are equal. They are all experiential beings. If the individual resolution experience is strong and it prompts numerous confirmation experiences, via interpersonal interaction, then it is only a matter of time before the interpersonal level of experience starts to sway in favor of the individual's developing set-of-experiences that comprise his/her philosophy or "way of being", and other individuals forming pairs, groups, and societies will experience similar moral determinations. Conversely, it is experience itself that determines group morality and not the power of the group. Group determinations of morality are themselves moral inasmuch as each member of the group's experience is intra- and inter-experientially consistent. In order to achieve this type of experience, assertive confrontation needs to be learned, permitted, and encouraged. Pressure to conform to hierarchically structured group values would only pervert experiential consistency, and once experiential consistency is perverted, the ultimate determination of the group regarding moral issues would be the result of political power rather than that of experience. Therefore, how we structure our groups is crucial to the determination of morality. I say this only to "round out" our discussion; I know full well that these contentions require a great deal of explication; that is the subject of another discussion altogether.

SOCRATES: To occur in the near future, I trust.

MASSAGE THERAPIST: That is my hope. It may be helpful, though, to apply these ideas, as sketchy as they are, to our sensual/sexual example of the massage therapist who delivers a veneration stroke atop the draping (sheet) over the genitals of a client. Let's say that the stroke initiates at the top of the forehead, the client lying supine with the sheet covering her body up to her neck, and it proceeds down her face, making very light contact with her skin, continuing inferiorly (toward her feet) over her chest, abdomen, pubic area, legs, and ending at her feet. This can be done with the fingertips or the entire hand as long as the touch is very light. This identical stroke is currently administered from head to toes (or shoulders to toes) while the client lies prone: it passes over the shoulders, back, buttocks (hips), legs, and feet. The question can be asked: if the sensuous light touching of sexually-related areas of the body (e.g. lower back, buttocks, upper thigh) over a draping is ethically acceptable, then why is that same touching over a draping of another sexually-related area of the body (i.e. the breasts of a woman) or the genitals (or pubic area) of each sex not acceptable? Since many ethical boards do not provide a rationale for their determinations, let's offer some possible reasons.

Reason 1: A woman's breasts are typically viewed in our culture as sexual objects, and not merely sexually-related objects; therefore, these objects are off limits to the touch, even over a draping, even if administered very lightly, because touching them purposefully in such a fashion would constitute a sexual act.

Reason 2: Nipples contain erectile tissue which, if stimulated, often produces stimulation in the genital area. Stimulation of the genitals constitutes a sexual act, even if done unintentionally.

Reason 3: Touching the pubic area, even if over a draping and not touching the clitoris directly, is prohibited because the pubic area is generally accepted as a sexual area of the body, and the purposeful touching of a sexual area constitutes a sexual act.

Reason 4: The penis of the male is a sexual organ (among other things) containing erectile tissue that, when touched, often results in sexual stimulation. Stimulation of the penis through purposeful touch, even if such stimulation is unintentional, is equivalent to a sexual act.

The main problem is determining just what a sexual act is. What criteria have to be met in order for an act to be sexual? And are these criteria separable from sensual, aesthetic, emotional, and intellectual criteria? I've already argued that sexuality is a sub-category of sensuality, that sensual sensation covers a wide range of sensations, i.e. all of those sensations pertaining to the five senses that are associated with pleasure, and that sexual sensations are a specific type of sensual sensation. A massage therapist "could" deliver a veneration stroke over the breasts (including nipples) or over the genitals of a client, while being sexually attracted to the client and feeling some amount of sexual stimulation in relation to the stroke without the "act" being sexual. Such an experience would be analyzed thus:

cognition: your entire body is venerable
affect   : veneration/pleasure
behavior : delivering hypnotic stroke
sense   : feel of body contour under draping, slight sexual stimulation
environ : massage room
"I"   : ownership

If the experience were sexual, the cognition would look more like "your body is sexy"; the affect supporting the cognition would be sexual desire (or something similar); the behavior might appear to be the same, but I would contend that at least the physiological behavior would be recognizably different. For instance, in venerating the body through touch, including sexual parts of the body, the massage therapist's finger tips and palms may be relatively dry, whereas sexual desire may co-exist with "sweaty palms". This is only one "possible" physiological difference. Also, I would contend that reflective experience, if unclouded by self-deception, would reveal, generally speaking, a stronger sexual stimulation, if not arousal, occurring in the massage therapist's sensorium (sensory field). In other words, the escalating tendency toward orgasm would exist in the developing set-of-experiences, whereas in the veneration-experience sensual pleasure deepens with the addition of the emotional pleasure of veneration. The sexual stimulation felt by the massage therapist (if any) is peripheral; it does not have the power or strength to prompt a sexual experience; it "serves" the stronger component of veneration and deepens it by including sexual parts of the body as venerable. The emotional and sensual pleasures of veneration stroking are **depth-oriented pleasures**, ends in themselves, satisfying in themselves; whereas sexual pleasure is **escalation-oriented**, expansive and building, satisfying in its outcome (orgasm) but often frustrating if its outcome is prevented. If this argument is sound, then the "act" of purposefully touching sexual areas of the body in massage would not be a sexual act.

SOCRATES: You know I'll have to play the devil's advocate here; or perhaps you're playing the devil's advocate arguing for such distinctions. If you are to remain consistent in your thinking, then a female therapist who administers a sensual veneration stroke to a male client could inadvertently prompt him to react sexually with an erection and even an orgasm - and all of this would not be a sexual-experience but rather a by-product of a veneration-experience? Does this not sound a little suspect to you?

MASSAGE THERAPIST: Put that way it certainly does. Perhaps an analysis of the client's experience might clarify this issue. Let's say a male client, lying prone, experiences sexual stimulation in response to friction stroking of his derriere. His experience could look like this:

cognition: oh, oh, what's that?
affect : surprise
behavior : body tensing a bit
sense : sexual stimulation/arousal
environ : massage room
"I" : ownership

Which quickly shifts to:

cognition: I'm getting sexually excited
affect : trepidation/pleasure
behavior : body tensing, muscles tightening, breathing pattern changing
sense : sexual arousal, hand motion on derriere
environ : massage room
"I" : ownership

Here the client is aware that he is sexually stimulated. He senses the sexual excitation, but the affect he feels is primarily trepidation or fear of embarrassment. Any sexual pleasure he feels is overridden by the strength of this trepidation. Even if the therapist, who, let's say, is not aware that he is sexually excited, delivers another friction stroke that prompts orgasm, the client's experience is still not primarily sexual. It is embarrassing. Any sexual pleasure he derives from his orgasm is overridden by embarrassment. Just as the massage therapist's sexual stimulation is overridden by sensual or sensual/emotional pleasure, so too is the client's sexual stimulation overridden by another affect. Even though orgasm has occurred, the experience is not primarily sexual. It is a **layered experience**, consisting of a focal and a peripheral affect. It can be represented thus:

cognition: knowing that orgasm is occurring

affect   : shock [pleasure]
behavior : orgasmic contractions, muscles tightening, holding breath
sense   : orgasmic sensation, hands on derriere
environ : massage room
"I"   : ownership

Here the cognition, behavior, sensation, and environment co-exist with two affects: shock and sexual pleasure, which will quickly be replaced by:

cognition: I had an orgasm
affect   : embarrassment [sexual pleasure]
behavior : muscles relaxing, breathing pattern returning
sense   : moisture in pubic area, hands on derriere
environ : massage room
"I"   : ownership

In the first experience sexual pleasure is greatly overridden by shock, in the second by embarrassment. A sexual "event" has occurred, but it would be inaccurate to call it a "sexual act". It is missing a necessary element: an *agented cognition*. In order for an act to be sexual, it must be *performed* as opposed to *experienced* by an individual. The cognition "knowing that an orgasm is occurring" is fundamentally different from "I am performing an orgasm", or, because of the difficulty in having a sense of control regarding orgasm, "I am acting in such a way as to bring about an orgasm". Without an agented cognition, the experience is not primarily sexual.

SOCRATES: Are you saying that if a woman is raped and her experience admits of no agented cognition, that is, she does not own herself in relation to the behavior occurring, then her experience is not primarily sexual?

MASSAGE THERAPIST: Exactly. The "act" may be considered sexual if by "act" we mean a specific interaction between two people, but the only person whose experience admits of agented sexuality is the rapist's. The victim may understand that a **sexual event** is occurring, but she is neither the author nor a voluntary participant in the event.

SOCRATES: The client, then, is a voluntary participant in a mechanical and sensual "act" but not in a sexual act.

MASSAGE THERAPIST: Yes. The sexuality, though certainly a component of the experience, and even a focal component for a period of time, does not consist of an agented cognition. No matter how sexual the "act" appears to be (e.g. incest), the respective experiences of the people involved in the act need not be sexual. Even in situations

where the rape or incest victim experiences some sexual pleasure, the overriding affect is not sexual. It may be terror, disgust, rage, numbness, etc. but not sexual pleasure.
SOCRATES: You seem to be using the term "act" to refer to an event between people, an interpersonal interaction, rather than an individual voluntary behavior. And you use "experience" to refer to a set of components of consciousness as owned, behavior being one of these components.
MASSAGE THERAPIST: Let me try to clarify. An **event** is an experience or set-of-experiences that occurs individually or interpersonally and consists of either focal or peripheral components that characterize it. Sexual stimulation in a client in a massage situation can be considered a sexual event in that the peripheral consciousness of the client consists of a sexual component. An **act** refers to an experience or set-of-experiences that occurs individually or interpersonally and consists of an agented cognition. A rape event consists of the agentless terror-experience of the victim and the agented sexual-experience of the rapist. If at least one of the participants' experience is agented, then the event can be referred to as an act, for that person. An experience, as I said, refers to a combination of cognition, affect, behavior, sensation, and the physical environment as owned.
SOCRATES: Therefore, a massage therapist can be involved in a sexual event without that event being a sexual act.
MASSAGE THERAPIST: Yes. The sexual event is a sub-component or sub-category of the main sensual (or mechanical) category.
SOCRATES: And a sexual-experience consists of a componential structure that is dynamic or escalating. But this experience can "serve" a stronger experience, e.g. a sensual-experience.
MASSAGE THERAPIST: Yes.
SOCRATES: Can the **weaker-experience** within the **stronger-experience** of this *layered-experience* be agented? That is, can the sexual excitation felt be the client who is receiving a sensual stroke be agented? And if it can, would that make the event an act in relation to sexuality?
MASSAGE THERAPIST: Socrates, you are truly the mid-wife of philosophical ideas. You challenge me to my intellectual ends. In response to your question I'd have to say this: The sexual aspect of the sensual experience can remain peripheral throughout the set-of-experiences or be focalized within the set-of-experiences without ever

being agented. The massage client (female, let's say) can be only peripherally aware of her sexual stimulation or be focally aware of it without ever being an agent in relation to it. She can also be an agent within her sensual-experience, but it is her sensuality that she is an agent of (e.g. cognition: "I want this pleasure to continue"). But once she becomes an agent of the sexual aspect of her sensual experience, her sexuality is focalized and the experience shifts to one of sexuality. We can only be agents of focal cognitions. The *course of experience* from peripheral, unagented sexuality to focal, agented sexuality might look like this:

cognition: this feels so good
affect   : sensual pleasure [sexual pleasure]
behavior : relaxed body [some blood rushing into genital area]
sense   : bodily sensations, hands on body [slight sexual stimulation]
environ : massage room
"I"   : ownership

Which would shift to:

cognition: that feels too good
affect   : concern, sexual pleasure [sensual pleasure]
behavior : body tensing a bit, breathing pattern changing [other muscles relaxing]
sense   : sexual stimulation [sensual stimulation]
environ : massage room
"I"   : ownership

Which shifts to:

cognition: oh, I like that sexual feeling (and I want more)
affect   : sexual pleasure
behavior : body tensing "inviting" more stimulation
sense   : sexual arousal, hands on body
environ : massage room
"I"   : ownership

The first two experiences are unagented; there is no "I"-as-agent in relation to the cognition. In the second experience the sexual pleasure increases; it moves from peripheral to focal consciousness. It is that to which the cognition "that feels too good" applies. But the focalization of the sexual component of consciousness does not make the experience agented. The client is just realizing that the sexual component is really there in experience, i.e. a "force to contend with". She is more concerned about it than pleasured in relation to it. But in her third experience her concern fades away and is replaced by a stronger sexual

pleasure, a sexually exciting bodily sensation, and an agented cognition. She now acts volitionally in relation to her focalized sexuality. For her experience to consist of an agented cognition in relation to a peripheral sexual stimulation, the experience would have to look like this:
cognition: I want this feeling to continue (grow)
affect : [sexual pleasure], sensual pleasure
behavior : [abdomen tensing, breathing pattern changing], other muscles relaxed
sense : [sexual stimulation], hands on body, sensual stimulation
environ : massage room
"I" : ownership

Here the cognitive element "this feeling" is misapplied. She identifies "this feeling" with sensual pleasure, and not with the growing sexual pleasure. It is the sexual pleasure to which the cognition "this feeling" should apply. Her abdomen tensing is not being cognized as applicable to her sexual pleasure; she is barely aware of it. The hands on her body is a focal sensation which alternates with her focal cognition. In other words, she is now aware of the therapist's hands on her body, now of her sexual feeling which she is cognizing or understanding as a sensual feeling. Her sexual excitation is overtaking her sensual pleasure, but she is not cognizing this as her experiential state-of-affairs. Rather, she is cognizing her sensual pleasure as focal. She is cognizing her sensual pleasure and therefore the agented aspect of that cognition (e.g. the "I want this to continue") is applied to the sensual feeling which is becoming peripheral, but it is the sexual excitation (that she understands to be sensual) that the cognition is experientially consistent with. She is, simultaneously, the agent of her sensuality (focal cognition) and her sexuality (stronger affect). It is only in this way, or some similar way, that I can see a peripheral component of experience being agented. So in answer to your question of whether or not such an experience can be called a sexual act, I'd have to say 'yes' inasmuch as its stronger affect is sexual excitation and its focal cognition is ambiguous or misapplied. If the agented cognition should apply to or be supported by the affect of sexual excitement rather than sensual pleasure, then the experience should be characterized as sexual and the agency of its cognition (even though misapplied) permits it to be called a sexual act.

SOCRATES: So the client can be sexually excited over and above being sensually stimulated without recognizing that sexual excitement for what it is. And she could "choose" to let or want the excitement to escalate while thinking that it is her sensual pleasure that is increasing in some way.

MASSAGE THERAPIST: I'd say, yes, the act is sexual though no one, including herself, realizes it to be so. But such an experience I've referred to previously as *mixed* rather than *layered*.

SOCRATES: Perhaps we should explore this distinction a bit further.

MASSAGE THERAPIST: If the client's experience consists of the following:

cognition: this feels good
affect   : sensual pleasure [sexual pleasure]
behavior : relaxed muscles [blood rushing into genital area]
sense   : hands on body, sensual stimulation [sexual excitement]
environ : massage room
"I"   : ownership

Then her experience is referred to as a layered-experience. Her cognition is supported by both sensual pleasure and sexual stimulation, but the sensual pleasure is stronger than her sexual excitement and the cognition applies primarily to the stronger affect. If her experience should shift to include agency at this point, it may look like this:

cognition: I want this to continue
affect   : sensual pleasure; [sexual pleasure]
behavior : relaxed muscles; [decreasing blood flow to genital area]
sense   : hands on body, sensual stimulation; [sexual stimulation decreasing]
environ : massage room
"I"   : ownership

She now is agented in relation to the "wanting to continue" (i.e. allowing this to continue), but it is the sensual pleasure that she wants to continue, which includes the sexual excitation amidst her sensual stimulation, but that excitation is not focal; and it is not that to which her agented cognition refers. Hence, the act is not sexual but sensual. Now if her experience were to shift to the following:

cognition: oh my, that's sexually exciting
affect   : sexual pleasure; [sensual pleasure]
behavior : muscles tensing, blood flowing to genital area, heavier breathing pattern; [other muscles relaxed]
sense   : sexual stimulation, hands on body; [sensual stimulation]
environ : massage room
"I"   : ownership

And is immediately followed by:

cognition: I shouldn't feel this
affect   : duty
behavior : hesitation, suspension of breathing pattern
sense   : sexual stimulation, hands on body
environ : massage room
"I"   : ownership

Which renders:

cognition: this feels good/I've got to stop this
affect   : sexual excitement/duty
behavior : muscles tensing in excitation and prevention, heavy breathing pattern continues and includes "prevention" signs
sense   : sexual stimulation increasing, hands on body/resistance increasing
environ : massage room
"I"   : ownership

Here the experience is compound. Two distinct experiences are opposed to each other: one sexual excitement escalating and the other resistance strengthening to match the rise in sexual excitement. At this point her agency is multiple: she wants the escalating excitation to continue and stop; she is ambivalent, but she is not "confused" or "mixed up" or "deceiving herself". But if her duty-experience had prompted:

cognition: that leg muscle feels good
afffect   : [sexual pleasure]; sensual pleasure
behavior : [muscles tensing in abdomen]; muscles relaxing in leg
sense   : [sexual excitement]; hands on leg, sensual stimulation
environ : massage room
"I"   : ownership

Then her focal consciousness shifts from her duty in relation to her sexual excitement to her sensual stimulation in her leg which constitutes attention away from her stronger sexual excitement. If this experience prompts:

cognition: I like the feeling in my leg (and want it to continue)
affect   : [sexual excitement]; sensual pleasure
behavior : [muscles in abdomen tensing more, muscles in leg tensing]; other muscles relaxed
sense   : [sexual stimulation]; sensual stimulation
environ : massage room
"I"   : ownership

She is the agent in relation to a cognition that is not supported by the stronger affect. Her agency is misapplied. Her stronger affect is sexual excitement; her stronger behavior is abdominal muscle contraction; her stronger sensation is sexual stimulation; but she is agented in relation to her cognition of wanting the "sensual" stimulation to "continue". The experience is intra-experientially inconsistent, i.e. mixed. As such she is engaging in a sexual act but would not (or could not in all honesty) admit it. Her experiential state-of-affairs consists of experientially objective sexual components that dominate the experience but are not cognized as such by the individual. So, in answer to your question, Socrates, I'd say that in a mixed-experience an agented cognition can be applied to weaker affect, behavior, and sensation, and a person can engage in a sexual act without knowing or admitting it, but the same cannot be said of a layered-experience unless the levels reverse their relationship and the secondary becomes primary, the primary secondary, in which case the agented component would apply to the stronger affect in each experience.

SOCRATES: Therefore a client can feel sexual excitement, even to the point of orgasm, without ever engaging in a sexual act.

MASSAGE THERAPIST: Precisely.

SOCRATES: Though future discussion might reveal examples to contradict or challenge your contention, I must admit that you seem to have met the challenge quite well.

MASSAGE THERAPIST: For now, possibly. But I, like you, am not sure of what the future will hold.

SOCRATES: Ok. Let's grant that our massage therapist, like the client, is engaged in a layered-experience: he is stroking the client sensually (or mechanically) while simultaneously feeling some peripheral sexual stimulation. His light stroke over the body of the client, which passes over her breasts and genital area, is a sensual and not a sexual act, because his agency rests with a sensual cognition which is supported by the stronger sensual affect, the stronger behavior, and the stronger sensation. His experience is intra-experientially consistent, and hence experientially right.

MASSAGE THERAPIST: Yes.

26. Group Levels of Experience and the Process of Morality

SOCRATES: But is this act moral? Let's say that the ethics board disagrees with you. The board maintains that any touching, except accidental or incidental touching, of the breasts (female) or genital area, even over a draping, constitutes a sexual act or sexual conduct.

MASSAGE THERAPIST: Inasmuch as the board is organized hierarchically it has power "over" its professional constituency. The board may be empowered by a more powerful organization (e.g. the state) or by its own professional constituency, i.e. voted into their hierarchically structured positions. Either way, the board's power is *unilateral*: "it" determines "for others" what is ethical and not ethical in the profession. Even if the board's structure is consensual (i.e. ethical decisions are made consensually), the determinations are unilateral if the board is empowered by others outside of its professional constituency (e.g. the state). Inasmuch as ethical determinations are unilateral or hierarchically derived, they skew the process of morality toward the experience of a select few and create a dominant-submissive moral structure. Inasmuch as ethical determinants are **equalitarian** and based on experience rather than power, they represent the morality of the profession.

SOCRATES: I know that this is the area to be discussed in detail at a later date, but I would like to ask some questions so that you might provide the outline of this area that you said you would.

MASSAGE THERAPIST: Go ahead.

SOCRATES: How do unilateral or hierarchically derived decisions "skew" the process of morality?

MASSAGE THERAPIST: Consider a basic hierarchical structure where decision-making power resides in one or several individuals; others' input into those decisions may or may not be invited or encouraged. If the experience of the decision-makers is intra-experientially consistent and strong, then the ethical determination is made, and the power of the hierarchical position is used, if necessary, to make sure that those with contrary opinions to that determination will eventually support the determination, if only behaviorally. What often happens in these situations is that intra-experientially consistent contrary opinions are usually not considered by the decision-makers, and if they are, they tend to be accepted or rejected inasmuch as they confirm or disconfirm the experience of the decision-makers. In hierarchies, experiential consensus, i.e. interpersonal experiential consistency among all members of the group, is not necessary. What is necessary is group-behavioral conformity. Such conformity consists of intra-experientially and inter-experientially inconsistent experience. The experiential structure of those conforming may be mixed as in:

```
cognition: I am acting professionally (by doing this)
affect   : [resentment]; duty
behavior : performing task subtly aggressively
sense    : environ
environ  : wherever
"I"      : ownership
```
The agented cognition applies to the weaker affect of duty; the stronger affect of resentment is not cognized for what it is as a component of an experiential state-of-affairs. This "mix" is reflected in subtly aggressive behavior. The experience is intra-experientially inconsistent and, hence, experientially wrong. Applied to moral situations, the experience is morally wrong.

SOCRATES: Are you saying that it is morally wrong for a person to suppress his strong feelings of rejection (resentment) so he could act out of duty to his boss?

MASSAGE THERAPIST: If the duty is not self-imposed, and the situation can be considered a moral one, then yes: the experience, and, hence, the behavior is experientially and morally wrong.

SOCRATES: And the same holds true for a person whose experience is compound, where the conflict is quite clearly understood for what it is.

MASSAGE THERAPIST: Yes. The person knows he doesn't want to do it, but he does it anyway. Here the experience might look like this:
```
cognition: I don't want to do this
affect   : dislike, resentment
behavior : performing task half-heartedly
sense    : environ
environ  : wherever
"I"      : ownership
```
The half-heartedness of the behavior supports the cognitive and affective components of experience, but the performing of the task itself does not. But at this stage of the set-of-experiences, the experience is only partially inconsistent. This dislike may fade as the behavior continues, thus resolving the partial inconsistency. But if the cognition and affect increase in strength, while the affect continues in a growing manner, the inconsistency increases. The set-of-experiences becomes more and more immoral inasmuch as this is a moral situation.

SOCRATES: It is difficult for one not to challenge your argument, my friend, but I will restrain myself so you can finish your outlining of this area.
MASSAGE THERAPIST: I appreciate your restraint.
SOCRATES: The upshot is, correct me if I am wrong, the more intra- and inter-experientially consistent experience is, the more experientially right it is; and if it is a moral experience, then the more moral it is.
MASSAGE THERAPIST: Yes.
SOCRATES: The more consistent individual experience is with others' individual experience, the more interpersonally right, and, hence, the more moral it is.
MASSAGE THERAPIST: Yes. Your insight into the process aspect of these ideas is commendable, considering what little I've said in this regard.
SOCRATES: I better take the compliment now, because after I get done scrutinizing this idea, you may want to retrieve it.
MASSAGE THERAPIST: I doubt it, but please proceed.

27. Experiential Morality vs. Other Moral Systems

SOCRATES: Your "method" or "system" of morality seems to be quite fluid and dynamic.
MASSAGE THERAPIST: Yes. This dynamic quality is an integral part of **experiential morality**.
SOCRATES: Would you describe this morality in your own words first, and then I'll question you on it.
MASSAGE THERAPIST: Yes. Morals are, first and foremost, experiences. Any given event within the empirico-phenomenal world can, at least theoretically, be subject to **moralitization**. Moralitization, or the process of making moral, can be characterized by any of the components of experience. Hume emphasized the affective component, claiming that the basis of morality rests with our feelings of acceptance and rejection, joy and repugnance, ecstasy and abhorrence. Kant emphasized the cognitive component (reason), claiming that reason alone can provide us with categorical imperatives upon which we can base a morality. Epicurus (and later the utilitarians) emphasized sensual pleasure and pain (and, later, happiness), claiming that these sensations guide us in determining right from wrong. Skinner emphasized the behavioral component, claiming that morality is the result of learned behavior or conditioning. Marx emphasized the environmental

component (i.e. matter and economics), claiming that morality is the result of changes in physical matter and economic circumstances. And most recently Wright emphasizes the environmental component (i.e. evolutionary genetics), arguing, in effect, that morality is the result of natural selection. At some point in ethical history, some component or combination of components of experience has served as the basis of morality, at least theoretically. Experientially, all components of experience are equal to each other; all are necessary for there to be experience. No component can be reduced to any other component. Each component "leaves its mark" on moralitization.

SOCRATES: Can you describe how each component "leaves its mark"?

MASSAGE THERAPIST: Examples: Rape is "felt" by many to be repulsive or abhorrent; reason, per Kant and Christian natural law, dictates that rape is the manipulation of one person for the satisfaction of another, or the treatment of a person as a means to an end, without his or her agreement; but such an intellectual approach to rape misses the affective potency involved in thinking about, let alone experiencing, it. Lying is "judged" to be wrong because it violates a principle of reason and undermines trust, which produces considerable social unhappiness, but people tend to find lying much less repugnant than rape. Some lies are considered to be morally quite acceptable, many rather innocuous, etc. Both rape and lying have their cognitive and affective components respectively, but those components do not characterize their respective experiences, as do the others. A massage in the afternoon, even if it involves a little sexual stimulation, is accepted as moral because it feels good and hurts no one. Giving money to the poor, even if its motivation is primarily egoistic, is recognized as a good thing to do. Getting a massage contains its behavioral component and giving to the poor contains it sensual component, but these components are peripheral in consciousness. Moralitization occurs on all componential levels of consciousness. No level has priority over any other, though philosophers and theologians have argued so in the past.

SOCRATES: Yes, I'd like to retrieve my comments on Augustine's emphasis on reason and revelation over desire. For Augustine reason has primacy over desire; it should control desire and point the way to the Eternal Law or God's determination of right and wrong. Even more so, Kant's reason is the inherent and supreme determiner of right and wrong. For Kant desire is virtually non-existent as a contributor to moral determinations.

MASSAGE THERAPIST: Exactly so. And that, I think, is their primary shortcoming. As I've already tried to show, reason is reducible to particular types of experiences in relation to each other, i.e. contradictory experiences within a circumscribed set-of-experiences, or two contradictory sets-of-experiences. Cognition is the primary component within the sets-of-experiences that "does battle" with desire, or the set-of-experiences dominated by affect. But the "triumph" of reason is not necessarily superior to the "triumph" of any other component of consciousness in determining morality. Love can override the coolest, most detached reasoning for determining proper action. Sexual desire can override sensually detached, Puritanical reasoning. Social action can override oppressive governmental reasoning. In other words, reasoning is an experiential process made up of components of consciousness in relation to each other and not some sort of superior faculty given to us by God or evolution so we can control our desires, prioritize our sensations, or direct our wills (behavior) so that we may "know God's will", "reach the Eternal Law", or simply determine right from wrong. Reason is just as faulty, just as prone to error, as is any other component of experience or set-of-experiences. Failing to recognize the importance of each component of consciousness in the process of moralitization results in an imbalance between componential structures of experience, either intra- or inter-experientially and interpersonally. Such imbalances prompt inconsistent componential structures which are equivalent to experientially wrong structures, which in moral situations, are equivalent to morally wrong experience.

SOCRATES: Can you give an example of how failing to recognize the importance of each component of consciousness results in an imbalance between componential structures of experience? And how such imbalances prompt inconsistencies?

MASSAGE THERAPIST: The Kantian stress on rationally derived moral principles locates moralitization in the component of cognition either intra-experientially (immediate cognition) or inter-experientially (through application of his universalization method). Whether or not we know what is right or wrong immediately or through a rational process over time, our knowledge is a component of experience; it is specifically the content of our cognitive component of consciousness. For Kant we can cognize our duty while we experience desire and either know immediately that our cognition is right and the desire wrong, or we can ask ourselves, "What if everyone acted upon such a desire whenever it conflicted with reason," and, based upon our answer, determine the rational course of action. Kant places reason over and above experience, something a priori that conditions experience, and, hence, we, as experiencers, must align our experience with reason if we are to determine right from wrong. In emphasizing reason in this manner, Kant rejects the importance of affect, behavior, sensations, and the physical environment as significant aspects of moralitization. Experientially, an intra-experientially consistent experience requires an affect, behavior, sensation, and an environment consistent with a cognition. Such consistency equals immediate rightness, equals moral rightness. There is no need to posit a priori conditions for experience, because experience is defined to include its own conditions inasmuch as we cognize them. Kant's a priori conditions of experience are cognitive constituents of experience or meta-experiential constructs. As cognitive constituents of experience they register in experience as cognitions. Example:

cognition: Lying is wrong because it is an example of treating people as a means to one's own end
affect : confidence
behavior : confident posture, etc.
sense : accompaniment
environ : accompaniment
"I" : ownership

Here lying is wrong not because of the reason stated; nor is it wrong because it violates some a priori principle which maintains that we should not treat people as means to our ends. Rather, the experience which consists in part of the cognition "Lying is wrong because..." is right because its componential structure is consistent. Experientially, a priori reason is nothing other than a simple, clear cognition supported by other components of consciousness. To make it more than that is to form a meta-experiential construct. Where such a construct is formed, cognition loses its equal componential status and reduces experience to a component of itself. Therefore, when we run into someone whose experience contradicts our own, or when we experience a contradiction within our set-of-experiences, we would, if we subscribed to the Kantian system, have to decide between what we have held to be a rational act (telling the truth) based on a rational principle (treating people as ends in themselves) and what we desire to do (tell a lie) based on egoistic or utilitarian principles. Such a compound experience might look like this:

cognition: tell a lie
affect   : concern for feelings of another
behavior : hesitation
sense   : accompaniment
environ : accompaniment
"I"   : ownership
And:
cognition: tell the truth
affect   : duty
behavior : hesitation
sense   : accompaniment
environ : accompaniment
"I"   : ownership

Here the Kantian has no choice other than to adhere to the "dictates of reason" if he is to do what is right. But how is he to determine which of the conflicting experiences reflects reason and which does not, other than by associating his current duty-experience with his past rational principle and affirming the duty-experience? And such would be fine if that is the way things worked. If all of our desire-experiences were weak in relation to our duty-experiences, then we would have little trouble in "acting according to reason". But such is simply not the case. A desire-experience may indeed outweigh a duty-experience and in addition be considered wholly rational. Therefore, a person may consider it wholly rational to lie under certain circumstances. Experientially, rationality is dynamic; it is a process of experience that is subject to intra-experiential, inter-experiential, and interpersonal experiential consistency. To make it into a basis for morality is to bias the importance of cognition and to skew the course-of-experience into the direction of pre-conceived principles. In our example, the Kantian would have to somehow deny the validity of his desire-experience and affirm the validity of his duty-experience when there is no possible way for him to do so. He cannot get outside of his experience to deny or affirm his experience. His denial or affirmation must be an experience itself, in relation to other experiences. If he were to deny his desire-experience when this experience is the stronger of the two conflicting experiences, then his experience is likely to be mixed, i.e. he will deny that which is more truly him and somehow justify that denial - only to have the experience surface again and again in the same or different form. If he were to deny the stronger experience and affirm the weaker and not be mixed in relation to them, then he would be blatantly lying.

He cannot determine that lying in this circumstance is wrong without experiencing his determination as a lie. Therefore, within the Kantian scheme of pre-determined or absolutist reason, we are often left with either mixed experiences or blatant lies in trying to resolve our conflicting experiences. The appeal to reason is, in effect, either an appeal to past experiences of what is rational or to a meta-experiential construct, which has no experiential basis.

SOCRATES: Let me see if I understand you. I'll use Augustinian reason. If I desire to have sex with another man's wife, and reason informs me that this desire is temporary and the hurtful consequences of the act would be long-lasting, then, according to you, given that my desire is stronger than my reason, or, more accurately, my desire-experience is stronger than my duty-experience, then any attempt to settle this conflict by choosing reason (or duty) over desire will end up either in a mixed experience or a blatant lie.

MASSAGE THERAPIST: "You" cannot simply "choose" the duty-experience. You don't have that kind of power. The duty-experience has its own strength and "you" cannot increase or decrease that strength; if the strength does increase or decrease, it is because it prompts other experiences that are increased or decreased in strength, or circumstances change which serves to increase or decrease the strength. When you affirm the existence of your duty-experience and deny or underassess the strength of your desire-experience, when in fact your desire-experience is the stronger of the two, your experience consists of an agented cognition that addresses or is supported by a weaker affect. Your experience is mixed. You are, in effect, giving "lip service" to a rational principle that in experiential actuality carries less weight in regard to you in this situation than does your desire-experience.

SOCRATES: It would be more moral for me to act on my desire and have sex with the other man's wife?

MASSAGE THERAPIST: I argue like this: When your experience resolves itself into an intra-experientially consistent experience, your behavior is part of an experientially right experience, and, hence, in our moral example, it is moral. Inasmuch as this intra-experientially consistent experience (i.e. resolution-experience) is confirmed by other experiences, your inter-experiential relationship is one of consistency, i.e. your resolution-experience is strengthened by confirmation experiences. Inasmuch as your inter-experientially consistent experience is consistent with the other person with whom you are interacting, your interpersonal experience is consistent (mutual level of experience). If you act prematurely, that is, if you have sex with the woman when you have not reached a functionally right level of experience, then you will experience guilt, remorse, or some other negative feeling. Your act will be judged as immoral and the experiential structure, which consists in part of your behavior, is consistent with your negative judgment.

SOCRATES: And if the course-of-experience resolves itself into a functionally right experience which prompts me to have sex with the woman? Then what?

MASSAGE THERAPIST: Then your experience would be intra-experientially consistent and morally right, for you, at this time. Then you have to see if future experience supports or confirms this rightness, i.e. if your partner's experience confirms your experience, and if your other pertinent mutual, group, and societal experience is consistent with your own.

SOCRATES: And if you live in a group and/or society that condemns such acts, then you're in for an up-hill battle to establish the moral rightness of such an act.

MASSAGE THERAPIST: Yes.

SOCRATES: If Kantian and Augustinian reason is reducible to components of experience and, hence, is subject to the dynamic flow of experience, then can I assume that Humean affect, Epicurian sensuality, and Skinnerian behavior, etc. are also reducible to components of experience and subject to the dynamic flow of consciousness?

MASSAGE THERAPIST: Yes.

SOCRATES: Could you just show me how this is so with Humean affect?

MASSAGE THERAPIST: Yes. X feels repugnance in relation to slavery events; Y feels confidence in their moral rightness. For either of them to appeal to their affect upon which to base their moral judgments to the near exclusion of the other components of their experience would result in a distortion of experience and a skewing of the course-of-experience into directions away from consistency. I may at one time feel confident about the moral rightness of slavery events, but over time, having experienced a number of disconfirmation-experiences, I may doubt the validity of my moral judgment regarding these events. Let's say that I experience these disconfirming experiences in a classroom setting; my peers disagree with me and argue their position in ways I had never considered. Their reasoning impresses me so much that my confidence in the moral rightness of slavery is disrupted. The seed of their reason is planted and takes root in me. My affect changes because of cognition-experiences. In other words, cognition-experiences prompt affect-experiences, as well as the reverse. If I maintain a Humean bias in this situation, I will tend to de-emphasize the rational validity of my experience and affirm the affective validity. I would affirm my confidence, e.g. I would act in a confident manner in relation to slavery discussions, but I would not feel much confidence. I would, in effect, cover my doubt and argue against anti-slavery arguments, possibly with great gusto, but the defense would be impotent, i.e. all flash and no substance. In adhering to the Humean bias, my experience is "locked into" past emotional justification for my moral reasoning. If my emotional justification is challenged by rational argumentation, I'll tend to reject the argumentation, form feelings in relation to those arguing in such a manner, and act so as to invalidate those arguments; and all the while my feeling of rejection toward slavery grows within me.

SOCRATES: Maintaining the Humean bias tends to blind oneself in regard to one's conflicting emotions which underlie one's morality; and maintaining a Kantian bias tends to blind oneself in regard to one's conflicting thoughts (or principles) which underlie one's morality.

MASSAGE THERAPIST: A succinct way of putting it, Socrates.

SOCRATES: I suspect that you can argue similarly in relation to the other proposed biases of morality, i.e. sensuality, behavior, and the environment. But how would you apply such an argument to the utilitarian theory of morality? Is utilitarian theory similarly biased?

MASSAGE THERAPIST: In utilitarian theory the happiness of all is the central criterion for morality. If happiness is an affect, which I maintain it is, then the theory is biased toward the affective component of experience. An advantage of utilitarian theory, though, is its interpersonal criterion. It requires that moral claims be based not simply upon one's own happiness but also upon the happiness of others. Experientially, this is an advantage over other theories in that moral claims require interpersonal levels of experience for their validity for anyone other than him or her self. It also has the advantage of being process-oriented. Since it requires many individual inputs, moral claims are subject to challenge, conflict, and contradiction. Experiential absolutes are more easily attained in utilitarian systems of morality than they are in deontological or divinely backed systems. But the drawback, as I said, is its affective bias. Experientially, happiness is only one component of experience. When inter-experientially conflicting situations arise, happiness will tend to skew the course-of-experience in a similar manner as do the other biases. For instance, if a woman experiences conflict over performing an act to save her own life while causing the death of "another life" (e.g. abortion), it is her own happiness that is of paramount concern and not that of all involved. Many may suffer in relation to her decision, but ultimately her view is that the decision is hers and that others' pain, though seemingly unavoidable, is not the direct result of her action. She does not understand her action to be the cause of their pain; they are pained because of who they are in this situation. If they weren't opposed to abortion, they might not be pained. Experientially, intra-experiential and inter-experiential consistency and some societal consistency may be all that is necessary to establish the morality of the experience. That is, she may be settled in herself that she is doing the right thing, the political and legal professions may affirm the legal right for her to do so, and the medical profession may supply the medical means of doing so. This may be sufficient for her to claim that the act is moral, even though it seemingly causes more pain than happiness within her group (i.e. family and friends). If she were to adhere to the utilitarian bias, she would tend to observe her stronger egoistic experience in utilitarian garb. She might deny her desire for personal happiness and affirm the idea that happiness of all should outweigh the pain of all and thus act in accordance with the weaker affect. She will bow to the needs of others and sacrifice her own needs, have the child, and bear the resentment that attends this while claiming the righteousness of self-sacrifice for the good of all.

SOCRATES: Her act of having the child under these circumstances is experientially inconsistent and, hence, morally wrong.

MASSAGE THERAPIST: Yes. Her experience is mixed, and this mixed experience prompts more mixed experiences. Thus she lives a life of growing resentment and hatred while trying to justify it on utilitarian grounds.

SOCRATES: And if she adhered to an experiential theory or model of morality?

MASSAGE THERAPIST: If her experience, which included the behavior of aborting (or allowing another to abort) the fetus is componentially consistent, then it is morally right for her at this time. If her subsequent experiences are primarily confirming-experiences, then her experience is inter-experientially consistent and, hence, morally right. If her experiences are strong and their consistency is maintained, at least functionally, in the face of the interpersonal experiences between her and her group(s), then her experience will continue to be consistent and morally right. If her inter-experiential consistency is maintained in the face of interpersonal experience between her and her society (laws, medical means, etc.), then her experience is still morally right. And, finally, if her inter-experiential consistency is maintained in the face of interpersonal experience between her and all of the societies of the world, if at all applicable, then her experience is morally right on a universal scale. In determining whether or not a given experience is morally right or wrong, the experientialist must consider the entire componential structure of the experience (resolution-experience), the structure of the entire set-of-experiences (resolution-experience plus confirmation-experiences), and the entire structure of interpersonal-experiences, which influence the development of the set-of-experiences (inter-experiential structures).

SOCRATES: If I understand you correctly, the experientialist may never really be able to determine whether or not anything is right or wrong, because the process involved is a continuous unending process. Also, multiple, even contradictory determinations of morality, can exist simultaneously. Individual intra-experientially consistent experiences can contradict each other, which would be similar to having two contradictory Kantian a priori principles of reason existing simultaneously. Group determinations can contradict individual and mutual determinations. And, to top it off, a single individual's intra-experientially consistent experience at one time can contradict her set-of-experiences that develops over time. Lastly, the experientialist position seems to be hopelessly relativistic, making the "process of moralitization" more important that the "content of morality", i.e. "how" we determine what is right and wrong more important than "what" we determine to be right and wrong.

MASSAGE THERAPIST: Let me consider your conclusions (criticisms?) one at a time. First, I agree that there is an unending quality to experientially determined morals: it is an on-going process, constantly subject to change, and the determinations certainly have a dynamic quality to them. But this in no way precludes ever reaching moral determinations. In fact, acts of reaching moral determinations increase within the experientialist model of interaction when compared to other models. Individual moral structures consist of intra-experientially and inter-experientially consistent experiences as well as (at times) inconsistent experiences. Intra-experientially consistent experiences form our absolutes in regard to morality and are confirmed and "solidified" by confirmation-experiences that help comprise our set-of-experiences regarding any given moral issue. When our group-experiences support our individual-experience, our absolutes become even more entrenched. The same absolutizing process increases as the larger groups, within which the smaller groups exist, support these absolutes. But the experientialist method of determining morality works for and against homogeneity simultaneously. By striving for individual experiential consistency and structuring our groups and societies to enable, encourage, and even require such consistency for their very existence, we create the basis for individual development and societal heterogeneity. And by striving for mutual, group, social and inter-societal experiential consistency, we create a basis for consensual interaction and social homogeneity. Maintaining a balance between an individually determined heterogeneous morality and an interpersonally determined homogenous morality is the natural outcome (or natural task) of experientialist ethics. Secondly, I agree with your conclusion that experientially determined morality admits of contradictory moralities that exist simultaneously between different individuals, groups, and societies, and sequentially within a given individual, group, or society. Empirical evidence already overwhelmingly supports the claim that such contradictions exist right now within and between individuals, groups, and societies. So too does empirical evidence support the claim that consistent moralities also exist in and between all levels of experience. The experientialist position does nothing to change the fact that moral contradictions and consistencies exist; it accepts it as a part of the process of moralitization. In fact, it is the balance between consistency and contradiction that drives the process. "Pure" consistency results in stagnation; "pure" contradiction results in chaos. A balance between consistency and contradiction results in a dynamic process of altering and grounding moral absolutes. Thirdly, an experientialist ethics requires both relativist and objectivist experiences in order to function. Intra-experientially consistent experiences (resolution- and confirmation-experiences) form the absolutist structure of experientialist morality. These experiences consist of components that comprise an objective state-of-affairs. Without these objective-absolutist experiences, we would not know who we are, what is real and what is not, etc. These experiences keep us grounded and provide us with the stability necessary to interact with others as experiential beings. Inter-experientially inconsistent or contradictory experiences form the relativist structure of experiential morality. Intra-experientially inconsistent experiences also add to the relativist structure but in a negative way. These self-deceptive experiences may serve as temporary bridges to constructive grappling with inter-experientially inconsistent experiences, but as far as I can see, they serve no other constructive moral purpose. They are, in fact, the basis of objective immorality within the experientialist perspective. But inter-experientially inconsistent experiences provide us with the "kick in the pants" necessary for us to realize our biases, expose our shortcomings, counter our oppressiveness, and remove our moral blinders. Inasmuch as we accept and grapple with the contradictions within our sets-of-experiences, we work through moral differences, alter our absolutes appropriately, and create moral consensus and mutual, group, societal, and inter-societal moral homogeneity.

SOCRATES: You're basically saying, then, that morals are part-and-parcel experiential existences, and for us to try to go beyond our experience in an attempt to establish moral absolutes or objective morals-beyond-experience is to create meta-experiential constructs, i.e. an exercise in "experiential futility".

MASSAGE THERAPIST: Yes.

28. Sex, Love, and the Moral Process

SOCRATES: Indulge me if you will. I'd like to apply our formal, theoretical discussion to a practical situation to see if some more light can be shed upon these ideas. I still have trouble with what I conceive to be your relativistic leanings. Let's say that our married man is sexually attracted to a married woman, and vice-versa, granting heterosexual orientation. They have enough interaction with each other to realize that they are attracted to each other in other ways also, i.e. in the areas of intelligence, personality, interests, etc. Also, they are aware that each is attracted in these ways to each other, which increases their attraction for each other. As these mutual feelings for each other increase or deepen, the man realizes that he's falling in love with the woman. At this point, Augustinian Christian morality is quite clear: lust after temporal things (e.g. flesh) is immoral. Not only is the act of adultery wrong but so too is the thought or desire to commit adultery because it is an example of lusting after temporal things. We should "lust after" or desire eternal things, i.e. things that cannot be taken away from us, e.g. wisdom, courage, fortitude, truth, (i.e. things that make us who we are). Christian morality offers us direction toward things that last, that persist over time, that determine our moral fiber or our character. But in your experiential view, intra-experiential consistency is the basis upon which to build a morality. Let's say that the man loves his wife and is sexually attracted to her, while simultaneously loving and being sexually attracted to this other woman. If his experience does not admit of conflict, then it is morally right for him at this time.

MASSAGE THERAPIST: Yes.

SOCRATES: The question arises: What about their respective vows to their spouses? If each vowed fidelity to each other, then are they not bound by their vow? And are they not breaking their vow? It seems that your criterion for morality, i.e. intra-experiential consistency, is a very immediate thing; it need not bother itself with past commitments or vows if such commitments do not surface in experience.

MASSAGE THERAPIST: I agree that intra-experientially consistent experience alone, i.e. as an independent experience, need not entail past commitments that bear on the experience in some significant way. But intra-experientially consistent experiences are not independent, isolated experiences. No experience is. It is the basis for morality inasmuch as it 1) is intra-experientially consistent, 2) is strong enough to prompt confirmation experiences that solidify its rightness, 3) withstands interpersonal experience, and 4) prompts confirmation-experiences on all applicable interpersonal experiential levels. (Whether or not a given intra-experientially consistent experience (e.g. resolution-experience) reaches the inter-societal level of experience is another issue altogether.) The point is that a given experience can be rendered moral or immoral at any level of experience and can be moral on one level while being immoral on another level at the same time. For instance, if the woman tells the man that she loves him, and her confrontation-experience is componentially consistent, then her experience is morally right for her at this time. If the man loves her but can't accept this experiential state-of-affairs, he may react quite negatively in relation to her self-disclosure. Perhaps he judges such a thing as professionally unacceptable or as a breach of his marital vow of fidelity. Either way, he denies his love for her and proclaims his professional or marital fidelity.

SOCRATES: If such were the case, his experience would probably be intra-experientially inconsistent or at least inter-experientially inconsistent, which would lead to intra-experientially inconsistent experiences. Either way, immorality would be an inherent aspect of the set-of-experiences.

MASSAGE THERAPIST: Yes. His intra-experientially inconsistent experience is experientially wrong and immoral, but the inter-experientially inconsistent experiences (i.e. set-of-experiences) need not be immoral. His experiences contradict each other, to be sure; he is ambivalent, confused, torn between several courses of action, but the experiences that constitute these contradictions are componentially consistent, at least functionally so. The morality of this situation is in the process of change. Absolutes are being altered. Identity is being changed. The man's intra-experientially inconsistent experience may look like this:

cognition : [I love her] [I shouldn't love her] confused thoughts
affect   : [love]   [duty]   anxiety
behavior :   anxious behavior
sensation : accompaniment
environ   : accompaniment
"I"   : ownership

Here his thoughts are "jumbled"; he is not debating with himself over whether or not he loves her; rather, he is confused, scattered. The thoughts or understandings "I love her" and "I shouldn't love her" do in fact occur in consciousness; they are parts of an actual experiential state-of-affairs. Likewise, his feelings are a mixture of love and duty (and, possibly, add to this fear). This blend constitutes his anxiety which is manifested in his anxious behavior. This experience, let's say, gives way to:

cognition : [I love her] [I shouldn't love her]; I don't love her
affect   : [dissipating love] [dissipating duty]; "controlled" anxiety
behavior : calming anxious behavior, more "directed" movements
sensation : accompaniment
environ   : accompaniment
"I"   : ownership

Here the new experience "pushes" the previous components into the far periphery so that they are unrecognizable. "Resolve" (a pseudo-control) supports the cognition "I don't love her", and there is no "I" associated with the peripheral [I love her, I shouldn't love her], i.e. no ownership recognized. The cognitions occur but are immediately overtaken by the new cognition.

SOCRATES: I understand that he doesn't "know himself"; he knows parts of himself, aspects of himself; but I've never heard of such experience being right or wrong, especially in the moral sense. He's confused, yes; ignorant of "who he is", yes; but I don't see him as immoral.

MASSAGE THERAPIST: I am not willing to attribute morality or immorality to him, per se, but I am claiming that the experiences are experientially wrong or inconsistent; and if we agree that this is a moral situation, then his experience is immoral.

SOCRATES: So an experience could be componentially consistent as a person commits adultery and the experience would be right and moral; whereas an experience that is componentially inconsistent as a person denies his love for another or some similar thing is wrong and immoral? I'm sorry, my friend, this is simply too foreign to my way of thinking.

MASSAGE THERAPIST: The way you've put it, Socrates, it is no surprise to me that it is "foreign" to you. Just because any experience could be rendered moral at any given time for any person does not mean that the behavioral component of that experience, i.e. the "act", is going to be determined as moral by everyone, not even by the person performing the behavior. More often than not, I will assume, even the person performing the behavior would be a part of numerous experiences that contradict the original-experience. All I am saying is that sometimes even what we would consider to be the most heinous of acts (behaviors) could be a part of a componentially consistent experience, an experience where everything "lines up", everything is "right", clear, and straightforward. To deny this would be tantamount to denying the very human-ness of the actor; for it is our componentially consistent experiences that serve as the basis for our identities, i.e. who we are. In many, if not most, cases, I would venture to say, the experiences which follow such componentially consistent experiences will be riddled with inconsistency and the set-of-experiences within which the experience is a part will render the "act" immoral. And if it happens that a given individual's set-of-experiences is inter-experientially consistent, at least functionally so, regarding what most would consider to be a human act, then the interpersonal levels of experience would come to bear upon this individual, in which case group, societal, or inter-societal determinations of morality would "prevail".

SOCRATES: But even if interpersonal levels of experience "prevail", it is still true that the individual experience and, possibly, the set-of-experiences within which the experience is a part, are morally right.

MASSAGE THERAPIST: For that individual at that time, or throughout that time, yes. Let me continue with your scenario to show

how this would happen. Our married man is sexually attracted to a married woman; he is also attracted to her intelligence, personality, and the fact that she is likewise attracted to him. Their appreciation for each other is mutual. He finds himself thinking about her quite often, and he realizes that her opinion of him is valuable to him. He enjoys the time he spends with her overall, and he values her thoughts and feelings not only in relation to himself but also in relation to the world. He realizes that he loves her. She is like his wife in some respects, different in other respects. She is her own person, with her own set of responsibilities and relationships, and so is he. She is now importantly included in his set of responsibilities and relationships; his love for her is not frivolous; it is not a self-indulgent, self-absorbed emotional pleasure for him, though it "is" certainly an emotional pleasure for him. He genuinely cares for her well-being and would respond to her ideas, feelings, cares, and interests as he would any person he loved, i.e. his wife, friends, family, etc. She has become integral to who he is. But let's say that throughout this development, he feels disturbed by his feelings for this woman. He thinks that he shouldn't feel for her like he does, that this type of feeling should be directed toward his wife alone. At this point, his experiences are conflicting with each other; he is part of a developing set-of-experiences that admits of inconsistency. He is engaged in a moral dilemma. His experiences with the woman tend to be componentially consistent; he enjoys being with her; he is not confused or conflicted when they are together. But when he notices that he is thinking about her quite a bit, that he may dress to please her when he knows he'll be seeing her, or that he takes pleasure in the thought or sight of her body, he feels pangs of guilt or has thoughts that he shouldn't be feeling or thinking this way. He becomes so confused that his receptivity to his wife is disturbed. That is, even when he is with his wife, the woman is there in his mind. Soon, he notices that he can't sleep well, his irritation-experiences increase, his energy level is inordinately high, etc. His relationship with his wife has always been honest; they disclose to each other their feelings, "good" or "bad", their ideas or thoughts, their sensations (pains and pleasures). He values their relationship; he values being honest to her and to himself. And he evaluates his "pre-occupation" with this other woman, though pleasurable overall, to be getting in the way of his *being present* to his wife. Therefore, he confronts the issue and discloses his perplexity to his wife. He tells her how he feels about this woman and that he doesn't want these feelings to interfere with his being present to her. He doesn't think he loves his wife any less because he loves the other woman. But he does at times feel pre-occupied and slightly guilty over his feelings for the woman, and these times have increased as his feelings have deepened. What is happening here experientially is that his componentially consistent experiences, which initially established the rightness of his relationship to the woman, are joined by conflicting experiences. Some of these conflicting experiences may be componentially inconsistent. I'll say that the guilt experiences tend to be componentially inconsistent: he has "I am immoral for having these feelings" thoughts while not feeling strong guilt to support them. He, in fact, feels slight guilt; his stronger feeling is his love for the woman and his desire to maintain his relationship with her. Inasmuch as he maintains the accuracy of his guilt and his duty to act "morally" by stopping the relationship (or something similar), his experiences are dominated by inconsistency, and immorality. Inasmuch as he "accepts" or maintains a set-of-experiences that admit of componential inconsistency, he is acting immorally.

SOCRATES: But the moral wrongness does not pertain to the feelings he has for the woman. That is, it is not necessarily morally wrong for him to love the other woman.

MASSAGE THERAPIST: No. The moral wrongness is inherent in the experience itself. It is a characteristic of componentially inconsistent experiences. It is not yet established whether or not his loving the other woman is morally wrong. It is only established that certain experiences, within which he is a part, are immoral in relation to his falling in love with the woman. Now let's say that these componentially inconsistent experiences are relatively few and that, for the most part, the experiences are consistent though conflicting. That is, he knows he loves the woman; he knows he loves his wife; he knows that he feels conflict in relation to the two knowledges; he knows that this conflict is disturbing his relationship with his wife. He has a history of discussing his problems with his wife; their relationship is firmly based on such disclosures, even when they might be disturbing. Therefore, he tells his wife about what is bothering him. Her reaction may vary, depending upon who she is in this situation. She may feel threatened, hurt, angry, or confident, understanding, and sympathetic.

SOCRATES: If I may interrupt a minute so as to play the devil's advocate, or perhaps, the "voice of reason": would a woman "ever" react confidently, understandingly, or sympathetically when she hears that her husband loves another woman?

MASSAGE THERAPIST: Yes. If she doesn't feel any threat that her husband will leave her for the other woman, that his feelings for her have not changed, and her understanding-experiences are strong enough to prompt confirmation-experiences that, as a set-of-experiences, will withstand interpersonal conflict (i.e. her friends and family criticizing her if they know), then she is likely to understand and even sympathize with her husband.

SOCRATES: You seem to be characterizing a rather unusual woman here.

MASSAGE THERAPIST: My argument is aimed at possibility rather than probability. Given our usual ways of passing on moral values from generation to generation, we tend to produce value systems that ground us in the world and in our selves while simultaneously limiting our possibilities of altering those value systems so as to be more experientially consistent. The experiential perspective we're developing, I believe, will help maximize experiential consistency and minimize experiential inconsistency, or, applied to morality, to maximize moral experiences and minimize immoral experiences.

SOCRATES: So the man's love-of-another experience is componentially consistent, just as it would be if he were not married.

MASSAGE THERAPIST: Yes.

SOCRATES: When he starts experiencing conflict either by experiencing pangs of guilt or realizing that his experiences with his wife are not componentially clear, i.e. his attention is split, he realizes he must confront the situation and tell his wife about his feelings for the woman.

MASSAGE THERAPIST: Experientially, what occurs at this point might be the following:
cognition: I love this woman
affect   : love
behavior : reflective comportment
sense   : accompaniment
environ : accompaniment
"I"   : ownership
Which is joined by:
cognition: Am I breaking my vow of fidelity to my wife?
affect   : trepidation (slight guilt)
behavior : worried comportment
sense   : accompaniment
environ : accompaniment

"I"   : ownership

We'll assume that this "inner struggle" persists for a period of time, woven between other experiences between the man and the woman and the man and his wife. He knows he loves the woman; there is no significant doubt about that. He also knows he loves his wife. In addition to this he knows he is not going to leave his wife for the other woman.

SOCRATES: How does he know this?

MASSAGE THERAPIST: He may not experience the thought of doing so, i.e. the thought never crosses his mind; or if it does, it is so weak that it quickly passes from consciousness and is evaluated as insignificant.

SOCRATES: In other words he experiences no conflict in relation to this idea or possibility.

MASSAGE THERAPIST: Right. But he does experience conflict in relation to the possibility of breaking his vow to his wife. This experience is significant enough to alter his course-of-experience and add a strong inconsistency to his set-of-experiences which addresses his relationship to his wife and the woman.

SOCRATES: When he was attracted to the woman, talked to her, etc., his experience prompted nothing in the way of significant conflict with his relationship to his wife.

MASSAGE THERAPIST: Right.

SOCRATES: But when he realized he loved the woman, such a conflict arose. He hasn't necessarily "crossed his moral line", but he's teetering on the edge.

MASSAGE THERAPIST: Yes. He doesn't see himself as guilty, but such a possibility looms over him.

SOCRATES: Therefore, because of the growing inconsistency within his inter-experiential structure, and because of who he is in this situation (i.e. disposed to telling his wife his problems), he confronts the issue with his wife.

MASSAGE THERAPIST: Yes. His conflict rests not with experience in relation to the woman but with experience in relation to his wife. It is his **relationship** with his wife that is conflicting, not his feelings for her. This relationship entails a vow of fidelity, a vow that the man assumed, at least to some degree, meant emotional fidelity, i.e. that he wouldn't love anyone else like he loved his wife, or if he did, then he would terminate such a relationship as quickly as possible. He now finds himself loving another woman, and such an experience, though intra-experientially consistent and strong, prompts experiences pertaining to his moral values. And these moral values are inextricably tied to his relationship with his wife. He is in the midst of a moral struggle, which is equivalent to a struggle between two conflicting intra-experientially consistent experiences. This amounts to a struggle for identity. The intra-experientially consistent experience of loving the woman conflicts with the duty-experience of maintaining his vow. Both experiences are componentially consistent and, hence, right and moral.

SOCRATES: Two conflicting moral rights are occurring simultaneously?

MASSAGE THERAPIST: In effect, yes. Two objective states-of-affair constituting two separate sets-of-experience are in conflict with each other.

SOCRATES: These are the inter-experiential inconsistencies that drive the dynamic of moralitization. They consist not of componentially inconsistent or mixed experiences but of compound experiences, i.e. conflicting componentially consistent experiences.

MASSAGE THERAPIST: Yes. It is these conflicts that offer us opportunity to confront the truth of the objective state-of-affairs, assert its truth to those with whom the truth is associated, grapple with the consequences of the assertion, and work through the conflict to produce a more consistent course-of-experience in relation to all pertinent levels of experience.

SOCRATES: How would this relate to the notion of levels of experience, exactly?

MASSAGE THERAPIST: The individual level of experience is in conflict. The value of emotional fidelity which, let's say, was internalized from the man's parents, church, and other social groups within which the man was raised has now come into conflict with his experience of loving another woman outside of his marriage. His individual level of experience is inconsistent in regard to this issue. One experience "says" it's wrong; another "says" it's right. Each experience is componentially consistent and therefore, right; but their relationship is contradictory. Experientially, experiences do not exist as separate and distinct isolable entities; they exist within contexts; other experiences precede and proceed from them. When one of the conflicting experiences is constituted in part by another person, then the conflict involves a mutual level of experience. In our example, each of the man's conflicting experiences consists in part of another person, i.e. loving the woman and married to the wife. Therefore, two mutual levels of experience are active simultaneously. Let's say that the man has not told the woman that he loves her; nor has he told his wife. The strength of each experience makes it very difficult for this man to maintain his usually consistent course-of-experience. The number and quality of his conflicting experiences rise beyond significance to the level of disturbing his life at home, his work, his sleep, etc. The two consistent yet contradictory truths create a good deal of tension and the man cannot alleviate this tension alone, though some of his efforts to do so are temporarily effective (e.g. he avoids the woman, works out at the gym, busies himself in work, drinks, etc.) Such individual efforts to alleviate the tension are doomed to fail, because the conflict does not exist on the individual level of experience. It exists on the mutual level, and in relation not to one but two people. Each person needs to be "dealt with". The experiential prescription: **acceptance:confrontation :grappling**. Acceptance refers to an evaluation-experience that affirms the validity of the experiential state-of-affairs. For our man it means he validates the fact that he loves the woman, that he fears that in doing so he is breaking his vow to his wife, and that he will hurt her because of it. Acceptance is equivalent to a settledness or a decision to tell the truth to those involved. Confrontation is the actual assertive communication of the man's experiential state-of-affairs to each of the others involved. In effect, he tells the woman that he loves her and his wife that he loves the woman. It is important that his acceptance-experience is strong enough to prompt a strong confrontation-experience. If his acceptance-experience is mixed, then he is merely deceiving himself and any confrontation he makes is ultimately destined to fail. (If he's slick at deception (self and other), he may allay the tension for a while, but it will inevitably return.) If his acceptance-experience is layered, then he stands the chance of balking in his delivery of the confrontation, e.g. feeling more guilt than confidence, indecision than decisiveness, etc. Optimally, his acceptance-experience is simple and componentially consistent. Combine that with a significant amount of strength and he's ready to make the assertive confrontation and deal with the consequences of it.

SOCRATES: And if he assertively tells his wife and she is hurt and angry and accuses him of infidelity?

MASSAGE THERAPIST: She could respond in a number of ways, depending upon who she is in this situation. If she and the man have a history of assertive confrontations, then the difficulty and pain involved tend to be easier to handle or "work through" than if their history excluded such confrontations.

SOCRATES: The more experience one has at assertive confrontation, the easier it is to do, and the easier it is to grapple with the consequences.

MASSAGE THERAPIST: Yes. So if she did respond by being hurt (i.e. she felt unloved or less loved than before), this could be remedied by his communicating that element of his experiential state-of-affairs that clearly indicates that he still loves her as much as ever and that he has no intention of leaving her for the other woman. And if he is not deceiving himself and his state-of-affairs is strong, it will prompt confirmation-experiences that will be expressed behaviorally to his wife as persistent and consistent love and affection for her. And if she gets angry and accuses him of infidelity, he is prepared to grapple with any disconfirming-experiences that the angry response might prompt. That is, her accusation of infidelity might "strike home" because that was part of his conflict and his acceptance-experience was not quite strong enough to absorb a "direct hit" without sustaining some damage. He will then go through more conflicting experiences where he might doubt himself, feel badly about loving the other woman, etc., but such grappling is usually short-lived, and eventually his confirmation-experiences will serve to strengthen his acceptance-experience, even if his wife continues to be angry or resentful toward him.

SOCRATES: Her anger will not "hit home". Her angry comments or assaults will not prompt him to feel guilty or morally wrong for loving the other woman.

MASSAGE THERAPIST: Exactly.

SOCRATES: Yet he doesn't ignore or avoid her angry expressions.

MASSAGE THERAPIST: No. That is a part of grappling. If he ignores or avoids her, he is not grappling with the response to the confrontation. His confrontation would then have been more of a "hit and run" confrontation, where he might applaud himself for his honesty but is not able or willing to work through the aftermath of his "honesty".

SOCRATES: The optimal type of confrontation is that which communicates one's experiential state-of-affairs as accurately as possible while being ready and willing to work through any disconfirmation-experiences that might occur in the wake of the confrontation. Our man would tell his wife that he loves the other woman, that he wants to include her in his life in some way, as one would a friend, but that his love for his wife was still in tact and his relationship to her still committed.

MASSAGE THERAPIST: Yes. Optimally, the marital relationship would not be threatened. But such an **individuation process** is not always characterized by such clarity and strength, especially within a culture that is struggling with its monogamous structure. Initial effects at individuation may be characterized by stumbling attempts to confront assertively, inaccurate or incomplete evaluations of acceptance-experiences, premature confrontations, and an inability to grapple effectively with repercussions of confrontations. In other words, in a society that does not provide an ethical/social means by which our man could maintain his love for the other woman through the development of a non-marital love relationship, the task of legitimizing such a relationship is difficult.

SOCRATES: But not impossible.

MASSAGE THERAPIST: Certainly not impossible.

SOCRATES: Could you elaborate on your notion of "individuation process"?

MASSAGE THERAPIST: Yes. An individuation process refers to a set-of-experiences composed of experiences that conflict with duty-experiences that reflect values developed throughout one's process of identity-development. A thorough explanation of the experiential position on identity-development is beyond the scope of this discussion, but I'll describe the process in relation to our example so you can more clearly grasp my use of the term.

SOCRATES: Fine.

MASSAGE THERAPIST: Our man married assumed that fidelity meant 1) no sexual activity with anyone other than his spouse and, possible less clearly, 2) no deep emotional attachments with other women, especially those to whom he is physically attracted. These assumptions form his value of fidelity; they are part of his **moral system**; they help define his **moral identity**; they are part of who he is. When he is initially attracted to the woman, he may or may not experience any conflict with his morality. Let's say his conflicting experiences are weak, passing, and insignificant at the beginning. They are overridden by the strength of the componentially consistent attraction-experience and confirmation-experiences in relation to the woman. When he finds himself thinking about the woman a lot, he may get concerned. His experience may vacillate from the pleasure-experience of thinking about her to the duty-experience of thinking he, a

married man, shouldn't be thinking in such a manner about another woman. At this point he may also have some guilt-experiences intertwined, but they, let's say, are weak. The individuation process has begun with the first weak conflicting experience. The contiguous pair of experiences might look like this:
cognition: she's got a beautiful smile
affect   : pleasure
behavior : reflective posture
sense   : work environment
environ : work
"I"   : ownership
Changing to:
cognition: I've got to get this (work) done
affect   : duty
behavior : resuming work
sense   : work environment
environ : work
"I"   : ownership
Here the "conflict" is germinal and probably not recognized as the beginning state of individuation.
SOCRATES: Are we to assume that he is physically attracted to the woman?
MASSAGE THERAPIST: Yes.
SOCRATES: Is the thought a sensual, sexual, aesthetic, or emotional thought?
MASSAGE THERAPIST: Let's say emotional. He is pleased about how her smile reflects her pleasure in relation to him; he is not at the moment "drawn into" the image of her mouth or lips (sensual); nor is he pleasantly "distanced" in relation to the image (aesthetic); nor is he cognizant of his own sexuality in relation to her mouth, lips, etc. (e.g. sexual).
MASSAGE THERAPIST: As his interaction with her increases, his attraction-experiences increase and diversify. He not only thinks of her emotionally but sensually, aesthetically, and sexually. The strength of his duty-experiences also increases, perhaps joined by some slight guilt-experiences when "caught" by his wife thinking of the woman. At this point he may be seeing that "something" is happening here; the conflict is becoming apparent. He may find himself concentrating more on work, but the concentration is somewhat forced. He may also avoid the woman a bit, but the avoidance is primarily in proximity only; he

continues to think of her or be aware of where she is. Since the attraction is mutual, she is experiencing her own set of conflicting experiences. Throughout the development of his sets-of-experiences, the man is continually judging his attraction-experiences. His judgment-experiences tend to confirm the rightness of his attraction-experiences, and disconfirm his duty-experiences.

SOCRATES: Though his duty-experiences are growing in number, his judgment-experiences in relation to them are unclear; they may look like this, if I may:

cognition: I shouldn't think about her so much [but why not]
affect : duty/doubt
behavior : strained reflective posture
sense : accompaniment
environ : accompaniment
"I" : ownership

And:

cognition: why not think of her, I like it, what's wrong with it
affect : resentment (over duty value)
behavior : resenting pose (possibly furrowed eyebrows, etc.)
sense : accompaniment
environ : accompaniment
"I" : ownership

MASSAGE THERAPIST: Yes. More doubt is experienced in relation to the duty-experiences as opposed to the attraction-experiences.

SOCRATES: Whereas if he were someone else, the duty-experiences could be strong and confirmed quite clearly.

MASSAGE THERAPIST: Yes. As the attraction-experiences increase in number and strength, the man, at some point, realizes that he loves the woman. This is equivalent to an acceptance-experience. He may vacillate for awhile afterwards, where contradictory experiences prompt periods of confusion, but eventually his confirmation-experiences solidify the validity of his acceptance-experience. At this point the resolution-experience expands to include himself in relation to the woman (because it is the woman whom he loves), and his wife (because it is his wife to whom he has vowed, though unclearly or weakly, his emotional fidelity). These experiences might look like this:

cognition: I love her (the woman)
affect : love
behavior : reflective posture

sensation: accompaniment
environ : accompaniment
"I" : ownership
And:
cognition: Loving her does not break my vow to my wife
affect : confidence
behavior : confident posture
sense : accompaniment
environ : accompaniment
"I" : ownership
SOCRATES: He has, in effect, altered (or clarified) the vow that he took at his wedding. This is equivalent to a resolution-experience. His moral dilemma has, in effect, resolved itself, at least on the individual level of experience.
MASSAGE THERAPIST: Yes. That understanding which constituted his vow was determined by previous experience and constituted part of who he was when he made the vow public and continued to constitute part of him up to this point where new experience has prompted a value-alteration and, hence, identity-alteration. He now sees clearly (or differently) that marital fidelity does not necessitate emotional fidelity or the loving of only one woman for the rest of his life.
SOCRATES: But could not such a resolution-experience be a rationalization? He actually desires to love this woman; he enjoys the emotional "high" it affords him; so he "talks himself into believing" that it's ok for him to love her.
MASSAGE THERAPIST: Yes, I think that is a possibility. But such an experience would be mixed, not simple; componentially inconsistent, not consistent. It might look like this:
cognition: It's perfectly fine for me to love this woman
affect : [doubt], confidence
behavior : somewhat anxious posture (or pseudo-calm)
sense : accompaniment
environ : accompaniment
"I" : ownership
The stronger affect (doubt) does not support the content of the cognition; the thought is thought (or spoken) weakly, i.e. without conviction. And this doubt is not given its full experiential actuality within subsequent judgment-experiences.

SOCRATES: Another case-in-point where self-knowledge equals morality and lack of self-knowledge equals immorality. At least such experiences form the building blocks of the process of determining what is moral and immoral.

MASSAGE THERAPIST: Yes. He is actually more doubtful than his cognition and behavior seem to indicate. Such a mixed experience could prompt a whole series of componentially inconsistent experiences. Since he lacks the conviction of his thoughts, he will probably not confront his wife with his resolution-experience. The thought of doing so would tend to be associated with either a weak affect (e.g. twinge of duty) or a stronger negative affect (e.g. trepidation or fear).

SOCRATES: He would be afraid to tell his wife.

MASSAGE THERAPIST: Yes. And these experiences may prompt a splitting of his mutual level of experience. He will tend to continue the emotional relationship with the woman, tell her he loves her, etc., all the while keeping this information from his wife.

SOCRATES: And rationalizing this split by thinking something like: "it might hurt her if she knew, so why tell her" or "she wouldn't understand what I'm doing, what my needs or wants are, etc., therefore, I shouldn't tell her".

MASSAGE THERAPIST: Yes, but it must be kept in mind that "he" is not rationalizing; rationalizing is a type of experience or set-of-experiences within which he is intimately and inextricably participating, and is responsible for inasmuch as there exists an agented cognition within his experiential structure. We're not to understand "rationalization" as an unconscious process whereby some mysterious ego-like force (a true "I") is trying to push itself into consciousness.

SOCRATES: It would refer to a conscious process of splitting sets-of-experiences that would be originally based on a mixed-experience or set-of-experiences.

MASSAGE THERAPIST: Exactly.

SOCRATES: And this would be immoral?

MASSAGE THERAPIST: Yes. Even though many of the man's experiences would be componentially consistent, at least functionally so, while with the woman, many of his experiences with his wife would not be consistent.

SOCRATES: Is this because he needs to address the situation with his wife?

MASSAGE THERAPIST: Yes. His mutual level of experience with his wife has been fractured; while the mutual level of experience with the woman may be much more consistent at this time.
SOCRATES: Which might lead the man to believe that his relationship with the woman is better than that with his wife.
MASSAGE THERAPIST: Yes.
SOCRATES: But this would be a mis-judgment?
MASSAGE THERAPIST: Overall, yes, but not at this point in time. It would probably be an accurate judgment. His relationship with his wife is becoming more and more inconsistent, more intra-experientially and inter-experientially inconsistent as well as (probably) interpersonally inconsistent or conflicting. The man is not confronting his wife. His relationship with the woman is undermining his relationship with his wife. He cannot integrate the experience into who he is because he is not addressing his relationship to his wife which is integral to who he is. His identity has been in part determined by his mutual level of experience with his wife. He has maintained his overall **integrity-of-experience** or experiential consistency on individual and mutual levels of experience throughout his relationship with his wife (we'll say) until now. It is his *relationship* with his wife that needs to be addressed.
SOCRATES: Does he think he's doing something wrong in loving the woman? Is he doubting himself? Feeling guilty? And this is what holds him back from telling his wife what bothers him?
MASSAGE THERAPIST: There may be some of these elements involved, but most of them are superseded by his resolution-experience and the confirmation-experiences that follow. His concern is not so much his own acceptance of himself but his fear of his wife's reaction. He is treading on new ground, and if he believes that his wife may react negatively to him or "disconfirm" the legitimacy of his own experiential rightness, then he will find himself in the position of having to deny himself expression of the love he has for the woman and resolve to remain emotionally "faithful" to his wife or persevere by seeing the woman despite his wife's objections.
SOCRATES: It seems to me that the first option is not a morally viable option. If he tells his wife and she in some sense "pressures" him to stop seeing her, his experience will remain inconsistent in relation to his wife. He may bear guilt, resentment, or some form of disagreeable resignation because he is at least behaviorally denying the validity of his own experience, i.e. resolution-experience and subsequent confirmation-experiences.

MASSAGE THERAPIST: You hit on a key point, Socrates. The denial of the validity of an objective set-of-experience is itself a mixed experience, and, hence, immoral. And it is upon this immoral foundation that a **denial set-of-experiences** develops, composed of numerous inconsistent experiences.

SOCRATES: The man would, again, be living a lie - at least in relation to this part of his life.

MASSAGE THERAPIST: Yes. Add to that the inconsistent experiences that are prompted in the future by such a denial and you have the extent to which the man acts immorally in relation to this issue.

SOCRATES: It seems like just about any rejection or denial of validity of one's "self" or one's componentially consistent experience is experientially wrong, and if a question of morality, immoral.

MASSAGE THERAPIST: Yes, and most noticeable when the consistent experience is strong. Within the experiential model, morality can no longer be understood as a static act-oriented phenomenon. Adultery is not a simple act that we can pin-point and say, "Ah, this is adultery and, hence, immoral, and this is not." Rather, it must be understood as an experiential process that may initiate with an attraction-experience that is componentially consistent and moral and end with a divorce that may also be componentially consistent and moral. And even to end it there is somewhat arbitrary, because the same or similar situation could arise again.

SOCRATES: What about the man's relationship with the other woman? Need he confront her with his feelings for her? And, because she is married, there is at least one other person involved; should he also know?

MASSAGE THERAPIST: The woman could be in the same or similar position as is the man. If she wants to maintain overall consistency in her experience with her husband, and this love of the man is prompting inconsistency, then she, like the man, needs to confront her husband, assertively letting him know that she loves the man, and then be prepared to deal with the consequences. The man and woman, on the other hand, need to confront each other with their feelings for each other if they are to maintain their own mutually consistent set-of-experiences.

SOCRATES: But they could decide to let their relationship cease, let the feelings for each other fade away, and resume their respective relationships with their spouses.

MASSAGE THERAPIST: If the love-experience or set-of-experiences is strong, then it will prompt a considerable amount of confirmation-experiences even after the relationship has ended. And though the thoughts of the other may diminish over time, the likelihood of the feeling disappearing is slim. A test of this strength might be a personal contact with the person, or even an anticipation of a personal contact; this may be all that it takes to rekindle the love. But if such a dissolution is self-imposed, for whatever reason, the diminishing love-experiences may seem as fond memories of a loved one and not as a source of inconsistency in experience. But I am not at all certain that this is possible.
SOCRATES: Inconsistency occurs if they would bow to the threats or guilt-inducing accusations of others, including those of their spouses.
MASSAGE THERAPIST: Yes. As a general rule: where resentment grows, so too does experiential inconsistency.
SOCRATES: From what you're saying, can I, at least tentatively, draw the conclusion that deception in general results in increased experiential inconsistency, whether intra- or inter-experientially or both, and, hence, immorality.
MASSAGE THERAPIST: Yes. There are deceptions that can be experientially consistent, but such consistency tends to be limited to individual and/or a circumscribed group of people. For example, deceiving one's enemy may be experientially consistent individually and between members of one's "side", but the consistency will break down when one is interacting with an experiential being and not simply "the enemy". Our man could deceive his wife and pursue an affair with the woman without "splitting his mutual level of experience" if his experience did not admit of his wife being an experiential being. But in such a situation, the mutual level of experience no longer exists in this area of their relationship.
SOCRATES: If he conceives of her as "the enemy", the destroyer of his happiness or some such thing, he could engage in experientially consistent experiences with the woman.
MASSAGE THERAPIST: Yes. But the determination of the morality of such experience is not limited to their intra- or inter-experiential occurrences.
SOCRATES: Yes, and this is the issue I'd like to pursue within the context of our example. Let's say that our man's love experiences are ontological (experiential states-of-affair), his conflicting experiences result in a resolution-experience of considerable strength. His previous

relatively unclear value of emotional fidelity is clarified and rejected. He rejects this value because of the strength of his experiential rightness, i.e. the strength and consistency of his experience in relation to his love for the woman, coupled with his honesty and confrontive capacity in relation to his wife. He, in fact, confronts his wife. He lets her know how he feels about the woman and how he feels about her, i.e. that he loves each of them and he wishes to stay married to his wife. All of these positions, I'll assume, have been confirmed by the man's experience prior to his confronting his wife. His wife, in turn, at first, let's say, feels a bit hurt, possibly angry, but knowing her husband as an honest and direct man, she doesn't think he's deceiving her about his wish to stay married to her. She doesn't feel the threat of his leaving her. (I guess I'll grant at least the possibility that such a reaction could occur, as long as their marital relationship is not threatened.) So the man can continue his relationship with the woman, enjoy her company, etc. without the wife overconcerning herself with that relationship. The woman would take as much time away from the family (if there is one) and the wife as would a male friend or a female friend to whom he was not physically attracted. At this point, I would assume that the moral rightness of this issue is established on the individual level by both people directly involved, i.e. the man and the woman's love-experiences are consistent and strong. They confront each other with their feelings and grapple, if need be, with the results of their confrontation. I'll assume that "confrontation" and "grappling" can be applied to communicating "positive" feelings towards others as well as "negative" ones.

MASSAGE THERAPIST: Yes. A **confrontation** refers to any communication of experience that is required for the growth and maintenance of a relationship, whether that relationship be personal or formal. It involves an **individuation identity process**, i.e. an assertiveness regarding one's experiential structure in relation to an opposing interpersonal experiential structure in the case of **separation confrontations** and in relation to a unifying interpersonal experiential structure in the case of **unification confrontations**. The two inform each other of their love for each other in a unification confrontation. But all confrontations run the risk of rejection or interpersonal disconfirmation from the confrontee. Such rejection, if experientially consistent, will, optimally, end in a successful grappling process on the part of the confronter, whereby he/she will realize the inaccuracy of his/her confrontation. Such rejection, if experientially inconsistent, will, optimally, end in the successful grappling process on the part of the confrontee, whereby he/she will alter his/her value, identity, absolute, and/or relationship with the confronter. In the rejection of a unification confrontation, (e.g. our man's profession of love being rejected by the woman), whereby the confrontation is experientially consistent, the rejection may result in grappling on the part of the confrontee, but such grappling is the result of a temporary disorientation. In our example, if the man's profession of love were to be rejected, when evidence pointed to its confirmation, he may be somewhat shocked or surprised, which would prompt him to reassess his experience and eventually reestablish his experiential consistency, confirming not her rejection but his own evaluation of her experiential structure.

SOCRATES: The rejection will set him back, possibly prompting him to doubt himself and/or doubt his understanding of the woman's feelings, but eventually he will re-confirm the validity of his assessment of her feelings for him, though possibly reassess or alter his overall understanding of the woman.

MASSAGE THERAPIST: Yes. It is the alteration of his understanding, which may entail an alteration of only some aspects of his understanding of the woman, that constitutes his grappling and produces growth in him in relation to her (even if the relationship terminates at this point). He may have been very accurate in his assessment of her feelings for him but inaccurate in other areas of his assessment of her.

SOCRATES: Resulting in the rejection.

MASSAGE THERAPIST: Yes.

SOCRATES: Well, let's say that the proper unification-confrontations are made and accepted by both the man and the woman. Their love for each other is individually and mutually right or moral. Let's also say that the proper confrontations are made between each of their respective spouses. Each spouse may grapple with the confrontations a bit, but overall neither is rejecting of the situation. Each spouse permits the relationship between the man and woman to continue.

MASSAGE THERAPIST: Ok.

SOCRATES: Now, let's say that the man and woman are physically attracted to each other and the thought of expressing their love for each other sexually seems quite natural to them. They've already opened their hearts to each other, but their emotions are only one component of their experiential being. They share their intelligence (cognition) through discussion, their emotion (affect) through love, and their behavior through interpersonal activity; why not share their sensuality and their bodies with each other? The physical attraction exists, so they wouldn't be deceiving each other. We've already allowed that the practical situation admits of time; let's say further that it permits any expense incurred; let's also say that because of contraception and each person's natural inclination to be careful regarding sexual matters, that impregnation is only a very slight possibility. Therefore, the heavy burden of pregnancy that would affect more people than just them is not a significant factor. The last and seemingly most significant inhibiting factors would be each of their respective values in relation to sex outside of marriage, their vows of fidelity in relation to their spouses and in relation to the groups sanctioning these vows (i.e. church and state).

MASSAGE THERAPIST: The individual level of experience is satisfied. Each person's set-of-experiences regarding any moral aspect of his or her relationship is at least functionally right.

SOCRATES: What determines whether or not their set-of-experiences is right?

MASSAGE THERAPIST: The respective experiential states-of-affair themselves.

SOCRATES: And who determines what those states-of-affairs are?

MASSAGE THERAPIST: The relativistic notion just won't settle down in you, will it?

SOCRATES: No, it won't.

MASSAGE THERAPIST: At this stage of the process of moralitization, the individuals involved, independently of each other, judge the rightness of their experience, but they don't have the power to "determine" its rightness. They don't create or construct their own experience; they don't choose any aspect of it, at least not in the traditional way we conceive of "choose"; they cannot get outside of experience to determine just what their experience is or will be. Their experience is right or wrong, partially right or partially wrong, etc. based on the componential structure of their individual experiences and their relationship with other experiences either contiguously, serially, or, in an issue-related set developed over time. They do not choose the power or strength of their experience; nor do they choose what experiences their experience will prompt. In this sense, experience is greater than they. Experience is not the power to which they must conform nor that which they must master, but that which they must recognize, accept, assertively act upon, and constructively grapple with.

SOCRATES: The initial attraction-experience prompts deeper attraction-experiences, which prompt conflicting experiences (interpersonally as well as inter-experientially), which eventually prompt the "recognition" and "acceptance" of the feeling of love in relation to the other, which prompts conflicting interpersonal and inter-experiential experiences, which prompt a resolution-experience and its own set of confirmation-experiences, which prompt an assertive confrontation-experience with one's respective spouse, which prompts a response that must be constructively grappled with.
MASSAGE THERAPIST: Yes.
SOCRATES: So the individual level of experience is satisfied at the points of 1) the acceptance-experience and 2) the resolution-experience.
MASSAGE THERAPIST: Yes. What follows each experience is interpersonal confirmation or disconfirmation of individual rightness. But such confirmation is not necessary for each person to confirm his/her experiences' own rightness, and such disconfirmation does not necessarily invalidate the rightness of his/her experience. In other words, **mutual confirmation** does not in itself determine the moral rightness of individual experience, but it does serve to strengthen it and ground it in a reality beyond individual experience. It is a confirmation of the validity of one's experience and evaluation of experience, i.e. one's identity. It generates one's identity on individual and mutual levels of experience. When the spouse is confronted, and grapples with and ultimately accepts the man and woman's state-of-affairs in each instance, a mutual level of experience is satisfied and the altered identities are further strengthened and grounded within the mutual level of experience.
SOCRATES: And all this could be occurring within larger groups to which these two belong, that bear upon each of their identities, and that may not confirm the rightness of their experience.
MASSAGE THERAPIST: Yes.
SOCRATES: So let's return to the physical attraction felt by our man toward the woman. He, quite frankly, wants very much to express his love for her in all ways that are available to him. The sexual urge is there, but he clearly understands his vow of fidelity to pertain to sexual activity, especially sexual intercourse, with anyone other than his spouse. It's true, let's say, that he has already "broken" this vow in a technical sense by engaging in masturbation and, once in a while, by conjuring images of another person while having sex with his wife, but such acts for him do not fall under infidelity. He figures that his

individual sex life is his own, a free and harmless pleasure; as long as his masturbation doesn't upset the course of his daily activities and that his sexual relationship with his wife is in tact, masturbatory pleasure is morally acceptable.

MASSAGE THERAPIST: So he is defining which sexual activities are to be considered within and outside fidelity boundaries.

SOCRATES: Yes.

MASSAGE THERAPIST: I suppose he does this also with looking at other women in a sexual manner, entertaining non-masturbatory but still sexual fantasies or images of other women, and possibly experiencing sexual arousal in some situations (e.g. company party, dancing with co-workers, etc.)

SOCRATES: Let's admit some of that, yes. So, according to what you've maintained so far, I would assume that the man is going to be a part of some contradictory experiences: his sexual desire-experiences are componentially consistent in themselves, but they tend to prompt conflicting componentially consistent duty-experiences. It seems that he should be able to resolve this conflict in a similar manner to his love-experience situation. After all, doesn't this sexual desire experience just prompt evidence of a clearer and more firmly entrenched moral value, i.e. sexual fidelity, and not something of a fundamentally different nature?

MASSAGE THERAPIST: What you're saying sounds reasonable to me.

SOCRATES: Well, if this is so, then he could, again, confront both the woman and his wife with his sexual desire for the woman and grapple with the repercussions of this confrontation.

MASSAGE THERAPIST: He could do that, yes, but, given what you've said, he may find that his confrontation is premature. He will have hurt his wife and, hence, his relationship with her without being ready to deal with the consequences of that hurt. Given only what you've said, the man's honest communication of his sexual-desire for the woman is not sufficient to constitute a full-blown confrontation. He has to go through the process of reaching an acceptance of himself or an acceptance of the rightness of his sexual desire for the woman. From what you've said, it sounds like he's approaching his wife for permission to have sex with the woman, a confrontation destined for failure.

SOCRATES: No, I didn't mean that at all. I'm just having difficulty seeing how he is going to get around this moral issue.

MASSAGE THERAPIST: If he "gets around" it, his experience is likely to increase in inconsistency and, hence, immorality.
SOCRATES: It just seems to me that you're moving in the direction of making it possible for this man (and woman) to "have their cake and eat it too". They can be married on the one hand and have love and sex with another person in addition to the love and sex they have with their spouses.
MASSAGE THERAPIST: Do you see something inherently or intuitively wrong or immoral in that?
SOCRATES: Yes! I'm sorry, my friend, but this is an issue from which I have difficulty separating my emotions.
MASSAGE THERAPIST: I'm sure you're not alone in that. Do you mind if I explore this with you a bit?
SOCRATES: Go right ahead.
MASSAGE THERAPIST: You were able to accept, at least to some degree, that the man's loving the woman was moral because he accepted the reality of it, confronted those whom he needed to confront, and grappled productively with the consequences of his confrontations. And there were no obvious or clear rules within any other groups in which the man participated that rejected the morality of his loving someone outside of his marriage. But with this sexual issue we have a fundamentally different situation. Moral codes, laws, and hundreds of years of established cultural values come to bear upon this issue.
SOCRATES: Yes. Loving a person outside of marriage is tolerable if not tragic, but if the love realizes itself in sexual union, then the immoral act of adultery is committed.
MASSAGE THERAPIST: Why is this act immoral? Why is it adultery? I know that the Christian tradition has maintained that such an act is immoral for the same reason we mentioned before in regard to lust or sexual desire in general being immoral, i.e. to lust after temporal things is immoral, or, to put it in the terms of our topic, sexual desire after the flesh is immoral. Is this what you mean?
SOCRATES: Put that way, my friend, the idea sounds a little silly. What is sexual desire if not desire for the flesh, or, specifically, the pleasures of the flesh. Admittedly, it is difficult these days to maintain the Christian doctrine that all sexual desire outside of marriage is immoral. Evolutionary ethics (Anders, Wright) maintains that males are in general genetically determined or at least disposed to "spreading their genes" or having sex with a variety of females, while females are determined or disposed to be more selective in their choice of sex

partners and tend to be less interested in sex overall. According to this theory, the pleasure derived from sex is the result of genetic mutations and exists universally (barring dysfunction) because it is effective in proliferating genes. Therefore, natural selection "favors" sexual desire (as well as selectivity) and sexual pleasure, i.e. these phenomena promote the proliferation of genes. From what I understand of your experiential point of view, it seems that I can draw some comparisons in relation to the Christian and evolutionary positions. First, if our man feels sexual desire for his wife, he is feeling "morally" according to the Christian doctrine and "productively" according to the evolutionary theory. Experientially, if his sexual desire-experience is componentially consistent and prompts inter-experiential consistency, then the feeling is moral, at least for him. But if the man feels sexual desire for someone other than his wife, he is feeling "immorally" according to Christian doctrine but still "productively" according to evolutionary theory. Experientially, if a sexual desire-experience for someone other than one's spouse is componentially consistent and prompts inter-experiential consistency, then the feeling is moral. Am I on track so far?

MASSAGE THERAPIST: I'd say so, yes.

SOCRATES: It seems that I can extend this feeling into action and use the same reasoning in relation to sexual conduct. The process of moralitization will also be similar to that discussed in relation to emotional fidelity. Conflicting experiences will occur where the man will desire sexual union and feel a duty to maintain his vow of sexual fidelity. But in this instance, because the man's understanding of fidelity is clear, his conflict is stronger. The strength of each set-of-experiences may very well prompt intra-experientially inconsistent experiences, but let's say that our man's understanding of himself is quite clear and that his conflict is primarily inter-experiential or compound. My first question is how is this inter-experiential conflict related to morality from the experiential point of view?

MASSAGE THERAPIST: Such inter-experiential conflicts are pivotal in the process of moralitization; they represent the first stage of the process. The conflict involves two componentially consistent experiences that contradict each other. Experientially, reason is a set of conflicting experiences that optimally results in a resolution-experience strong enough to prompt confirmation-experiences that solidify the rightness of the resolution-experience. Reason is not a cognitive faculty employed in deciding between right and wrong, as if right and wrong is already given or determined by some extra-human force. Reason holds no sway over desire; as a set-of-experiences, it "consists" in part of desire. The man's conflict lies between experiences, both of which he is an integral part.

SOCRATES: The sexual-desire experience is therefore more akin to evolutionary theory in that it is not immoral in itself, though it may not be considered "productive" either.

MASSAGE THERAPIST: Inasmuch as the sexual desire-experience is componentially consistent, it is moral. So too is the duty-experience. Both experiences are moral. The duty-experience, which is traditionally recognized as the "voice of reason" is only a different experience from the desire-experience that contradicts it. Whether it indicates the right or moral "way to go" over and above the "way of desire" remains to be seen. And our man cannot determine which is right simply by "deciding" or "choosing" one over the other. As already shown, such a decision is impossible for him to make; he doesn't have the power to do so. The experiences of which he is an inextricable part must "go their course". He must "live out" the conflict. Such a process may involve his approaching the subject with his wife indirectly, e.g. a theoretical discussion of sexual infidelity; or it may involve a series of avoidances of the woman or his wife; or ambivalent behavior, pre-occupation, etc. The man may try to stop seeing the woman altogether and "fortify" his long-held values. But if his love-experience and sexual desire-experience are consistent and strong, then such a move will only be an avoidance of the truth and, hence, will itself be a move in the direction of immorality.

SOCRATES: Experience becomes mixed or inconsistent as the man moves away from the woman; he is deceiving himself, denying a truth which lies in his consistent experience in relation to the woman.

MASSAGE THERAPIST: Exactly.

SOCRATES: Therefore, in order to moralize this situation, the man must accept the truth or objective state-of-affairs of his sexual desire-experience, confront the woman and his wife much like he did with his love-duty conflict, and grapple with the consequences.

MASSAGE THERAPIST: Yes.

SOCRATES: But in this case he may be "biting off more than he can chew". Like you said, the force of group values, social values, and hundreds of years of cultural training come to bear upon this situation. Even if his wife understands and accepts his loving the woman, she may have great difficulty accepting the sexual aspect of his love for her. Her experience may be a componentially consistent repulsion of her husband's sexual desire-experience in relation to the woman. And such a repulsion-experience may be strong enough to prompt confirmation-experiences that solidify the repulsion and overtake any conflicting love-experiences that might occur, in which case divorce may ensue.

MASSAGE THERAPIST: I certainly couldn't deny that possibility. If the social probabilities against extra-marital sexual involvement (which includes family, friends, church, and state) is strong, then even if the wife is accepting of his sexual expression of his love for the woman, she may not be able to tolerate the rejection-experiences of those close to her, e.g. her family and friends who may know about her husband's relationship with the woman.

SOCRATES: Conflicting experiences often occur in response to the rejection-experiences of others.

MASSAGE THERAPIST: Yes. And you've hit upon what I see to be the crux of moralitization in relation to interpersonal levels of experience. Our identity or who we are is developed, sustained, and altered based on the interplay between the individual intra- and inter-experientially consistent experiences and the conflicting or contradicting experiences of those close to us (e.g. family, friends). For example, when our parents reject a componentially consistent experience in which we smack a sibling for taking our toy, they influence who we are. Difficulties arise when the rejection is aimed not at the **expressive level** of our experience (i.e. the behavior) but at the **evaluative level** (i.e. evaluating the rightness of our experience). In such instances, the experiential state-of-affairs is negated by those upon whom we are dependent. The rightness of our retaliatory act is not confirmed but rejected, i.e. "we" are not confirmed but rejected. Such interpersonal power can result in a variety of mixed or inconsistent experiences, and much time will have to be spent in recognizing and accepting the inconsistencies for what they are, confronting those who need to be confronted, and grappling with the repercussions of our confrontations. But since this is taking us too far afield, I'll have to limit this aspect of our discussion to these statements. Perhaps we can finish our discussion on identity development from the experiential point of view at a later date.

SOCRATES: That would be fine.

MASSAGE THERAPIST: As it applies to our discussion, the wife may accept the man's sexual desire for the woman not as a threat to his desire for her but as an expression of his love for the woman, thus separating one passion-relationship from another, but her acceptance may be weak. For instance, she may say rather spontaneously to her mother that her husband is spending the afternoon with the woman. Her mother's rejection of the rightness of such an activity may prompt conflicting experiences in relation to the wife. These conflicting experiences are in some way relayed to the man, thus prompting his own conflicting experiences. If the man's evaluation of the rightness of his passion for both women is strong and he is able to separate the relationships and their attendant responsibilities, then he is in position to assert himself in relation to his wife.

SOCRATES: What form would such an assertiveness take?

MASSAGE THERAPIST: Like other assertivenesses it would be an accurate rendering of his experiential state-of-affairs. For instance, he may tell her that he loves and is passionate toward both her and the woman but wants to be married to her and not to the other woman. He wants to maintain his relationship with the other woman "and" his marriage to her, without breaking his vow of fidelity. He, therefore, wants to alter his vow of fidelity.

SOCRATES: He wants to re-negotiate the terms of his vow, so to speak.

MASSAGE THERAPIST: A very business-like way of putting it but essentially accurate. We can assume that he took his mutual vow in good faith, i.e. he and his wife were committed to virtually the same thing - sexual exclusiveness. Let's also assume that his vow as experienced was at least functionally right, functionally consistent. But vows are only certain types of experiences, i.e. types which bind us to future courses-of-action. They are promises, and as such are to be held binding, unless and until such binding cannot be supported by intra- and inter-experientially consistent experiences. That is, once the vow becomes a source of experiential contradiction, and the contradictions prompt componentially inconsistent experiences, it is time to address the legitimacy of the vow and "negotiate" its alteration so as to promote experiential consistency, rather than to promote mixed experiences and, hence, experiential immorality. In reference to our example, this means that the man's experience of love and sexual desire is at least functionally consistent. He experiences no wrong in loving a woman aside from his wife and wanting to express that love for her sexually; he experiences no wrong in loving his wife and wanting to express his love for her sexually; he experiences no wrong in wanting to remain married to his wife and upholding his marital responsibilities while he simultaneously maintains his loving relationship with the woman. But he does experience it as wrong to act against his vow. His conflict is clear. To deny the legitimacy of his experience in relation to the woman would be to deny the evaluative level of his experience, i.e. to deny himself. To deny the legitimacy of the evaluative level of his experience in relation to his vow to his wife is equally to deny himself. Again, he is in position to moralitize. He may at first opt to act in accordance with his vow and keep his sexual distance from the woman, but if the strain of such action prompts physical, psychological, or emotional distress or points strongly in the direction of mixed experiences (e.g. having sex with the woman and covering it up to his wife), then he will have to act in the direction of acceptance:confrontation:grappling. In other words, he can 1) physically, psychologically, or emotionally deteriorate under the stress, 2) "split" himself into the covert lover of the woman and the overt lover of his wife, or 3) integrate himself through acceptance:confrontation:grappling.

SOCRATES: The process of moralitization is intimately connected to the development of the identity.

MASSAGE THERAPIST: Yes. And the **moral identity** is equivalent to the **integrated identity**, which is equivalent to a consistent set-of-experiences regarding any given moral issue.

SOCRATES: The **split identity**, if I may so name it, seems to characterize most of what constitutes adultery. The sexual acts that are performed against one's vows and relationships, whether loving or not, are carried on clandestinely. You've already maintained that the clandestine nature of or deception involved in adultery is intra-experientially inconsistent, sometimes in a complex sense where the adulterer is deceiving himself, and sometimes in the compound sense where the adulterer is simply lying. The complex situation automatically admits of immorality, but how does the compound situation admit of immorality, if at all?

MASSAGE THERAPIST: It does admit of immorality. Though the compound experience may consist of two functionally right conflicting experiences (i.e. the lie and the recognition of the truth), the full rendering of the experiential state-of-affairs is being withheld from the other person involved. The other receives the lie which is only half of the experiential state-of-affairs. Hence, the consistency of her experience rests upon a half-truth, experientially speaking (i.e the lie being accepted or experienced as fully justified and, hence, right, by the adulterer). In other words, the grounds for maintaining a mutual morality have been removed; interpersonal experiential consistency has been violated. So though the adulterer may feel fully justified in engaging in his sexual acts with another woman, his justification is individual at best, possibly mutual in relation to the woman who might feel as he does, but that mutuality will not extend to his wife or anyone who is not supportive of his actions. And since his wife is a necessary component of his experience and integral to who he is, he needs to confront and work through the experiential state-of-affairs with his wife in order to restore mutual consistency with all pertinent or relevant experiential beings. In addition to the dis-integration of the mutual level of experience regarding this issue between him and his wife, his actions and subsequent deception have dis-integrated the grounds for experiential consistency between him and the groups within which he lives. He has broken his vow (violating church code, let's say), and the law (violating social code). The breaking of the code and law does not in itself make the act immoral; such violations can be wholly moral (e.g. Ghandi, Jesus, etc.) What makes the act immoral is the dis-integration of the mutual grounds for experiential consistency. Even if our man were to engage in sexual intercourse with the woman whom he loved without first confronting his wife with the truth, he still can be considered as acting morally, or at least less immorally, if he is convinced that he must inform his wife of his experiential state-of-affairs. It is the "process" of moralitization that supersedes the "content" of morals in this instance. The man's experience of sexual union with the woman is componentially consistent but only because he is committed to confronting his wife with the truth. If his commitment is self-deceptive and he postpones the necessary confrontation, his experience is actually mixed and, hence, immoral. But if the sexual union was what was needed for the man to actually know that this is what he really desired, what he thought was right, then its actuality serves as a clarification of the direction of moralitization. It is movement in the process toward integrating identity and individual and mutual experiential consistency.

SOCRATES: Are you saying that the man must have sex with the woman in order to act morally in relation to his wife?! Such a thing sounds like the grossest of rationalizations for illicit sexual conduct that I've ever heard!

MASSAGE THERAPIST: Only if you see morality as primarily content-oriented and fail to see its process-orientation. From the **content-orientation of morality** the sexual union between the two people outside of their marriage is a breaking of their marital vow of fidelity, in their minds, in their spouse's mind, in their church's "mind", in their society's "mind"; and they will have to bear the consequences of their acts on all levels of interpersonal interaction. That is, if upon hearing the truth, wife decides to divorce the man on the grounds of infidelity, the full weight of the law is on her side and the man will suffer the consequences. But where the process-orientation of morality is considered, we can see how the man might not be in position to confront his wife with his sexual desire in relation to the woman until he knows clearly that a sexual union with her is a consistent expression of his love for her, despite his vow to his wife. Optimally, the man would confront his wife prior to breaking the vow, but such is not always the case. The process-orientation recognizes the difficulty in integrating identity, especially when such integration is done in the face of mutual, group, and societal pressure, without side-stepping the necessity of that integration. Some people will integrate prior to breaking vows or promises; other will not. Such an explanation certainly does not justify the breaking of a vow; it merely gives reasons for why some people will break vows before they are ready to accept, confront, and grapple with the consequences of their confrontations. Nor does this explanation absolve the person from responsibility for his breaking the vow; experientially, he is fully responsible inasmuch as he is an agented cognition within his own experience.

SOCRATES: But it does say that, under these circumstances, it is more moral to break a vow of fidelity, renegotiate one's marital vows, integrate oneself and reestablish consistency in experience on at least individual and mutual levels of experience than it is to break the vow and cover it up or to keep the vow and deny the truth of one's experience in relation to another experiential being.

MASSAGE THERAPIST: It is the least of the three evils.

SOCRATES: But immoral nevertheless.

MASSAGE THERAPIST: Yes.

SOCRATES: Whereas it is entirely moral to accept that one loves and sexually desires a person other than one's spouse, to assertively confront the relevant individuals involved with this truth, and to grapple with the consequences of the confrontation.

MASSAGE THERAPIST: Yes.

SOCRATES: What if the assertive confrontation with the wife produces considerable pain on her part, even though the man doesn't technically have sex with the other woman? Just knowing that he wants to have sex with her hurts her. Wouldn't it be more moral of him to

simply stop seeing the woman, maintain his vow to his wife, and allow his passion to die down and eventually fade away?
MASSAGE THERAPIST: Not if it would entail the denial or rejection of the rightness of his experience. That is, if he were to stop seeing the woman because he thought that that would be the most moral thing to do while feeling passion for her and evaluating that experience as right, then his not seeing her constitutes an inconsistent experience, i.e. a denial of what he experiences to be right.
SOCRATES: He, again, would be living a lie.
MASSAGE THERAPIST: Yes.
SOCRATES: And, hence, he would be acting immorally.
MASSAGE THERAPIST: Yes.
SOCRATES: And possibly even justifying his immorality by thinking himself nobly moral in sacrificing his own pleasure for the sake of his marriage.
MASSAGE THERAPIST: Possibly.
SOCRATES: But what choice does he have in acting morally? The consequences of assertive confrontation, even if worked through on the mutual level with his wife (a difficult task at best), will certainly entail the force of family, church, and state. Does the issue have to go any further than the mutual level of experience? Could the couple sustain such a love relationship outside of their marriage as long as no one else knows about it? Would it be anyone else's business?
MASSAGE THERAPIST: It is possible, it seems, to contain the issue at the mutual level as long as considerable discretion is used, but once discretion shifts into deception, then we have the beginning of experiential inconsistency and the beginning of a dis-integrating mutual relationship. For instance, if the wife's mother suspected that the man was seeing another woman, she might discuss this with her daughter (the wife). Does the wife deny that it is happening so she can avoid the rejection she knows will be forthcoming? Or can she grapple with the repercussions of an assertive confrontation or revelation of the experiential state-of-affairs? How one deals with these situations is an indication of the strength of one's acceptance-experiences. If the wife has doubts about the legitimacy of her husband's rightness in maintaining his extra-marital love relationship, then the pressure of the rejection she feels from her family alone may prompt conflicting experiences that may overwhelm any belief she had in the rightness of her husband's actions. Her inconsistent experiences will, in turn, affect the man, possibly to the point of a marital ultimatum, i.e. "stop seeing

her or I'll divorce you". The man will probably, again, experience contradictory experiences until some mutually agreed upon resolution is determined, mutual between wife and man, and man and woman, or the marital relationship dissolves because the man would not be willing or able to deny the rightness of his experience in relation to the woman to the extent requested or demanded by the wife.

SOCRATES: You do realize, my friend, that you're actually maintaining that a man (or woman) could have a moral extra-marital love relationship that could bring about the painful dissolution of his (or her) marriage.

MASSAGE THERAPIST: I'm well aware of that, Socrates.

SOCRATES: All right. If the man's assertive confrontation with his wife regarding his feelings of love and the sexual expression of that love toward the woman results in his wife's acceptance of an alteration of their marital vows so that the man's sexual involvement will not be construed as a breaking of that vow, then how would that altered vow be understood, and by whom would it be understood to be binding in its new form, what group levels of experience would be involved, and what would their involvement be?

MASSAGE THERAPIST: Let's say that the altered vow would be understood as a promise to be as honest as possible in relation to oneself and one's spouse regarding the truth of one's experience, to disclose that truth in a non-aggressive, assertive manner, and to grapple with the repercussions of the disclosure, i.e. to stay with the spouse throughout the process. In short, it would be a vow to maintain the marital relationship through mutual efforts toward union and self-integration.

SOCRATES: So the phrase "to be true to him/her in good times and in bad" would mean *to be truthful to oneself and to one's spouse*" and *to be faithful in one's commitment to the marital relationship*". These definitions are closer to the meaning of fidelity, at least in our example, than is anything having to do with love and/or sex outside of marriage.

MASSAGE THERAPIST: Yes. The first two definitions of "being true" are difficult to achieve but at least the difficulty is pointed in a positive, self-integrating direction rather than in a negative, self-denying direction. If the emotional disposition to love someone and to be loved by someone is an inextricable part of experience (which I maintain it is), then it does not suddenly disappear when one gets married. The same holds true for physical attraction. When we get married, these aspects of our experiential being don't suddenly focus themselves upon only one individual. We are still drawn to those who stimulate our senses, our emotions, our intellects, and our bodies. We are still drawn to those whom we stimulate sensually, emotionally, intellectually, and physically. We are still prone to loving others when these stimulations are mutual and to expressing our love sensually, which includes sexually. To deny these dispositions is to deny aspects of our experiential being, i.e. our "selves" in relation to components of experience. Must we experience these attractions (emotions and sensations) in relation to others outside of our marriage? No. Must we act in consonance with the direction these attractions point us? No. The attractions may not be strong; the circumstances may not be conducive to acting in consonance with them; our spouse's responses may be too severe for us to even entertain an assertive confrontation; we may have jobs that don't permit much exposure to others who might attract us in this manner. There may be all sorts of reasons why we aren't stimulated by others or act in accordance with our stimulations. But when those feelings do occur and are sufficiently strong to prompt deeper feelings, and the environment is conducive to the strengthening of those feelings, then to deny the validity or refuse to recognize the strength of these experiences is equivalent to self-deception and identity dis-integration. To act as if they don't exist or are evil or bad is to engage in various forms of inconsistent experiences where our behavior is not consistent with our thoughts, feelings, and sensations. But to accept the truth of these feelings, to disclose this truth to others whom the feelings pertain or involve, and to be prepared to grapple with or work through the repercussions of these disclosures is a positive (though certainly not easy) self-integrating direction to travel. It is self-affirming rather than self-negating, confirmation-inducing rather than guilt-inducing. Duty now applies to looking at ourselves honestly, disclosing ourselves to relevant others effectively, and working to deal productively with the repercussions of our disclosures instead of denying our feelings and sensations, avoiding situations where we might feel those feelings more strongly, or diverting these feelings into other channels (e.g. physical exercise, work, etc.)

SOCRATES: It doesn't sound like you're arguing against the institution of monogamy per se, nor in favor of adultery per se, but your moralitization of extra-marital love relationships, at least under certain conditions, seems, if it were adopted as common practice, to undermine monogamy and promote adultery.

MASSAGE THERAPIST: Viewed from the traditional point of view, I understand exactly what you're saying, but viewed experientially, monogamous marriage, at least in modern western culture, refers to a particular social, economic, psychological, and emotional *relationship* that will, optimally, though certainly not necessarily, sustain itself until death. It also, importantly, provides a strong structure in which to raise children. When the relationship is threatened, that which threatens it is conceived as evil, bad, or immoral. When loving someone outside of the marital relationship is felt as threatening to the relationship, then "rejecting" emotions rally to ward off the threat. Jealousy is an emotion that surfaces in response to a perceived threat to a relationship, whether that relationship is between same sex friends, homosexual partners, or heterosexual spouses. When we like someone and enjoy his or her company, "we" are affirmed, at least in part, by him or her. He or she provides us with confirmation-experiences of who we are as experiential beings. When we love someone to whom we are not sexually attracted, and he or she loves us, then we are affirmed wholly by them and we affirm them wholly, though our bodies are affirmed non-sexually. Our identities are mutually confirmed, despite our differences. When we love someone to whom we are sexually attracted, and he or she loves us, then we affirm and are affirmed wholly by them, and our bodies are affirmed sexually. All of these affirmations are aspects of our experiential being; all address who we are; and in order for us to be who we are, we need all of these aspects of who we are to be affirmed, by ourselves and by significant others, but only in ways that we ourselves, as experiential beings, determine as appropriate. When a threat to the experiential course of self-affirming experiences occurs, we naturally rally to ward it off. But if our defensive responses to a perceived threat are quelled by the consistent and persistent maintenance of the relationship, then the emotions subside and the threat disappears. If our man loves and sexually desires his wife and the experiences which are partially constituted by these feelings are consistent and strong (persistent), then he will continue to love and sexually desire his wife, even if he simultaneously loves and sexually desires another woman. And his consistent and persistent love and sexual desire for his wife will serve to allay her felt threat of having that identity-affirming course of experience end for her.

SOCRATES: My friend. I have no doubt that you honestly believe what you're saying.. But I think you are either ignoring some fundamental aspects of human nature or you expect too much from the average human being, or both. I'll draw on evolutionary theory to support my opinion that neither men nor women in general would accept your argument. Evolutionary theory maintains that female jealousy involves primarily the threat of abandonment or desertion and secondarily that of sexual infidelity, whereas male jealously involves primarily the threat of sexual infidelity and secondarily that of abandonment. Emotional attachments by the man to a woman outside of marriage are more feared by the wife than are sexual liaisons because of their strong connection to abandonment. Abandonment would jeopardize the proliferation of genes because of the inadequate resources, both economically and emotionally, that abandonment causes. Emotional attachments involve time and money, i.e. resources that are diverted away from family. Prolonged emotional attachments will increase this diverting of resources as well as increase the likelihood of abandonment. Hence, it would not be in the wife's genetic interest to accept her husband's extra-marital love relationship, no matter how consistent and persistent he is in his love and desire for her. Likewise, it is in the man's genetic interest to ward off threats to the proliferation of his genes by reacting emotionally (jealously) to wife's sexual infidelity. He may accept her emotional infidelity because it doesn't severely threaten his chances of pushing his genes into the next generation, but he will not accept her sexual infidelity.

MASSAGE THERAPIST: I'm familiar with the theory, Socrates, and I'm curious about several issues. Let's say that a woman has genes for jealousy. The jealousy occurs in consciousness in response to certain types of environmental cues, or, if you prefer, perceived threats. Let's say that she sees her husband talking to an attractive woman at a party. She "notes the occurrence" and continues to interact with others. Would you say that her genes are acting up at this point?

SOCRATES: I'd say that she is aware of the sexual-emotional attraction situation between her husband and the woman.

MASSAGE THERAPIST: She's going to check back now and then to see how things are going and not because she wants things to go well for her husband but because the situation poses at least a very slight threat to her.

SOCRATES: I'll accept that.

MASSAGE THERAPIST: But what kind of threat are we talking about here? How is her husband talking to the woman? Is his interest in her overtly sexual and wife's noting of the occurrence is the first step toward a jealous rage on her part, or is his interest in her more diverse, i.e. physical, intellectual, emotional, etc. and wife's noting of the occurrence is the first step in a course-of-action for him that will end up

in his abandonment of her for the other woman? Since the evolutionary theory maintains that abandonment is the primary female fear, let's get to that point as quickly as possible, and say that the wife's noting of the occurrence is the first sign of emotional threat.
SOCRATES: Fine.
MASSAGE THERAPIST: Why does she feel threatened by her husband talking to an attractive woman at a party?
SOCRATES: I'm not sure what you mean?
MASSAGE THERAPIST: Does she feel threatened because her genes are causing her to feel threatened? Or might she feel threatened because she's unsure of what might happen emotionally between her husband and the woman? Or possibly because she knows her husband is vulnerable to attention from attractive women? Or perhaps because her self-confidence is particularly low at this point in her life and she's distorting the implications of the situation?
SOCRATES: The theory accounts for the human tendency or disposition for women to feel threatened in these situations. Individual psychological or environmentally determined factors may certainly bear upon the situation, but the general tendency toward feeling threatened is genetically determined. Such a theory accounts for the wide-spread occurrence and persistence of the feeling amongst humans of all races, creeds, and cultures. The difference in feelings could be accounted for by many non-genetic factors but only in relation to the genetic. That is, at some point, in some situations, nearly all people will experience such a threat. The woman who does not experience the threat at the party will experience it in other situations, should those situations arise.
MASSAGE THERAPIST: It is natural or genetically-determined for a female to feel threatened by emotional abandonment, i.e. by the loss of emotional attachment or love.
SOCRATES: Yes.
MASSAGE THERAPIST: Is this not so of men also?
SOCRATES: Yes, but they tend to feel it less acutely, less severely than women.
MASSAGE THERAPIST: So if the party situation were reversed, the man would be "noting the occurrence" of his wife talking to an attractive man as the first step toward a sexual encounter between them rather than the forming of an emotional attachment leading to eventual abandonment.
SOCRATES: Yes.

MASSAGE THERAPIST: And some men will experience the threat in such situations and some will not. But those that do not will probably feel it in other situations.
SOCRATES: Yes.
MASSAGE THERAPIST: And these men may also feel some threat of emotional abandonment; and the women may also feel some threat of sexual encounter.
SOCRATES: Yes.
MASSAGE THERAPIST: If it is natural, or determined by the nature of our genes, to feel threatened in some emotional/sexual situations but not in all such situations, and if in specific situations some of us may feel threatened while others of us don't, then can I conclude that it may be quite difficult to determine exactly which situations will cause all of us to feel threatened? I may be threatened by my wife's slow dancing with an attractive man, whereas such a thing wouldn't be a matter of concern for another man. Can we say that all men would feel threatened by their wives having sexual intercourse with another man?
SOCRATES: No. Some cultures permit wife-exchanges; some subcultures permit wife-swapping. Some men who are sexually incapacitated may allow their wives to have sex with other men, and other men have agreements with their wives that each of them could engage in sex outside of the marriage. And these activities do not seem to prompt undue threats to their marriage.
MASSAGE THERAPIST: Then some men are capable of not feeling threatened when their wives have sex with other men.
SOCRATES: Yes.
MASSAGE THERAPIST: Are we to conclude from this that these men are genetically different from other men?
SOCRATES: I know of no empirical research to bear this out.
MASSAGE THERAPIST: Then it seems to me that who-feels-threatened-about-what is probably an individually determined, situation-based phenomenon.
SOCRATES: Perhaps.
MASSAGE THERAPIST: We may very well possess the genetic structure which permits us to feel threatened in regard to emotional/sexual situations, but just which situations will provoke the feeling in whom is probably a relative matter.
SOCRATES: Perhaps.
MASSAGE THERAPIST: Also, could the "fact" that we possess such a genetic structure mean that just because we might feel threatened

in a certain situation that we would have to feel threatened in all similar situations? Could we not, let's say, become more familiar with the situation and/or the people composing it so that the threat will eventually subside if not disappear altogether? For instance, a man might feel threatened when his wife befriends a man at her work, but as he becomes more familiar with the situation and sees that his wife has no difficulty emotionally or sexually in maintaining the friendship, and it doesn't significantly disturb his home life and his sexual interaction with his wife, then couldn't we say that he has *worked through* his feelings of threat? That though possibly genetically-based, such feelings might be more like steps in developing trust rather than static, unchanging limits on human emotion?

SOCRATES: I admit that what you say sounds reasonable, but given the overwhelming evidence of human jealously and often times the destructive behavior that attends it, I prefer to think conservatively and regard human nature as genetically incapable, except in rare circumstances, to overcome this jealousy.

MASSAGE THERAPIST: I'm not asking that you give up that notion. I'm asking that you entertain the idea that human jealousy serves the evolutionary "purpose" of stimulating us to defend our genetic partnership from destruction. But it is the partnership or relationship, i.e. the continuous flow of confirmation-experiences in regard to oneself as an experiential being, and not the exclusivity of the emotional attachment or sexual behavior that is threatened. The woman's threat may well be emotion-based, but it is not the fear of her man's falling in love with someone else per se that ultimately threatens her, but his radical alteration of his relationship to her, his physical, emotional, and sexual abandonment of her, or his transference of love from her to someone else. The man's threat may well be more sex-based, but it not his fear of his wife's having sex with another man per se that ultimately threatens him, but her radically altering her sexual relationship to him, i.e. the transference of sexual desire from him to another man. If she were to persist in her love and sexual desire for him, then the threat of "sexual defection" would be minimized. Just as the husband would feel more comfortable with his wife's male friend when he realizes that the friendship is not a threat to his marriage (and sexual partnership), so too will he feel more comfortable with his wife's love relationship.

SOCRATES: You realize, my friend, that what you are saying will strike a hefty majority of the male population in our culture as at least unlikely and at most altogether repugnant.
MASSAGE THERAPIST: I'm well aware of that too, Socrates. That's why I'm arguing this case as a possibility rather than a probability, at least for this period in time. But I am arguing straightforwardly that as we, men and women alike, become more proficient at the process of acceptance:confrontation:grappling, we will be able to work through threatening situations and realize our integrity as not primarily determined by our emotionality (love) or sexuality in relation to one person but by all aspects of our experiential being in relation to a number of people in our lives simultaneously. If we are, as I contend, experiential beings, then we are emotional as well as sexual beings. How we relate ourselves to others, and what partnerships or relationships we find ourselves in (e.g. family, society) or choose to be in (e.g. friendships, marriage) constitutes the interpersonal aspect of our experiential being (people being a part of our environment). Because we form a particular relationship with a person does not mean that we can funnel or channel aspects of our being toward that person alone, as if other people won't attract us, like us, or love us, and we them. Rather than deny the validity of our dispositions to love others and be loved by them, and to express our love to them sexually when sexual attraction co-exists with the love, we need to find more effective ways to accept these dispositions as valid or at least potentially valid, to assertively confront relevant others, and grapple with the consequences. If in doing so we succeed in reducing the threat of emotional abandonment and sexual defection, integrate our identities by re-establishing consistent individual and mutual experience, and alter social and moral customs to be more consistent with the integrating process, then, it seems to me, we will have taken the first step necessary in dealing constructively with our more powerful emotions and urges rather than finding more "creative" ways to feel the emotions and express the urges clandestinely and deceptively. And, paradoxically, such an integrating process would serve to perpetuate monogamy as a social, economic, emotional, psychological, and sexual relationship between two people that will persist over time.
SOCRATES: Minus emotional and sexual exclusivity.
MASSAGE THERAPIST: Yes.
SOCRATES: My friend, I admit, I admire your optimism. Or, perhaps, I am sympathizing with your naiveté. You're assuming that we

human beings are capable of using this identity-integrating method effectively, when empirical data, I'm sure, bears out that accepting our experience as it is constituted rather than avoiding, denying, and rationalizing it "away" is a difficult task as best, not to mention the difficulty in assertively confronting others in regard to the truth of ourselves and dealing with the consequences of our assertiveness.

MASSAGE THERAPIST: I never said it would be easy. I'll be the first to admit that such a process is difficult and sometimes painful. But as the skill of implementing the method is learned and effectively applied to actual situations, the difficulty decreases. As the difficulty decreases, the number of times using the method increases, which serves to decrease the difficulty even more, i.e. it results in a positive, self-affirming, self-integrating circle, rather than the vicious circle of self-denial and deception. Also, I've selected extra-marital love relationships to explore the connections between the levels of experience and the process of moralitization rather than to show how the identity-integrating process can be used effectively. In applying the method to extra-marital love relationships, I'd assume a great deal of practice and mastery of the process. Such an area of self-acceptance and confrontation is generally opposed by many groups and societies. Hence, I realize the difficulties involved in applying the method in this area.

SOCRATES: But you won't let that stop you.

MASSAGE THERAPIST: Of course not.

SOCRATES: I thought not. Ok. Let's say that our husband and wife have a good deal of identity-integration process experience. They are able to confront each other, grapple with their confrontations, and they even reach a mutual agreement in regard to the alteration of their marital vows to permit extra-marital love relationships as long as each experiences only marginal threat. Let's even say that they overcome the problem that could arise as they implement their new vows and achieve mutual inter-experientially consistent experience. Are extra-marital love relationships, as you've conceptualized them, moral?

MASSAGE THERAPIST: As I've described them, and at the individual and mutual levels of experience involving those whose impact on the identity of the people involved is significant, I'd say, yes, they are moral for all those involved.

SOCRATES: And if the church, let's say, to which they belong condemns the act as adulterous, and their society would recognize it as adultery if divorce were to ensue at some point down the road?

MASSAGE THERAPIST: If the church or any other groups to which they belonged knew about and condemned the act, then the individuals would have to be able to grapple with this. The church's condemnation, if not a significant part of the experiences constituting their relationship, may very well become a part of it, even if only in subtle rejections from fellow church-goers or clergy. Their knowing would be similar to an assertive confrontation, even if they found out from a third party. To challenge such a time-honored institution as monogamy by eliminating its sexual-emotional exclusivity component while retaining the monogamous relationship as the primary relationship in all ways, i.e. practical, emotional, sexual, financial, etc., and to assert the rightness of their love relationship, all involved would have to be ready and willing to grapple with the social repercussions of their assertive confrontation, whether they actually make the confrontation (tell others) or not (someone else tell others.) Groups can react in a variety of ways to such a confrontation: they can formally bar the individuals from participation in the group (as would professional groups), excommunicate them (as would a church), or informally ostracize or "close ranks" and snub them (as would acquaintances, co-workers, or would-be friends). And, as already mentioned, families and friends can also reject them in a variety of ways. But within a democratic, pluralistic culture, they might find enough outside acceptance to make their lives bearable if not happy. Now the question: if society in general condemns the behavior as immoral, does that make it immoral? Only for society in general. Certainly not for those engaged in the behavior. The small group could establish itself as a morally viable group unto itself. The experiential contradiction would lie between the small group and other groups; within the individuals constituting the small group, experience is functionally consistent.

SOCRATES: Let's say that society in general adheres to the principle of fidelity in marriage, where fidelity means emotional and sexual exclusivity. Some members of society believe that the principle is basically given to us (or commanded) by God (i.e. supernaturalists); others hold to it as an intuitive truth (i.e. deontologists). Our newly "formed" group challenges the principle with a principle of its own. Let's refer to it as the **principle of honesty in marriage**. Our small group says it is better or more moral, on principle, to tell the truth about one's experiential state-of-affairs when such states-of-affair bear directly upon the experience (and identity) of another (others), even if this truth causes the other pain and would possibly break up the marriage.

MASSAGE THERAPIST: Forgive me for interrupting, but I think I should stop you before you go too far with this. I'd say that there is a conflict here, but it is between experiences and not principles. A principle is nothing more than a particular type of experience. As such it is subject to change. We may adhere to a principle intuitively; experientially, this intuition may be cognitive, affective, behavioral, or sense-physical. For instance, stealing our neighbor's property may strike us as intuitively wrong though we may not be repulsed by it (cognitive intuition), whereas we might feel repulsed by child molestation (affective intuition). But given certain circumstances, these intuitions are alterable, at least in degree if not fundamentally. For instance, we may tolerate if not sympathize with the man who has been "beaten down by society" when he steals the property of the rich. Likewise, a man who has been molested since childhood, and who is battling within himself not to molest others and to remain within the law, may be less repulsive and more pitiable than the man who is conceived as a sexual predator. Also, in many cultures, sexual situations between adults and children were (are) part of the acceptable sexual practices within these cultures. Therefore, what constitutes molestation is subject to experience. Principles and intuitions are not always "served up to us whole and strong"; they often develop over time (e.g. the principle of anti-slavery was not always as strong as it is today in our culture, and for some it isn't even a principle but a perversion of morality). Therefore, I think you need to reduce these principles to experience before we can understand them within the framework we're developing here. At one time the man's intuition dictated that emotional and sexual interaction with someone other than one's spouse was wrong. That intuition was challenged and eventually overridden by his experience of loving the woman. Further experience confirmed the rightness of his love for her over the rightness of emotional exclusivity, i.e. his intuition changed due to the strength and consistency of his confrontation experiences in relation to loving the woman. The same thing applies to his intuition of sexual infidelity.

SOCRATES: And I suppose you'll still maintain that there exists an objective quality to all this change going on, and that the objectivity lies within the structure of experience itself.

MASSAGE THERAPIST: Yes.

SOCRATES: And if our small group should influence others and more and more people come to hold these new principles or experience these new intuitions, then do we have the co-existence of two opposing moralities, at least in regard to this issue?

MASSAGE THERAPIST: Yes.

SOCRATES: Then how is this conflict resolved, if it is resolved at all?

MASSAGE THERAPIST: Through the evolution or process of experience, through the method of acceptance:confrontation:grappling, and through identity-integration in relation to others.

SOCRATES: So the morality of extra-marital emotional and sexual involvement is not something to be determined by a particular individual, group, or group of groups (society), or the totality of all known groups (inter-society) but by all (each and everyone) of these experiential beings participating in some experiential way with the issue. We need not achieve mutual rightness to determine individual rightness, but mutual rightness serves to confirm and strengthen individual rightness. If our small group influences change in other groups, then the group level of experience serves to confirm the rightness of mutual and individual levels. And the same applies to the societal and inter-societal levels of experience. And, all the while, other conflicting intuitions or principles may be developing within the whole experiential structure that may or may not significantly alter these new moral values.

MASSAGE THERAPIST: I'd say you have aided me significantly in clarifying my own thinking, Socrates.

SOCRATES: If each experiential being participates in the process of moralitization in relation to a given moral issue, and if this process consists of acceptance, confrontation, and grappling, then it seems to me that it would behoove us to organize ourselves in such a way as to promote or encourage this process. It seems that our current hierarchical structures do more discouraging than encouraging of this process. But that is for another time.

MASSAGE THERAPIST: Yes.

INDEX

Abandonment, 211-215
Absolutes, 84, 87, 113, 171, 173-175
Acceptance:confirmation:grappling, 205, 215, 219
Acting-experience, 44
Agented act, 50
Agented cognition, 51, 52, 64, 67, 73, 141, 155, 156, 158, 159, 161, 163, 169, 190, 206
Agentless behavior, 49, 50
Anders, T.., 199
A priori principle, 167, 173
Assertive confrontation, 76, 79, 80, 84, 121, 151, 184, 185, 197, 206-209, 217
Assertive-experience, 78, 79
Assertiveness, 76, 78, 194, 203, 216
Augustine, St., 10, 18, 165
Characterizing experience, 73
Christian metaphysics, 11
Christian morality, 10, 11, 18, 20, 23, 175
Choice, 31, 32, 34, 39, 40, 45, 46, 49, 108, 109, 168, 200, 207
Cognitive component, 15, 16, 48, 49, 71, 73, 124, 164, 166
Cognitive periphery, 37, 77
Cognitivization of self, 16
Cognitivized "I", 18, 47-49, 51, 54, 57-59, 69, 70
Component of consciousness, 15, 17, 18, 29, 32-39, 41, 42, 45-47, 53, 77, 86, 90, 95, 96, 107-109, 122, 126, 155, 165, 166
Component of experience, 2, 7, 9, 16, 18, 26, 34, 53, 58, 59, 71, 75, 81, 96, 99, 104, 117, 119-123, 125, 126, 132, 158, 163-165, 170, 209
Componential Structure, 69, 86, 93, 95, 96, 98, 106, 110, 123, 133, 137, 156, 166, 167, 173, 176
Components of consciousness as owned, 37, 96, 109, 126, 156
Confirmation experience, 55, 60, 68, 74, 75, 77, 94, 115, 120, 127, 151, 169, 170, 173, 174, 176, 181, 185, 186, 188, 191, 193, 197, 210, 214

Compound ambivalent experience, 23
Compound experience, 21, 22, 24, 69-72, 100, 167, 183, 204
Conflicting courses of action, 38, 44
Confrontation, 59, 60, 75, 76, 79-85, 150 151, 176, 184-186, 194, 195, 197-199, 202, 204-209, 215-217, 219
Consensus, 52, 162, 175
Consistency over time, 79, 95
Consistent-discontinuous-consistent model of experience, 105
Content-orientation of morality, 211
Content unit of experience, 106
Contiguous experience, 25, 112
Continuous inter-experiential bond, 106
Contradiction-experience, 74
Conviction-experience, 71
Decision-experience, 44, 117
Denial set-of-experiences, 48, 168, 192
Depth-oriented pleasure, 153
Desire-controlling thought, 26
Desire-experience, 69, 70, 106-108, 112-114, 168, 169, 198-200, 201, 202
Determining experience, 98
Disconfirmation experience, 55, 127, 170, 185
Discontinuous inter-experiential bond, 105
Dominant-submissive moral structure, 162
Duty-experience, 62, 64, 66-70, 89, 90, 106, 107, 112-114, 160, 168, 169, 183, 186-188
Effective level of satisfaction, 83
Egoism, 165, 167, 172
Emotional pleasure, 153, 154, 179
Empirico-phenomenal world, 82, 164
Epicurus, 164, 170
Equalitarian structure, 162
Eroticism, 121, 123
Escalation of intensity, 136
Escalation-oriented pleasure, 153
Ethical code, 8, 133, 150

Evaluation experience, 84, 85-88, 93, 127, 184, 188, 189
Evaluative aspect of experience, 90, 93, 95, 100, 104, 106, 111, 114
Evaluative level of experience, 202, 204
Evolutionary ethics, 12, 165, 166, 199-201, 211, 212, 214, 219
Experience-in-general, 94
Experiential absolutes, 84
Experiential being, 1-3, 7, 8, 12, 19, 39, 83, 99, 120-129, 133, 149, 151, 174, 193, 195, 205, 206, 209, 210, 214, 215, 219
Experiential component(s), 7, 68, 83, 88, 90, 97, 110
Experiential consistency, 1, 2, 92, 100, 116, 117, 122, 124, 127, 151, 162, 168, 172-174, 176, 181, 191, 195, 200, 203, 205
Experiential constructs, 97, 98, 167, 175
Experiential contradiction, 7, 10, 66, 67, 87, 203, 217
Experiential morality, 164, 174
Experiential state-of-affairs, 51, 52, 54, 55, 60-64, 66, 67, 69, 70, 72, 74-82, 84-87, 90, 91, 113, 118, 126, 134, 141, 142, 158, 161, 163, 176, 177, 184, 185, 202-205
Expressive level of experience, 202
False conviction-experience, 71, 164
Focal consciousness, 13, 14, 23, 33, 36, 37, 48, 57-59, 61-63, 66-69, 77, 90, 112, 145, 146, 148, 157, 160
Functional acceptance, 84-86, 88, 106, 121
Functional equanimity, 80
Functional-intuitive scale, 115
Functional rightness, 86, 88
Free will, 26, 28, 29, 31, 32, 34, 35, 39-44, 46, 108, 109, 113, 115
Grappling, 79, 175, 184, 185, 194, 195, 202, 204, 215, 219
Group level of experience, 117, 150, 219
Hume, D., 13, 18, 164, 170, 171
"I"-as-agent, 47-50, 157
"I"-as-ownership, 37
Identification memory, 37, 70, 105

83
Identity, 19, 59, 72-74, 82, 83, 87, 101, 113, 115, 125, 177, 183, 186, 189, 191, 194, 195, 197, 202, 204-206, 209, 210, 216-218
Identity-experience, 73, 74, 82,
Immediate experience, 29, 35, 37, 39, 42, 44, 47, 50, 63, 69, 76, 81, 98, 122
Inconsistent experience, 7, 68, 124, 173, 175-177, 180, 190, 192, 200, 202, 208, 209
Independent self, 108
Individual level of experience, 116, 117, 119, 121, 123, 127, 132, 183, 184, 189, 196, 197
Individuation identity process, 194
Individuation process, 186, 187, 194
Initial-experience, 110-112
Integrated identity, 204
Integrity of experience, 191
Intra-experiential consistency, 22, 65, 67-69, 86, 89, 91-93, 105, 110, 111, 116-118, 122, 128, 161, 162, 167, 169, 170, 173, 174, 176, 182, 183
Intra-experiential level of experience, 105, 118
Intra-experiential inconsistency, 66, 68, 71, 90, 91, 161, 163, 175-177, 200, 204
Intra-experiential split, 67, 68
Inter-experiential consistency, 92, 116, 117, 122, 124, 172, 173, 200
Inter-experiential contradiction, 67, 87
Inter-experiential level of experience, 59, 105
Inter-experiential inconsistent experience, 22, 68, 122, 162, 174-177, 191
Inter-experiential ontology, 59, 69, 143
Interpersonal experiential consistency, 122, 127, 162, 168, 205
Interpersonal level of experience, 128, 144, 151
Inter-societal level of experience, 116, 117, 119, 175, 176, 178, 219
Intuition experiences, 86, 106
Intuitive acceptance, 121
Judeo-Christian tradition, 97
Judgment experience, 52-62, 64, 78,

79, 89-91, 93
Kant, I., 164-171, 173
Layered experience, 154, 156, 159, 161
Level of experience, 116-129, 150, 151, 170, 176, 183, 189-191, 193, 196, 197
Love relationship, 186, 207-209, 211, 215-217
  non-marital, 186
  extra-marital, 207-209, 211, 216, 218
Marx, K., 164
Memory experience, 14
Meta-experiential construct, 51, 87, 96, 97, 108, 114, 167, 169, 175
Moral conviction, 45
Moral identity, 186, 204
Moral system, 6, 7, 10, 22, 164, 186
Moralitization, 164-167, 173, 174, 183, 196, 200, 202, 204, 205, 209, 216, 219
Motivational power of experience, 106, 107, 110, 112
Mutual confirmation, 117
Mutual level of experience, 116, 118-120, 122-128, 144, 170, 183, 194, 190, 191, 193, 197, 205-207, 217
Mutual resolution, 80, 81
Mutually assertive interaction (process of), 75
Objective experiential consistency, 124
Objective reality within experience, 51
Objective state-of-affairs, 51, 52, 54, 55, 60-67, 69, 70, 72, 74-82, 84-87, 90, 91, 113, 118, 126, 127, 134, 141, 142, 158, 161, 173, 174, 176, 177, 183-185, 197, 201-205, 207, 218
Orgasm, 101, 131-133, 136, 143-145, 147, 148, 153-155, 161
Peripheral consciousness, 37, 58, 59, 66, 70, 90, 120, 156
Periphery of consciousness, 9, 58, 60, 65, 74, 77, 90, 112
Persistence of experience, 106, 110, 112
Physical attraction, 8, 20, 131, 134, 136, 146, 196, 197, 209
Physical environment, 1, 2, 7, 14, 16, 17, 20, 21, 26, 56, 81, 96, 98, 100, 104, 156

Physical world, 1, 123, 125
Primary component of experience, 120, 122, 123, 124
Primatize, 2, 8, 120
Principle experience, 120
Principle of fidelity, 87, 119, 217
Principle of honesty in marriage, 218
Process of experience, 38, 81, 82, 168, 219
Process of morality, 95, 108, 161, 162
Process orientation of morality, 205, 206
Process unit of experience, 106, 117
Prohibitive experience, 42-44
Prompting experience, 110
Pseudo-identity-experience, 73
Quality of experience, 94, 95
Quantity of experience, 94, 95
Reason, 32, 40, 42, 44, 70, 108, 109, 112-115, 121, 164-173, 180, 200, 201
Reason experience, 44
Rejection-experience, 202
Resentment, 5, 82, 163, 172, 188, 191, 193
Resolution-experience, 84, 115, 116-118, 120, 127, 169, 173, 176, 188-191, 193, 197, 200, 118
Responsibility, 46-52, 64, 206
Responsibility-experience, 48, 51, 52
Right(ness):wrong(ness), 86-87, 90, 92-95, 100, 105, 106, 110
Russell, B., 17, 18
Scope of effect, 121, 128
Self-affirming experience, 209, 210, 216
Self-as-soul, 11
Self-as-who-we-are, 11
Self-judgment experience, 56-60, 62, 64
Self-reflection, 12-18, 41, 47, 49, 56, 58, 59, 63-65, 68, 69, 73, 79, 99, 104, 108, 109, 111, 113, 135-137, 140
Self-reflective experience, 13, 16, 18, 49, 56, 59, 63-65, 68, 73, 79, 99, 104, 109, 111, 113, 135-137, 140
Self-restraining thought, 22, 26
Sensual attraction, 131, 132, 136, 139
Separation confrontation, 194

Series of experiences, 42, 57, 59, 63, 65, 76-78, 138, 139
Set structure, 86
Sets of components of consciousness, 32, 35, 37, 38, 77, 86, 95, 107, 109
Sexual arousal, 140-145, 148, 149, 154, 157, 198
Sexual attraction, 102-104, 97, 131-136, 139, 141, 142, 215
Sexual event, 155, 156
Sexual experience, 6, 94, 118, 132, 136, 142, 145, 146, 149, 153
Sexual infidelity, 201, 211, 219
Sexual interest, 85, 101-103, 133, 136, 143-145
Sexual stimulation, 133, 137, 139, 142, 143, 145, 147, 148, 152-154, 156-161, 165
Single course of action, 38
Skinner, B.F., 164, 170
Societal level of experience, 117, 176, 119
Soul, 10-12
Split identity, 204
Strength of experience, 95, 106, 100
Stronger experience, 156
Super-human moral code, 87
Third-person point of view, 40, 43
Threshold of action, 57, 110
Trans-experiential function of ownership, 42
Truth, 76, 78-81, 124, 125, 183, 184, 201, 204-206, 208, 209, 216, 218
Unification-confrontation, 195
Utilitarianism, 164, 167, 171, 172
Veneration stroke, 149, 153, 154
Ways of understanding, 30
Weaker experience, 156
Who she is in this situation, 16, 39-41, 49, 70, 140, 180, 184
Who he is in this situation, 54, 108, 113, 182
Who I am in this situation, 6, 58, 63, 77
Who we are in this situation, 44, 92
Whole human being, 7, 8
Will as concept, 18, 45, 47
Will as faculty, 26, 28, 29, 34, 36
Willed experience, 44
Wright, R., 165, 199